MASCULINITY AND
POPULAR TELEVISION

For Paul

EDINBURGH UNIVERSITY PRESS

Rebecca Feasey

MASCULINITY AND POPULAR TELEVISION

© Rebecca Feasey, 2008

Edinburgh University Press Ltd
22 George Square, Edinburgh

Typeset in 10/12.5 pt Sabon
by Servis Filmsetting Ltd, Stockport, Cheshire, and
printed and bound in Great Britain by
CPI-Antony Rowe, Chippenham, Wilts

A CIP record for this book is available from the British Library

ISBN 978 0 7486 2797 4 (hardback)
ISBN 978 0 7486 2798 1 (paperback)

The right of Rebecca Feasey
to be identified as author of this work
has been asserted in accordance with
the Copyright, Designs and Patents Act 1988.

CONTENTS

1. INTRODUCTION: THEORISING MASCULINITIES ON THE SMALL SCREEN

Television studies is the new and growing academic discipline that emerged out of a diverse range of sociology, politics, film, media and cultural theory departments during the late 1970s and early 1980s. However, even though television studies was originally understood as the populist subfield of existing disciplines it has more recently gained critical renown and respectability in its own right. After all, the history and pervasiveness of television, the virtually unlimited number of programme choices available, the sheer reach of the medium and the ability to access and archive previously ephemeral texts has appealed to a recent generation of scholars and students who not only accept, but more importantly, embrace the small screen.

The discipline appeals to a broad cross-section of the academic community, and as such, extant literature spans such distinct and disparate areas as market reforms in television production (Deakin and Pratten 2000), television and cultural policy (Ouellette and Lewis 2000), television and consumption (Dickinson *et al.* 2001), the role of the audience (Hill 2002), the privatisation of public television (Hoynes 2003), television's impact on global culture (Mathijs and Jones 2004) and television stardom (Jermyn 2006). And yet, irrespective of the broad scope of such research, the topic that has dominated and continues to dominate the burgeoning field is that of gender roles and sex role stereotyping.

However, if one considers that the term 'gender studies' has until very recently been synonymous with women's studies, and that literature on the representation of gender in the mass media tends to focus on an examination of femininity and a woman's role in film, advertising and the magazine sector, then it will come as no surprise to find that existing research on representations of gender on television is dominated by work seeking to expose or unmask the depiction of women on the small screen. Such work has looked to explore the depiction of the matriarch in the prime-time soap opera (Madill and Goldmeier

2003), the single girl in the situation comedy format (Dow 1996), female empowerment in contemporary animation (Rowe Karlyn 2003), the kick-ass heroine in the fantasy teen and science fiction text (Projansky and Vande Berg 2000), the doting good woman in the hospital drama (Philips 2000), the abrasive female detective in the cop show (Creeber 2001), the trivialisation of the female athlete in sporting coverage (Brookes 2002), the exhibitionism of women in reality programming (Pozner 2004), the depiction of the domestic goddess in lifestyle television (Hollows 2003a) and the objectification of the female in television advertising (Lavine, Sweeney and Wagner 1999).

The continued interest in the representation of women is due in part to television's status as a domestic medium that was aimed at a female consumer during the early 1950s, and in part to the influence of the second-wave feminist movement that emerged in the late 1970s. Feminist television theorists were originally concerned with exploring depictions of femininity on the small screen, and as such, they chose to overlook the representation of masculinity, machismo and the man's role because 'deconstructing images of men may have . . . divert[ed] attention from the feminist work that still needed to be done on women' (MacKinnon 2003: 8). However, although such research provided valuable insights into the depiction of femininity, feminism and a woman's role, it also meant that masculinity and male heterosexuality continued to be understood as fixed, stable, unalterable and therefore beyond enquiry. However, even though 'femininity may be more readily understood as a constructed category (because of its association with things like make-up, hairstyles [and] clothing), masculinity [is] equally socially constructed' (D'Acci 2005: 379). Therefore, we must acknowledge that masculinities, like femininities, are created by the cultural environment rather than by biology or nature, and as such, it is important that the representation of men and masculinities be open to the sorts of questioning that has for so long applied to women and their femininities.

I refer to the plural masculinities rather than the singular masculinity because masculinity itself must be understood as 'fluid, time-related and variable across cultures and eras as well as subject to change over the course of a person's life, and within any given society at any one time' (Hakala 2006: 57). In this way, a study of masculinities rather than the more monolithic masculinity allows for an examination of the myriad and multiple ways in which masculinity can manifest itself both on and off screen. However, although it is important to point to the multiplicity of masculinities available and foreground the social construction of the gendered identities being presented, it is also necessary to highlight the ways in which different models of masculinity have been said to form a hierarchy of acceptable, unacceptable and marginalised models for the male.

Robert W. Connell developed Antonio Gramsci's seminal work on Italian class relations and coined the term 'hegemonic masculinity' to describe those white, heterosexual, competitive, individualist and aggressive men in the paid labour force who dominate the moral, cultural and financial landscape (Connell 1995: 77). The hegemonic male is said to be a strong, successful, capable and authoritative man who derives his reputation from the workplace and his self-esteem from the public sphere. In short, the hegemonic definition of manhood is 'a man in power, a man *with* power, and a man of power' (Kimmel 2004: 184).

This model of masculinity is said to be the ideal image of the male against which all men are judged, tested and qualified, so much so in fact that hegemonic masculinity has 'become the standard in psychological evaluations, sociological research . . . self-help and advice literature for teaching young men to become real men' (Kimmel 2004: 184). Indeed, even though this narrow image of masculinity may only ever be embodied by mythical figures, legendary heroes and a very small number of men in society, 'this does not . . . lessen its credibility as a standard of masculinity to which men are supposed to aspire' (MacKinnon 2003: 115). As such 'many men live in a state of some tension with . . . hegemonic masculinity' (Connell 1998: 5). Moreover, even though black and Asian masculinities, lower-class and anti-sexist masculinities, effeminate, gay, elderly and pacifist masculinities may all be said to command less political power, wealth or prestige than the hegemonic male, very large numbers of men are complicit in sustaining this hierarchic model. After all, while some men enjoy the fantasy of such powerful masculinity and others enjoy the displaced aggression that comes with 'gay bashing' or 'racist attacks', all are said to benefit from the institutionalisation of men's dominance over women which is at the heart of hegemonic power (Carrigan, Connell and Lee 1985: 592). Michael Kimmel makes this point when he tells us that being a man means 'not being like women', irrespective of the age, ethnicity, class, race or sexual orientation of the male in question (Kimmel 2004: 185). In this way we are told that 'anti-femininity lies at the heart of contemporary and historical conceptions of manhood, so that masculinity is defined more by what one is not rather than who one is' (ibid.: 185).

There exists a broad range of work on the representation of masculinities, the portrayal of the hegemonic order and the relationship between masculinity and domesticity in the popular media, be it Hollywood films (Fradley 2004), muscular action stars (Huffer 2003), men's lifestyle magazines (Benwell 2003), advertising (Hakala 2006) or sports (Whannel 2002). Likewise, there exists a wealth of recent research on the sociology of masculinity concerning masculinity and materiality, masculinity in crisis, sexuality, male power, identity, the politics of masculinity and the male role in management (Whitehead 2002). That said, there is little to account for the array of masculinities seen on the small screen and no single defining text that is dedicated to the way in which the presentation of masculinities on contemporary television programming can be seen to adhere to, negotiate or challenge the hegemonic hierarchy.

For example, even though Miranda Banks presents some truly enlightening work regarding the representation of American heroism in the teen male melodrama, the author does so in a volume dedicated to the wider area of adolescent programming (Banks 2004). Likewise, when Kenneth MacKinnon presents a history of masculinities, the male sex role and machismo on the small screen, this work is only one section of a text that is dedicated to the examination of the male in the broader media landscape (MacKinnon 2003). In this same way, Nickianne Moody offers an insightful consideration of masculinity, science and technology in popular 1980s programming, although such work exists in a broader examination of the action series which addresses issues such as consumption, audience responses, fashion and popular culture (Moody 2001). The point here is simply that although existing literature on the representation of masculinities on television appears fascinating, it always remains a brief examination within a wider academic terrain. As such, this work can never fully develop the complexities and potential contradictions at stake in this particular area of investigation.

Although theorists have been keen to examine the representation of women on television since the 1970s, explored the depiction of masculinities in a range of popular cultural arenas and started to unmask, deconstruct and theorise the myriad representations of men on the small screen, this volume is ultimately addressing an existing although still much overlooked area of investigation as it seeks to examine the representation of men, masculinities and the male role in a wide range of fictional and factual television genres.

This book will present a detailed textual reading of a variety of masculinities from contemporary British and American programming, including the representation of men as friends, fathers, heroes and martyrs, and consider the ways in which such figures can be understood in relation to wider social and sexual debates of the period. And this examination of masculinities is crucial, not because such representations are an accurate reflection of reality, but rather, because they have the power and scope to foreground culturally accepted social relations, define sexual norms and provide 'common-sense' understandings about male identity for the contemporary audience.

Each chapter will introduce the history of a particular genre and briefly outline the representations of gender that have been seen in such programming before looking at the ways in which masculinities are being constructed, circulated and interrogated in relevant televisual case studies. In this way, readers are encouraged to acknowledge significant changes in the portrayal of masculinities and a man's role on the small screen, with Chapters 2 to 8 looking at the representation of masculinities in a diverse range of popular fictional genres and Chapters 9 to 12 seeking to unmask male roles and responsibilities in a number of factual or 'infotainment' texts, concluding that contemporary programming forms a consensus as it investigates, negotiates and challenges the power, authority and patriarchal control of the hegemonic male.

Chapter 2 examines the construction of masculinity in the supposedly feminine genre of soap opera, paying particular attention to ways in which masculine gossip, the blurring of the personal and private sphere and issues surrounding paternity can all be seen to negotiate the stereotypical male role in *Coronation Street* (1960–), *Emmerdale* (1972–) and *EastEnders* (1985–); Chapter 3 considers the depiction of the male in both the straight situation

comedy and what has been termed the 'gaycom', suggesting tha
tation of male friendship, homosociality and homosexuality are
if not more important, than heterosexual relations in shows
(1994–2004), *Coupling* (2000–4) and *Will & Grace* (1998–2(
then goes on to look at the problematic fathers and father–son ᵣₑₗₐ
that dominate adult animation, concluding that programmes such as *The Simpsons* (1989–), *King of the Hill* (1997–) and *Family Guy* (1999–) are situated so as to present alternative and potentially subversive representations of family, friendship and masculinity on the small screen.

Chapter 5 is concerned with the representation of the adolescent male in the teen television drama, paying attention to the ways in which supernatural shows such as *Roswell* (1999–2002) and *Smallville* (2001–) draw on the alien motif in order to educate young men about male behaviour, appropriate gender roles and the confusions surrounding the adolescent experience; Chapter 6 explores the potential for inverted sexual dynamics in the science fiction and fantasy genre, focusing on shows such as *Farscape* (1999–2003) and *Firefly* (2002–3) as they can be seen to present the very real possibility of a culture beyond gender differentiation and sex role stereotyping; Chapter 7 examines the changing role of the doctor-hero in the new hospital drama, looking at the way in which an early image of infallible masculinity has been replaced by more tortured and tormented images of the male in shows such as *ER* (1994–) and *House* (2004–). Chapter 8 then goes on to look at issues of gender, power and aggression in the traditionally masculine police and crime drama, concluding that the structuring male hero in shows such as *24* (2001–) and *Spooks* (2002–) has to sacrifice domestic duties and family commitments for the good of his professional career and for the greater good of society.

Chapter 9 examines the depiction of the celebrity athlete in contemporary television sports coverage, paying particular attention to the ways in which figures such as David Beckham remind us that the dominant, aggressive and competitive male is merely a historical and cultural construct that can be exploited or negated in the current cultural climate; Chapter 10 considers the ways in which the viewing public has been seen to quite literally cast their vote for a particular version of emotional adult masculinity in *Big Brother 8* UK(2007); Chapter 11 considers the representation of masculinity and the male role in lifestyle programming, looking at the ways in which programmes such as *The Naked Chef* (1999), *The Naked Chef 2* (2000) and *Queer Eye for the Straight Guy* (2003–6) reclaim domestic labour and household tasks as masculine leisure activities rather than feminine or burdensome chores. Chapter 12 then goes on to explore those concentrated images of masculinity that are evident in a range of contemporary television adverts, considering the ways in which male grooming, car and beer commercials can be seen to negotiate earlier images of the competitive individualist in favour of a softer and more understated image of the male. The concluding chapter will present a synthesis of the analyses offered throughout the book, restating the case for considering the representation of masculinities on the small screen before looking at the future of masculinity in contemporary programming and pointing to future research directions.

Although this volume seeks to cover a wide range of television genres and programme titles, I am aware that readers will question the inclusion of some texts and the exclusion of others, to which I will comment that I have deliberately chosen a range of contemporary shows that proved popular with audiences and that are accessible in archival form. I have included a range of both British and American programmes due to the fact that Britain and America are similar countries that share a common language, cultural heritage and advanced economic state, and more importantly, because many of the programmes that are drawn on throughout the volume have created a cultural impact on both sides of the Atlantic. Furthermore, I have included a short synopsis of relevant shows throughout the work so that readers are able to familiarise themselves with the case studies being presented here, irrespective of their particular locale. And it is to these programmes that I now turn . . .

2. SOAP OPERA: THE MALE ROLE IN THE WOMEN'S GENRE

INTRODUCTION

Soap opera has traditionally focused on the home, the family, domestic tribulations and the strong woman, and as such, it has long been said to appeal to the female viewer. However, more recently, the genre has tried to extend its audience by bringing in a range of central male characters as a way to attract the man in the audience and a wider range of television advertisers. With this in mind, this chapter will introduce a short history of the soap opera and briefly consider the representation of women in the genre before looking at the changing depiction of masculinities in a range of popular British prime-time shows such as *Coronation Street*, *Emmerdale* and *EastEnders*. I will pay particular attention to the ways in which masculine gossip, the blurring of the public and private sphere and issues surrounding paternity can all be seen to negotiate traditional representations of hegemonic masculinity and the dominant male role. Although I will be mapping out the key codes and conventions of the most popular British soap operas, I would ask the reader to consider my propositions against a wider range of both British and American texts. After all, the wider genre shares similar formal elements such as popularity and longevity, an unending nature, a basis in daily and family life, an appeal to female spectators and a presentation of contemporary social concerns.

An examination of masculinity in soap opera is crucial due to the fact that a relationship can be said to exist between the representation of men in the domestic drama and the status of men in the wider population. For example, while Peter Salmon sees prime-time soaps acting as a 'social barometer' for the wider romantic, sexual, familial and domestic concerns in society (Salmon cited in Hobson 2003: 50), Dorothy Anger informs us that these popular texts have an impact on our lived environment because they 'send messages about appropriate or expected behaviour' (Anger 1999: 110). Such an examination is necessary because such programmes are consistently the most watched shows on British terrestrial television, with audiences reaching between 7 and 11 million for *EastEnders*, *Coronation Street* and *Emmerdale*.

HISTORY OF THE GENRE

Soap opera began on commercial American radio in the 1930s, with daytime shows such as *Painted Dreams* (1930–40), *Ma Perkins* (1933–60), *The Guiding Light* (1937–56) and *Woman in White* (1938–47). Such shows were given the title 'soap' by the American press because they were sponsored by detergent companies such as Procter and Gamble (who advertised their products during the programme) and 'opera' due to their tendency to over-dramatise all manner of household concerns. Therefore, soap opera can be understood at its most basic level as a serialised drama that focuses on a range of family affairs, personal relationships and friendships. These domestic dramas proved extremely popular with female listeners who were isolated in their homes, and by 1940 soap operas represented 90 per cent of all commercially-sponsored daytime broadcast hours (Allen 2005: online). The genre remained popular with the female audience when it moved to television in the 1950s, and shows such as *Search for Tomorrow* (1951–86), *Love of Life* (1951–80) and *The Secret Storm* (1954–74) established the soap opera as a regular part of the daytime television schedules.

STORIES OF HEART AND HEARTH

Feminist television criticism has routinely informed us that this daytime, and more recently prime-time drama, appeals to the female viewer due to its representation of strong female characters (Brown 1994: 49–51), its commitment to problem solving and intimate conversations (ibid.: 54–5) and its open-ended narrative structure (ibid.: 58). However, although soap opera has been applauded for its commitment to female characters and the familial experience beyond crude and rigid stereotypes, such work tends to overlook the representation of the male in the genre. The little work that does exist on the depiction of masculinities tends to draw on rigid and unchanging social types such as the sensitive new man, the decent husband, the romantic hero and the villainous bastard.

FROM DECENT HUSBANDS TO VILLAINS: STEREOTYPICAL REPRESENTATIONS OF MASCULINITY

While Nicholas Abercrombie argues that all men tend to be either weak and unreliable or devious and immoral in soap opera (Abercrombie 1997: 52), Jane Root suggests that most of the male characters are either 'sad or bad; sorry problem-boys ripe for nurturing or shallow, glamorous, matinee idol types' (Root 1986: 67). While Mary Ellen Brown refers to soaps sensitive 'new man' as someone who listens to wives, mothers and girlfriends and 'who embodies many of the cultural characteristics of the social construction of women' (Brown 1994: 54), Peter Buckman introduces the 'decent husband' as a man who offers emotional support to his wife and children and someone who 'represents the cornerstone of hearth and home that we are all taught to revere' (Buckman 1984: 42). Likewise, we are told that the 'romantic hero' is a handsome yet flawed bachelor (ibid.: 54) and that the 'villain' is a wealthy man who gets to 'bed all the pretty girls [and ignore] the social rules and graces that all the good people have to abide by' (ibid.: 61). However, although one might look to critique such theorists for drawing attention to a number of predictable and unsophisticated male stereotypes, it is worth noting that at the time of their writing, these characters were rarely central, significant or fully-developed protagonists in their own right, but rather, supporting players for the females who dominated the genre. Peter Buckman hints at the simplicity and superficiality of these male characters when he says 'thumbs up or thumbs down, and on with the next' (ibid.: 42). Therefore, although we have been told that 'soap characters cannot be stereotypes because we know the characters too well' (Hobson 2003: 83), one might suggest that this rule has only previously applied to the leading ladies of the genre in question.

Male characters and masculine narratives

Since the late 1980s and early 1990s, prime-time soap operas such as *Coronation Street*, *Emmerdale* and *EastEnders* have made a conscious effort to negotiate such masculine stereotypes by presenting a more diverse range of male characters including 'boys, youths, young men, twenty-somethings, thirty-somethings, older men, sons, fathers, brothers, husbands [and] lovers' (Hobson 2003: 98), or to put it more succinctly, 'every manifestation of the masculine has become a major part of the genre' (ibid.: 98–9). It is not simply that more male characters are seen in the genre, but rather that 'more space and arguably more sympathy' (Geraghty 1991: 6) is given to those men who are presented. Therefore, male characters are no longer mere supporting players, but are viewed as powerful and complex leading protagonists in their own right (Root 1986: 72). As evidence of this shift, it is worth noting that many of today's media and screen studies students seem genuinely bewildered by the idea that soap opera could be thought about as a woman's genre (Gauntlett and Hill 1999: 226).

Furthermore, not only are male characters being seen as complete, fully-rounded figures, but the genre's 'feminine' focus on problem solving and intimate conversations has been supplemented by more 'masculine' plotlines which deal 'more regularly with the public sphere and emphasise the male grip on themes of business and work' (Geraghty 1991: 168). We are told that 'arguments became more violent, rows seemed louder and physical force [is] no longer a rare phenomenon' in the contemporary domestic drama (ibid.: 173). And it is precisely this combination of male characters and traditionally masculine narratives that is said to be bringing a new male audience to this long-running genre. Therefore, although the male audience and advertisers were 'traditionally suspicious of the genre' (Buckingham 1987: 16), both are now turning to the soaps (Hobson cited in Brunsdon 2000: 127). And yet, although many of today's soap operas are keen to include all manner of kidnappings, car chases and violent beatings in order to appeal to the male audience (Hobson 2003: 138–9), it is not necessary to condemn the genre for exploiting such seemingly patriarchal plotlines. After all, active and aggressive narratives can be used to show the male protagonist working through marital concerns, challenges to family loyalties and the pressures of male friendship. Indeed, Christine Gledhill makes the point that masculine action tends to represent 'unexpressed and often unexpressible male emotion, which needs a melodramatic climax to break out' (Gledhill 1997: 380). Therefore, the most dramatic transformation in the soap opera is not necessarily the inclusion of masculine storylines *per se*, but rather the challenge to hegemonic masculinity that arises from seeing men express (albeit in a somewhat spectacular manner) their innermost thoughts and feelings.

Talking men

Although I have suggested that men have been seen to express their thoughts through action and aggression in the contemporary soap, Dorothy Hobson goes a stage further by suggesting that men have actually started talking to one another in the genre, and 'not just talking in a socially expected sense, but having conversations with each other. Talking about their *feelings*' (Hobson 2003: 99). However, although Hobson is keen to suggest that 'men moved into the position of being characters who are involved in sharing their emotions with other men' (ibid.: 100), there are still many examples of men's inability to talk and of men's awkwardness in sharing confidences in the domestic drama.

For example, when Grayson Sinclair/Christopher Villiers finds out about Perdita Hyde-Sinclair/Georgia Slowe's fifth consecutive miscarriage, he tries to reassure his wife that children are not as important to him as she is. However, rather than speak from the heart about this tragic event, Grayson jokes that her miscarriage is not a problem because she was the best wife that he could get at short notice on his budget. And when she scolds him for his total lack of sensitivity, he comments that 'I'm not very good at this sort of thing, I usually have a vet to look after the animals' (*Emmerdale* 18/09/2006: ITV1). When Violet Wilson/Jenny Platt tells her friend Sean Tully/Antony Cotton that she is worried about her relationship with Jamie Baldwin/Rupert Hill, she asks him to talk to her boyfriend and find out if he wants to end their liaison. However, when Violet says 'when you're out tonight, will you talk to Jamie?', Sean's quick response is 'well I was going to communicate by smoke signals'. When she asks again for him to 'really talk' to her boyfriend, Sean cannot help but comment that 'blokes don't talk' and reminds her that meaningful conversations should be left to girlfriends, wives and mothers. However, Sean feels so guilty about letting his friend down that after several drinks with Jamie, he finds the courage to communicate with him about his relationship with Violet, however, after Sean warns him that 'we're going to get to the bottom of this, even if it takes all night' we cut to a sleeping Jamie, unable and unwilling to share an intimate conversation with his closest male friend (*Coronation Street* 22/09/2006: ITV1).

Likewise, when Billy Mitchell/Perry Fenwick finds out that his newborn baby daughter is suffering from Down's Syndrome, he finds himself unable to speak to his wife, his male friends or even his extended family about his heartache. The character finds himself struggling to support his family either financially or emotionally, but rather than admit to this or try to seek help, he simply puts on a brave face as he visits mother and baby in hospital, before finding himself confused and alone on a London underground train. When the train hits a small delay, Billy finds himself pacing the carriageway, snarling at strangers and talking to himself in a way that starts to alarm the other passengers. When a man sitting opposite politely asks him to 'sit down and read the paper mate', Billy explodes with rage and challenges the stranger to a fight. If one remembers that masculine narratives are said to appeal to the male audience, one might expect to see an aggressive altercation between the two men. However, rather than turn the aggressive dialogue into a violent brawl, the heated exchange actually morphs into a heartfelt sequence wherein Billy reveals his distress at his baby's disability and the stranger in question confesses his pain after the sudden death of his sister-in-law. The scene sees both men at their most aggressive, and their most vulnerable, with both shedding tears of grief and sorrow before shaking hands and going their separate ways. And yet, however moving this scene appears to be, it simply demonstrates Billy's inability to talk openly and honestly with his own friends and family about his feelings, and points to his inability to separate such intimate talk from physical aggression (*EastEnders* 17/09/2006: BBC1).

The aforementioned sequences suggest that men make a conscious effort to avoid intimate conversations, and as such, one might look to challenge the genre for its presentation of stereotypically taciturn masculinity. However, that said, there are a number of researchers who tell us that men and women have different biological brain structures and it is these differences which form different patterns of communication. For example, developmental psychopathologist Simon Baron-Cohen suggests that the 'natural wiring' of the female brain demands a capacity for empathy and emotion, whereas the 'natural wiring' of the male demands an interest in systems and in how things work (Baron-Cohen cited in Cohen 2004: 2). We are told that the separation in the male brain of language function in the left hemisphere and emotional activity in the right could explain men's inability to express their inner emotions. After all, according to such research, the female brain has the advantage of emotion in both hemispheres which suggests that women enjoy more connections between language and emotion. In fact, Baron-Cohen goes as far as to suggest that autism (a disorder in which sufferers demonstrate an indifference to other people and a profound difficulty with communication) is simply an 'extreme version' of the male brain (ibid.: 3). Likewise, neuropsychiatrist Dr Louann Brizendine has pointed to profound differences in male and female communication patterns, informing us that a woman uses about 20,000 words a day due to the fact that talking actually activates the pleasure centres in a woman's brain whereas men use only 7,000 because they are programmed to be laconic (Brizendine cited in Newland 2006: 33). The point here is that if a woman's brain has unique chemical and structural characteristics that underpin traits such as compassion, empathy and loquaciousness, then one might have to consider the possibility that the modern male is struggling to be caring and empathetic because he is 'hard-wired' to be emotionally reserved and uncommunicative (ibid.: 32). Commenting on Brizendine's work, Martin Newland notes that 'women have an eight-lane super-highway for processing emotion while men have a small country road' (ibid.: 33) and that 'thanks to the unique chemical make-up of her brain, a woman tends to know better what others are feeling, while a man can't spot an emotion unless someone actually cries or threatens him' (ibid.: 33).

However, although developmental psychopathologists and neuropsychiatrists are continuing to explore essentialist notions of gender identity, decades of feminist scholarship has critiqued such work, concluding that gender is a social construction and that sex roles are learnt, acquired and internalised. After all, feminist thinkers routinely tell us that the brain is the most androgynous of organs, and that men and women possess interchangeable emotional, intellectual and psychological traits, so that any conversational differences between the two is simply a matter of sex role stereotyping and cultural conditioning (Cashmore 2005: 162). Indeed, we are told that 'men are socialized to be ambitious competitors, estranged from their feelings and their needs for intimacy, while women are socialized to maximize their empathy and minimize their aggressive autonomy' (Leverenz 1986: 457). Therefore, although a wide range of feminist critics and social scientists might point to significant differences between male and female communication patterns, they tend to find that 'the differences are due, not to brain organization, but to cultural determinants . . . influenced by the different expectations people have about males and females' (Cashmore 2005: 162). Fischer and Manstead make it clear that although women experience emotions more intensely than their male counterparts, and express these emotions more overtly than the male 'these gender differences were directly caused by sex-role socialization' (Fischer and Manstead cited in Walton, Coyle and Lyons 2004: 402). To put it more succinctly then 'the reason why men and women are not equal is *not* because they are different biologically, but because they are treated differently' (Cashmore 2005: 162). Moreover, recent research offers a significant challenge to those who continue to talk about gendered communications because such work refutes the notion that women are more verbal than men. For example, Janet Hyde informs us that 'women don't interrupt more than men, nor are they more talkative or empathetic in conversation . . . or any better or worse at verbal reasoning', concluding that any difference in language use between men and women is statistically negligible (Hyde cited in Herbert 2007: 40). Hyde informs us that there is little distinction between male and female talk, and as such, any evidence of differences between the two must be related to environmental or societal rather than biological or physical causes.

However, although the men of soap opera appear uncomfortable when talking about their emotions and ill at ease when revealing their vulnerabilities and disappointments to other men, the very fact that the central male protagonists are trying to convey their intimate thoughts and feelings goes some way towards negotiating existing cultural stereotypes and breaking down longstanding distinctions concerning male and female communications. Audiences and advertisers alike might be seen to respond to such awkward images of the male in the domestic drama as a generation of men struggle to challenge earlier sex role stereotyping and negotiate the emotional reserve of the hegemonic male.

PUBLIC AND PRIVATE MEN

Soap opera can be seen to challenge the power of hegemonic masculinity by encouraging men to talk to other men, and in this same way, the genre can be seen to negotiate this hierarchic model of the male by blurring the boundaries between the public sphere and the domestic realm. After all, even though society has long been 'accustomed to the gendering of the public and private spheres – of men earning their reputation and deriving their self-esteem from the public, of women confined and assessed within the private' (Clare 2001: 129), soap opera struggles to distinguish such traditionally gendered spaces. Many of the genres most dramatic moments occur when seemingly private moments, such as an extramarital affair or family feud are played out in public. Those characters who are seen working in the drama tend to work in the domestic or service industries (be it pubs, market stalls, launderettes, hair salons, nail bars or nightclubs), where they are regularly seen in conversation with both work colleagues and other friends and family members. The point here is simply that the line between the 'working' public space and the 'domestic' private space has become obscured in the genre and 'even more permeable' in the wider social context (Hanke 1998: 79).

For example, when we see Grayson and Perdita discussing their potentially serious financial concerns, this conversation is carried over from their shared family home to the local pub, the Woolpack. And even though the pair are heard commenting that both their marital and financial affairs should be kept quiet to save any social embarrassment, they continue to discuss these matters in the full view (and earshot) of the wider community (*Emmerdale* 26/09/2006: ITV1). Likewise, when Violet and Sean are seen sharing a private conversation about sex and relationships over drinks in the Rovers Return Inn, we see the pair finish their drinks, walk behind the bar and take up their positions as part-time bar staff. And although the friends have moved from paying customers to paid employees, their private conversation continues, without the use of either hushed voices or cryptic codes here (*Coronation Street* 22/09/2006: ITV1). Christine Geraghty comments that 'soaps find it virtually impossible to use work settings which deny or suppress the emotional needs of individual characters or locations in which conversations cannot take place', and the fact that Violet and Sean have managed to 'colonise the public sphere and claim it for the personal' (Geraghty 1991: 53) is testament to her claim. Furthermore, while Stacey Slater/Lacey Turner and Ruby Allen/Louisa Lytton share breakfast in the extended Slater household, they reveal their private feelings about their current relationships with Bradley Branning/Charlie Clements and Sean Slater/Robert Kazinsky respectively. We see these young women talking in the comfort and privacy of their own home, and as such, we can understand why they are willing to talk about such personal issues as pregnancy and abortion. However, although one might expect such intimate conversations to stay within the confines of the safe domestic sphere, their intimate conversation actually continues when the friends go to work, setting up a clothes stall on the bustling Walford market. When friends and customers appear on the scene, they are simply encouraged to join in this most personal of conversations (*EastEnders* 18/09/2006: BBC1).

Soap opera characters tend to conduct their most private and intimate conversations in a wide range of communal locations, and as such, there is little privacy for the men and women of the genre (Mumford 1995: 52). Indeed, it is this lack of privacy that leads existing theorists to conclude that these programmes are redefining the boundaries between public and private locations. In short, 'there is no "private" sphere in the soap opera community because there is no privacy' (ibid.: 49). While the genre clearly brings personal relationships into the public or work arena (Geraghty 1991: 54), it can also be seen to deal with working relationships as if they were personal.

Because the owners of the Woolpack are sisters and sparring partners, the lines between family disputes and business differences become blurred, with an innocent enough question about a wine order resulting in a screaming argument about their teen experiences in front of a busy bar room (*Emmerdale* 26/09/2006: ITV1). Likewise, the bar staff in the Rovers Return Inn are treated as family, sharing confidences with one another, and helping the employers out at a moment's notice as if 'for a friend' (*Coronation Street* 26/09/2006: ITV1). Likewise, when we see Jake Moon/Joel Beckett take over the running of the Scarlet nightclub, he combines his role as manager with that of unofficial guardian of the teenage Ruby, the owner's daughter, so that discussions about hiring and firing staff routinely end up being about the suitability of current or future boyfriends for the young woman (*EastEnders* 17/09/2006: BBC1).

Coronation Street offers one of the most explicit examples of the blurring of the public/private sphere and of working/personal relationships in a recent storyline that draws on both the business world and the domestic arena. When Danny Baldwin/Bradley Walsh returns from holiday to find that he has a new business partner in the shape of Liam Connor/Rob Collier, his barely concealed irritation is compounded when he discovers that Liam is dating Frankie Baldwin/Debra Stephenson, his ex-wife. Danny continues to have strong feelings for Frankie, however, rather than actually reveal his true emotions, he makes it his business to interfere in her new relationship, in both the public and private sphere. For example, when Frankie and Liam go on a quiet date in the local pub, deliberately away from friends and work colleagues, it is not long before they are rudely interrupted. While the new couple are discussing the pros and cons of a trip to the cinema, Danny walks over to their table and, without being invited, joins in their conversation. Danny then offers to buy 'the two lovebirds a drink', to which Liam comments 'if I was you Danny, I'd be too scared to make this lovely gesture . . . I mean I'd worry about looking weak or as if I felt threatened or something like that, but if it's not a problem for you . . .'. Danny then comments that it is 'not a problem for me sunshine' before ordering the beverages (*Coronation Street* 25/09/2006: ITV1). The ensuing banter makes it clear that Danny is distressed at seeing his ex-wife with a new, attractive and younger partner, while Liam seems genuinely concerned about upsetting his new employer. However, rather than deal with these issues in a suitably private space, these business partners only make it as far as the busy office before confronting such concerns. And even then when the men do manage to talk about their 'complicated' situation, it has to begin as a work-based discussion concerning who 'puts the hours in' before leading onto the more personal issue of their mutual feelings for Frankie. These men do not dwell on the potential seriousness of the emotional entanglements here, but instead turn the conversation into a scene of sexual oneupmanship with Danny telling Liam that he must feel 'like George Lazenby in the company of Sean Connery' to which the younger man replies 'well the age thing is a factor yeah but I suppose I'd be more like the new one, Daniel Craig' (*Coronation Street* 25/09/2006: ITV1). Both men resort to adolescent insults over age, impotency and mastery, and as such, it is clear that they each fear being dominated by a stronger man and forced to relinquish their position in the hierarchy of masculinity. However, what is even more interesting here is the fact that this sequence, like many work-related scenes in the genre, supports Christine Geraghty's claim that public power relations are 'either ignored altogether or translated into personal relationships' in the prime-time soap opera (Geraghty 1991: 56).

Although such scenes might be seen as a way of maintaining the genre's 'femininity' by having work and business-based storylines played out in terms of personal conflict between families, friends and lovers (MacKinnon 2003: 69), such scenes could also convincingly demonstrate the ways in which the male is seeking to take over the private sphere. Therefore, although the genre's 'intermingling of work and family relationships could lead to women taking on a greater role at work than might have been expected because they carry into the public world the skills they use in the personal sphere' (Geraghty 1991: 62–3), the aforementioned sequence reverses this position so that men are seen to take over the private arena, insisting that because the personal and the public sphere are so closely linked, those actions that are acceptable in one arena are equally as appropriate in another (ibid.: 63).

FATHERHOOD AND PATERNITY

The ways in which the male characters deal with working relationships as if they were personal might be seen to demonstrate the ways in which the male is vying to take control of the private sphere. And, as further evidence of the male's growing power in this domestic arena, it is relevant to look at the genre's representation of men as fathers. After all, although the genre routinely depicts the financial and emotional stories of lonely single mothers, soap operas are also keen to depict the trials and tribulations of the single father, be it Tom King/ Kenneth Farrington after the death of his wife years previously (*Emmerdale* 19/09/2006: ITV1), Ashley Peacock/Steven Arnold after his wife is put in a psychiatric ward for postnatal depression (*Coronation Street* 17/09/2006: ITV1) or Billy Mitchell after his wife refuses to see their Down's Syndrome daughter (*EastEnders* 16/09/2006: BBC1). Therefore, when we hear Carl King/Tom Lister tell his on-off girlfriend that his father is

> the man who gave me everything . . . after my mum died . . . he was the one who sat on my bed after I'd had a rough day at school, or when my marriage broke up and I lost my kids, he was the one who tried to make things better when I cried like a baby.
>
> (*Emmerdale* 19/09/2006: ITV1)

Such scenes demonstrate the significance of 'relationships between fathers and their children' in the domestic drama (Hobson 2003: 138). Even though the single father is sometimes seen to be 'uneasy in handling personal relationships, somewhat baffled by his children's needs, and confused about how to handle his own role' (Geraghty 1995: 79), the fact remains that even if he struggles to bring up his children, he is at least ostensibly in control of the private, domestic sphere.

However, rather than take the representation of such fathers as evidence of the genre's commitment to the male as homemaker, it is worth noting that the ways in which the soap opera draws on issues of paternity can be seen to challenge the importance of the fatherly role. After all, Laura Stempel Mumford comments that 'the attribution of paternity is something of an obsession' in the genre (Mumford 1995: 94). The theorist comments that the 'prominence of storylines involving secrets or mistakes over paternity, and the importance characters attach to discovering who has fathered a particular child' are evidence of the fact that paternity is a defining characteristic of the soap opera (Mumford 1995: 94). And one only has to think of such recent storylines as Cain Dingle/Jeff Hordley discovering that he is the biological father of teen tearaway Debbie Jones/Charlie Webb (*Emmerdale* ITV1), cheating Charlie Stubbs/Bill Ward finding out that he is the true father of Shelley Unwin/Sally Lindsay's unborn baby (*Coronation Street* ITV1) and Zoe Slater/Michelle Ryan finding out that the man that she has been calling her dad for over a decade is in fact her uncle (*EastEnders* BBC1); to realise that 'if it is possible to describe soap operas as being "about" any one thing, they are about paternity' (ibid.: 94).

The genre's commitment to issues of paternity can be understood as one more way in which the contemporary soap opera is challenging 'traditional definitions of masculinity' (Buckingham 1987: 111), and as one more way in which the genre has 'tried to be socially responsible and dramatically relevant by addressing social concerns of the day' (Anger 1999: 126). After all, while Robin Baker informs us that 10 per cent of the British population are not genetically related to the men they grew up calling father (Baker 2008: online), Jeanette Papp tells us that the figure for the Western World is nearer 15 per cent (Papp 2008: online). Moreover, even though 'elaborate legal, social and religious barriers have been raised in an attempt to ensure the "fact" of paternity . . . the very existence of these regulations only serves to underline the profound anxiety that surrounds the issue' (Mumford 1995: 96).

Such questions of paternity position the female character in a position of control in the soap opera genre, because only she has 'the power to name, or to misname the father' (Mumford 1995: 111). And therefore only she has the power to control the inheritance of status, property and businesses. However, it is worth noting that although the paternity mystery may threaten to destroy those families involved, more often than not, the familial disruptions are only temporary, and the paternity mystery actually goes towards reinforcing family networks, thus re-establishing male potency and male power over the domestic arena (ibid.: 98). Therefore, even though Rodney Blackstock/Patrick Mower was originally horrified and unable to cope with the discovery of his gay son Paul Lambert/Matthew Bose, recent episodes have shown the two men bonding in both the domestic and business arena (*Emmerdale* ITV1). Likewise, when Fred Elliott/John Savident discovered that Ashley, the young man he thought to be his nephew was in fact his biological son, he actually moved in with the man in question in order to encourage father–son bonding (*Coronation Street* ITV1). When Ian Beale/Adam Woodyatt discovered that it was he and not his friend Garry Hobbs/Ricky Groves who was the biological father of baby Bobby, the man was happy to bring his new-found son into the family home (*EastEnders* BBC1). Therefore, if one agrees with Anthony Clare that men earn their reputations and derive their self-esteem from both the public and private world, as both breadwinner and master of their own house, then the fact that the majority of paternity mysteries in the soap opera end in the reconciliation of the father and child is important here (Clare 2001: 129).

PATRIARCHAL SOAPS

Although British and American soap operas share formal and thematic elements such as an open-ended narrative and the focus on family life, there are clear distinctions between the two. Indeed, one might even go as far as to suggest that the changes that have appeared in prime-time British soap opera since the late 1980s and early 1990s have long been part of the American prime-time genre. For example, although much writing on British soap opera has tended to focus on the role of the matriarch and the strong woman, these features can be seen to contrast with those prime-time American soaps that appear dominated by patriarchal authority. Tamar Liebes and Sonia Livingstone foreground the rule of the father in the genre by telling us that 'there is a mutual invasion' of the domestic and business world in the American soap opera 'so that each is used for gaining points in the other' (Liebes and Livingstone 1998: 11). We are informed that programmes such as *Dallas* (1978–91), *Dynasty* (1981–9) and their respective spin-off series *Knots Landing* (1979–93) and *The Colbys* (1985–7) routinely focused on a central male protagonist as the head of an extended family and business empire, be it John Ross Ewing Jr/Larry Hagman, Blake Carrington/John Forsythe, Gary Ewing/Ted Shackelford or Jeff Colby/John James, and that such men were in a continual struggle to keep control over both their family affairs and business matters. From this perspective, the male hero is engaged 'in a continual struggle to keep control over the family, to bar entrance to unsuitable entrants and keep inside the family space those who belong there through birth or marriage' (Geraghty 1991: 69). However, rather than separate this family figure head from the business world, we are told that the male soap hero is turned into a 'single entity in which the separate spaces of home and office are merged' (ibid.: 65). Although we see the patriarchal American soap hero fighting to assert control, the genre makes it clear that he must fail to reach absolute power in both the domestic and working sphere, with either a business attack challenging domestic harmony or vice versa (ibid.: 63). Domestic harmony challenges business success and an 'attack' to the business world can endanger the domestic arena.

With this in mind, the contemporary British soap opera can be seen to be borrowing from earlier American productions. After all, when Tom King was recently kidnapped and held to ransom by the callous Sadie King/Patsy Kensit and murderous Cain Dingle, this patriarch tells his sons not to part with the ransom money, because he would rather die than jeopardise the family business. However, when youngest son Carl pays the kidnappers to ensure his father's safe return, instead of thanks, his father and elder brother deride his actions and blame him for putting their hard-earned business in peril (*Emmerdale* 19/09/2006: ITV1). Likewise, when we see that Danny's business with his new partner and his relationship with his ex-wife are both a success, the conventions of the genre make it clear that either the business or the new romance must be tested, and in this case the test comes in the shape of an affair between Frankie and Danny's biological son (*Coronation Street* 20/10/2006: ITV1). In this same way, Ian Beale can be seen as either successful local businessman or caring husband, but the man cannot be seen as both simultaneously. Therefore, because his recent business ventures (as owner of both the local café and chip shop) are considered a relative success, his relationship must be seen to be challenged, in this case by the revelation of his wife Jane Collins/Laura

Brett's infidelity (*EastEnders* 5/10/2006: BBC1). *Emmerdale, Coronation Street* and *EastEnders*, like their earlier American counterparts, appear concerned with representing 'the precariousness of patriarchal power' (Geraghty 1991: 163), and as such, one might suggest that they are once again positioning soap opera as a woman's genre.

Conclusion

This chapter has briefly outlined the ways in which the British and American soap opera share similar formal and thematic elements, the ways in which the British daytime and prime-time soaps have a long history as a woman's genre and the ways in which the contemporary dramas have been revised and updated in order to appeal to the male in the audience. The chapter pays particular attention to the increase in rounded male characters, the blurring of the personal and private sphere, the dominance of paternity mysteries and the negotiation of patriarchal authority that has long existed in the American prime-time soaps. However, the changes in the British soaps should not simply be seen as one more example of the Americanisation of popular culture, but rather as a 'way of taking a health check' on male–female relationships, male friendship, fatherhood and financial concerns in contemporary British society (Salmon cited in Hobson 2003: 50).

3. SITUATION COMEDY:
HOMOSEXUALITY AND MALE
CAMARADERIE

INTRODUCTION

Situation comedies have been categorised as those humorous classical narrative shows that use regular characters, a routine setting and variations of the same plot over, over and over again. Such shows were first heard on American radio in the 1920s, and the genre remained popular with audiences when it transferred to the small screen in the late 1940s and early 1950s. In fact, the genre has lost little of its appeal over the intervening years, with sitcom continuing to dominate the contemporary television schedules (Mills 2005: 57).Throughout the genre's long history, the sitcom has tended to focus on both the home-based drama of family comportment in shows such as *My Family* (2000–) and the workplace drama of sexual exploration in programmes such as *Scrubs* (2001–), with recent shows such as *Joey* (2004–6) looking to combine the couch-centric family with the flirt-centric concerns of the workplace (Hartley 2002: 67). After all, family and home, work and authority 'are common areas of experience and most people are able to recognize the humour that results in friction between people forced to live or work together' (McQueen 1998: 58). Indeed, it is because of the genre's focus on relationships in the home, the workplace and the community that the sitcom tends to be 'examined for the way it reflects changes within society' (Mills 2005: 8).

This chapter will briefly outline the history of the situation comedy before considering the ways in which the genre has been seen to comment on a range of social and sexual concerns from the 1920s to the present day, paying particular attention to the representation of the male in contemporary comedy programming. Even though extant research suggests that heterosexual relationships are at the core of this particular genre, this chapter will examine programmes such as *Friends, Coupling* and *Will & Grace* in order to suggest that the representation of male friendship, homosociality and homosexuality are as important, if not more important than heterosexual relations in the contemporary sitcom. It is worth noting that even though the sitcom has a long and successful history on British television, the genre's prevalence on American screens far outweighs that of its British counterpart (Mills 2005: 57), and as such, this chapter will be examining a number of long-running American programmes that have been imported to and proved popular with the British audience. This is not to say that programmes such as *Butterflies* (1978–83) are not fascinating for their commentary on appropriate sex and gender roles for women (Andrews 1998: 50–64), or that shows such as *Steptoe and Son* (1962–74) or *Men Behaving Badly* (1992–9) are not relevant for their depiction of a particular version of misbehaving masculinity (McQueen 1998: 59), but simply that the popularity of contemporary American sitcom dominates on both sides of the Atlantic.

HISTORY OF THE GENRE

The sitcom was first heard on American radio in the mid-1920s, with programmes such as *Sam and Henry* (1926–7) and *Amos & Andy* (1928–43), and the format remained a staple on US radio in the 1930s and 1940s with shows such as *The Aldrich Family* (1939–53), *Blondie* (1939–50) and *The Life of Riley* (1944–51). The format remained popular with the American public in the late 1940s and early 1950s when it transferred from radio to television. Television sitcoms such as *The Goldbergs* (1949–55), *Mama* (1949–56) and *Beulah* (1950–3) were keen to present examples of urban, ethnic and working-class families dealing with life in America (Morreale 2003: 2–3). However, by the mid-1950s and 1960s, programmes such as *The Donna Reed Show* (1958–66), *The Dick Van Dyke Show* (1961–6) and *Bewitched* (1964–72) were more concerned with the representation of married life in the idealised middle-class suburbs, with *I Love Lucy* (1951–7) providing a clear transition between the ethnic and domestic context here (ibid.: 4). Although this 'Hi Honey I'm Home' format continued to be popular throughout the 1960s, shows such as *My Three Sons* (1960–72) and *The Andy Griffith Show* (1960–8) modified the format by focusing upon the everyday situations of a widowed father struggling to raise his children (ibid.: 87).

However, it was not until the 1970s that the genre could be read as 'socially relevant programming that addressed contemporary issues and concerns' (Morreale 2003: 151). After all, while *The Mary Tyler Moore Show* (1970–7) advocated the politics of liberal feminism by featuring a professional single woman both in and beyond the home, *All in the Family* (1971–83) showcased a range of previously taboo issues such as death and alcoholism, rape and menopause for the viewing public. Likewise, *Maude* (1972–8) dared to feature such controversial topics as divorce and abortion, and acknowledged that single-parent families had become commonplace in society (ibid.: 152).

Although the 1980s saw a number of offbeat, dysfunctional and irresponsible families in shows such as *Mama's Family* (1983–90), *Roseanne* (1988–97), and *Married . . . with Children* (1987–97), we are told that these programmes were not trying to debunk traditional family values so much as 'desperately trying to hold on to them under a tidal wave of societal change' (Crotty 1995: 10). In this way, the comedy of anger, insult and outrage was being used not to attack the family *per se*, but rather to challenge 'TV's sentimentalized portrayal of it' (Zoglin 1992: 33).

The 1990s saw the genre redefine friendship as the new pseudo- or quasi-family unit in such popular programmes as *Seinfeld* (1990–8), *Friends* and *Spin City* (1996–2002). And yet, perhaps more importantly for the sake of this particular chapter, the 1990s also saw the emergence of what Stephen Tropiano refers to as the 'gaycom' (Tropiano 2002: 245), with programmes such as *Ellen* (1994–8), *Will & Grace* and *Normal, Ohio* (2000–1) featuring gay characters in conventional situation comedy spaces. And although there are clear distinctions between the sitcom and the gaycom here, what the programmes have in common is their desire to reach the sophisticated, twenty- to thirty-something viewers with their representations of 'young . . . unmarried, urban and upscale characters' (Morreale 2003: 248).

With this short history in mind, the sitcom must be credited with mediating historical change due to the fact that the genre has presented such ideologically contentious themes as alternative families, race relations, gender roles and sex and sexuality, albeit in a safe and familiar popular television format. While Paul Wells tells us that the sitcom has managed to 'smuggle' in challenging ideas under the guise of humour (Wells 1998b: 181), Darrell Hamamoto goes further to suggest that the situation comedy has 'offered oppositional ideas, depicted oppression and struggle, and reflected a critical consciousness that stops just short of political mobilization' (Hamamoto 1989: 2).

MEN, MASCULINITY AND HOMOSOCIALITY

According to Karen Walker, the dominant cultural ideology about friendship informs us that 'women are more intimate and talk in their friendships, whereas men engage in activities and do not share feelings' (Walker 1994: 252). Therefore, we are told that 'it becomes important for men to be able to go out or do things with each other, go to the pub or go fishing together' in order for men to feel a sense of loyalty or camaraderie with other men (Seidler 1992: 22). However, rather than see such activities as sites of male intimacy or nurturing, it is worth noting that 'the male bonding that reportedly occurs in the pub, on the sports field and terraces, in clubs and in the workplace' (Clare 2001: 87) and the 'mixture of drinking, brawling, bravado, sexual posturing and social misbehaving in which young men indulge and find friendship and affection' (ibid.: 87) are all devoid of any real intimacy. Even though these activities encourage men to spend time in male company, they do not encourage men to let down their 'emotional barriers' and express their 'innermost thoughts and feelings' (ibid.: 87).

Men are not encouraged to develop close friendships with other men because of the hegemonic hierarchy which demands that they 'can and should be self-sufficient' (Bentall 2004: 5). The point here is that if men are to develop in-depth male friendships they would have to 'risk rejection and vulnerability by opening up to friends and by expressing emotions and feelings' which they are, society tells us, ill-equipped to do (Nardi 1992: 7). Therefore, men are seen to avoid close male friendships in order to avoid any 'threats to self-sufficiency, self-esteem, and independence' that come with such networks (ibid.: 7). In fact, we are told that men are only ready to share themselves in the most 'desperate or extreme situations' (Seidler 1992: 21). David Bentall makes this point when he tells us that contemporary men are raised to believe the myth that 'security is not found in close relationships, but in solitude' (Bentall 2004: 8) and that because of this 'men purposefully work to distance themselves from their emotional needs, as those around them frown on any who would dare to admit a need for support' (ibid.: 8). Hence, it is easier for men to have friendships if they hide their social, familial and sexual problems from other men:

> [A]fter all, our closest friends need never know about the difficult issues that inevitably occur in all our lives. At the office, we talk about the weather, the stock market, or who's going to win the playoffs. We all know that life is more than raindrops, bank accounts, and championships – yet even friends struggle to get past this basic level of communication.
>
> (Bentall 2004: 68)

Irrespective of whether one agrees with the feminist critics or the developmental psychopathologists, men are said to be unable to develop close friendships with other men because they are, or at least present themselves to be 'inexpressive, rational and competitive' creatures (Cohen 1992: 115), devoid of those caring and nurturing characteristics that enable women to articulate their feelings. We are told that competition is 'the mark of most male relationships' in business, sport, academic life, romance and other social situations (Clare 2001: 205) and that all male friendships are based on 'unspoken relationships of power and subordination' (Seidler 1992: 29). Existing work goes as far as suggesting that men can make an effort to improve their position in masculine social hierarchies by using such 'markers of manhood' as occupational achievement, wealth, power, status, physical prowess and sexual success with women (Kimmel 2004: 186). It is soon evident that 'men's lives are highly organised by relations *between men*' (Flood 2003: 2) and that macho bravado is performed for the approval of other males. Michael Kimmel makes this point when he comments that 'other men watch us, rank us [and] grant our acceptance into the realm of manhood' (Kimmel 2004: 186).

Furthermore, existing work on the representation of male friendship on television informs us that 'most entertainment limits friendship to a bunch of guys hanging out together, going to the bar, or watching a game', suggesting that such images fail to depict homosociality as anything other than 'superficial interaction' (Bentall 2004: 4). We are told that the television sitcom shows men as 'lazy and boorish, living to watch the games and trading competitive insults with each other' (ibid.: 5). With this in mind then, the sitcom is said to treat male friendship as facile and superficial, which in turn invites 'society as a whole to give up on the expectation that male friendships can ever be more' than emotionally detached bravado (ibid.: 5).

However, although the case for such facile male friendships appears compelling, it is worth noting that heterosexual men do seem to value such friendships, to the point where they will prioritise homosociality and homosocial bonding, with male friendships taking priority over male–female relations (Flood 2003: 4). Moreover, in 'heterosexual men's sexual cultures, there are a variety of . . . sexual practices which can serve to . . . cement bonds between men' such as watching strip shows and exchanging pornography (ibid.: 8). Although men may not always be comfortable with intimate, nurturing and caring friendships, they do actually have other 'natural tendencies that can help them in pursuing genuine friendship' such as frankness (Bentall 2004: 94). After all, such directness 'may be an advantage in probing beneath the emotional surface, getting issues on the table quickly, and then dealing with them constructively' (ibid.: 94).

FRIENDS AND COUPLING: HOMOSOCIALITY AND HETEROSEXUALITY IN THE STRAIGHT SITUATION COMEDY

This consideration of male friendship as either facile or frank brings me to the representation of homosociality in the contemporary situation comedy. It is my point that although shows such as *Friends* and *Coupling* can be seen to depict men as competitive and emotionless characters who bond over sports, porn and sexual conquests, I would suggest that a more detailed examination of these friendships go beyond 'watching a game, playing golf, or going out for a few drinks' (Bentall 2004: 3). In fact, one might suggest that the contemporary sitcom presents male friends who can talk honestly about their careers, their dreams for the future, or the problems that they currently face in an intimate (albeit humorous) manner.

Friends is the long-running popular American sitcom centred around the lives, loves and occasional occupational concerns of six twenty- to thirty-something friends living in New York, with palaeontologist Ross Geller/David Schwimmer, computer programmer Chandler Bing/Matthew Perry and actor Joey Tribbiani/ Matt Le Blanc as the male leads. Ross and Chandler have been friends since college while Joey becomes Chandler's new roommate at the outset of the first series. The programme can be seen to rely on dominant cultural ideologies about male friendships when an awkward silence between new roommates Chandler and Joey is saved by the appearance of *Baywatch* (1989–2001) on their television set. Although Chandler has never seen the skimpily clad lifeguards in the show before, it only takes a few moments for him to begin admiring the female characters as they run across the sand in their trademark red swimming costumes. Both men immediately find themselves sitting quite comfortably together on the sofa, beer in hand, complimenting the women on screen. In fact, the television drama becomes such an important part of their subsequent male bonding that they set their oven timer to tell them when their favourite programme is on (3:06 'The One with the Flashback'). Furthermore, when Joey moves out of the apartment, an equally awkward phone call between these now best friends is again saved by the oven-timer reminding them that the show is about to begin (2:17 'The One where Eddie Moves in'). However, even though we may applaud these men for their depiction of a developing friendship, one might suggest that these characters bonding over their mutual objectification of women is problematic because such objectification is understood to be not only a superficial take on male relations, but 'the very essence of what hegemonic masculinity means' in society (Bird 1996: 129).

When Ross tells his friends that he is feeling depressed because it is the anniversary of the first time that he and his lesbian ex-wife consummated their relationship, Chandler and Joey arrange to take him to watch a New York Rangers hockey game in Madison Square Garden (1:04 'The One with George Stephanopoulos'). Likewise, when Ross is trying to impress his new partner he agrees to play a game of rugby with some of her old male school friends even though he is ill-equipped to play such a brutal game, simply because he feels that he must prove his manhood in front of such physically powerful men (4:15 'The One with All the Rugby'). When Joey and Chandler are unable to agree on the design of their new dinner table, the room mates decide to forego a traditional piece of kitchen furniture in favour of a foosball table (1:12 'The One with the Dozen Lasagnes'). In this way, the table provides a constant social and sporting activity for the men in the series, an activity which the characters are seen playing throughout the show's long history. In fact the table is a permanent feature of the small apartment until is has to be demolished in the final ever episode, although not before both Joey and Chandler have said their heartfelt goodbyes to the plastic men, telling them that they have given the room mates 'so many great times' (10:18 'The Last One, Part 2'). From this estimation, the programme continues to foreground current cultural stereotypes of men's friendships as being based on shared social activities and the sporting arena rather than any real intimacy and emotion.

However, although the programme is seen to foreground stereotypically sexist and sporting images of male friendship, including predictable male back-slapping (2:16 'The One where Joey Moves Out') and repeated viewings of *Die Hard* (7:06 'The One with the Nap Partners'), the show can also be seen to negotiate such images in favour of male intimacy and genuine friendship here.

Vegard Iglebæk suggests that the relationship between Joey and Chandler can be seen to widen the degrees of acceptable personal disclosure between men by 'representing new ways of men dealing with each other' with emotionality and feeling as the foundation of the relationship (Iglebæk 2000: 2). For example, Chandler and Joey can be seen to hug affectionately more often than they back-slap one another (2:19 'The One where Eddie Won't Go'), Joey, Ross and Chandler actually talk about the importance of their friendship (4:22 'The One with the Worst Best Man Ever') and they even buy each other meaningful presents, be it plastic spoons (2:16 'The One where Joey Moves Out'), gold jewellery (2:14 'The One with the Prom Video'); reclining leather chairs (2:15 'The One where Ross and Rachel . . . You Know') and a pet chick and duck (3:21 'The One with the Chick and a Duck') twice (10:17 'The Last One, Part 1'). The point then is simply that although hugging, sharing intimacies and the 'exchange of gifts reflects a pattern more recognised as central to women's friendships' (Iglebæk 2000: 6), it is precisely these intimate, expressive and emotional acts which provide the basis for the men's friendship in the series. Although I am not suggesting that such socialising represents a radical new form of male friendship, I am suggesting that it represents a progressive representation of heterosexual men's friendships on the small screen. After all, although male relationships are often 'expressed through roughhousing and banter, intimacy kept at bay with male bravado' (MacKinnon 2003: 38), *Friends* can be seen to challenge the strict borders that 'tend to structure much of men's social interaction' (Steinberg, Epstein and Johnson cited in Iglebæk 2000: 7).

And yet, although Joey and Chandler's relationship can be understood as a positive take on dominant cultural ideologies surrounding male friendship, it is necessary to challenge Iglebæk's claim that we are 'witnessing new attempts to expand male, heterosexual behaviour for personal disclosure with other men, without worrying too much about homosexuality' (Iglebæk 2000: 1). After all, *Friends* is peppered with negative gay references, and Joey and Chandler's conversations in particular are littered with subtle homophobic jokes (1:15 'The One with the Stoned Guy'). Indeed, while Joey and Chandler look shocked, hurt and insulted to be mistaken for a gay couple when babysitting for Ross's young son on a city bus (2:06 'The One with the Baby on the Bus'), Ross appears uncomfortable when his son starts playing with his first Barbie doll (3:04 'The One with the Metaphorical Tunnel'). Ross and Chandler look ill at ease when Joey asks them to help him practise for a gay kiss (2:24 'The One with Barry & Mindy's Wedding'), Ross looks awkward when a young male student declares feelings for him (7:18 'The One with Joey's Award') and this same man then refuses to hire a male nanny for his daughter because the 'manny' seemed too in touch with his emotions (9:06 'The One with the Male Nanny'). Therefore, although theorists such as Stephen Tropiano have commented that 'homosexuality is never turned into a joke on *Friends*' (Tropiano 2002: 216), I would suggest that homosexuality is (on occasion) presented for comic value in the series. A brief examination of the only gay male character that appears more than momentarily in the series reveals the way in which the programme reinforces longstanding cultural stereotypes. Steve Zahn plays Duncan, a gay ice-dancer who seems to conform to societal expectations that demand gay men be smart, funny and creative with a penchant for throwing 'great academy award parties' (2:04 'The One with Phoebe's Husband'). However, the fact that this character reveals his latent heterosexuality, commenting that he went to straight bars in college and 'experimented' with women exploits those longstanding negative stereotypes which view homosexuality as nothing more than a passing fad or experimental phase (Gross 2001: 74).

We are told that young men avoid intimacy and close male friendships for fear of being labelled homosexual, by society in general and by other men in particular (MacKinnon 2003: 8). Vito Russo says it best when he says 'now if only people wouldn't assume that all those loving brothers were as queer as three-dollar bills, men could hug without having nightmares' (Russo 1987: 70). Likewise, David Bentall informs us that the one thing that 'keeps men, especially young men, from pursuing in-depth male friendships today is the modern cultural inference that any close male relationship must have a sexual dimension' (Bentall 2004: 8–9). It is the fear of homophobia that has led contemporary young men to deny the importance of male friendships (Lehne 1989: 416–29). Although Chandler, Ross and Joey are less than pleased to be read as homosexual (1:08 'The One where Nana Dies Twice'), they do genuinely care for one another and can be seen to take the necessary time to nurture their friendship. In this way, *Friends* can be seen to present a potentially positive representation of male bonding because these men do not let societal fears of being labelled interrupt or destroy their intimate relationships.

Likewise, *Coupling* (a programme that viewers routinely refer to as a British version of *Friends* and a programme that was subsequently produced in America) is a hybrid sitcom centred on the lives, loves and occasional occupational concerns of six twenty-something friends living in London, with Patrick Maitland/Ben Miles, Steve Taylor/Jack Davenport and Jeff Murdock/Richard Coyle as the central male protagonists of the series. *Coupling*, like *Friends*, can be seen to both challenge and confirm dominant cultural stereotypes concerning contemporary male friendships. After all, although the programme appears dedicated to presenting pornography, lap-dancing and masturbation as sites of male bonding between these central characters (1:01 'Flushed'; 3:01 'Split'; 3:07 'Perhaps, Perhaps, Perhaps'), with Lara Croft's *Tomb Raider* (1996) being presented as a shared sporting activity for the men in the show (3:01 'Spilt'), the programme also depicts these men as close friends, able to converse about such intimate problems as sexual performance anxiety (1:01 'Flushed'), impotence (2:04 'The Melty Man Cometh'), commitment (1:06 'The Cupboard of Patrick's Love') and childbirth (4:06 '9½ Months'), albeit in a humorous fashion. And yet, *Coupling* is keen to remind us that its leading protagonists are heterosexual men, with 'naked women, stockings, lesbians and Sean

Connery dressed as James Bond' acting as 'the four pillars of heterosexual society' throughout the show's brief history (1:04 'Inferno'). The male characters are heard commenting that 'we are men . . . we have only one word for soap, we don't own candles, we have never seen anything of any value in a craft shop . . . we do not even know what . . . pot pourri is' (3:06 'The Girl with One Heart'). Therefore it is clear that the programme is setting up distinctions between the heterosexual and his gay male counterpart, with sexual activity and physicality defining the former, and stereotypically 'sissy, untough, uncool' images defining the latter (Leverenz 1986: 455). Likewise, when Patrick comments that 'I'm 33, single, with neat hair . . . even I think I'm gay' (2:07 'Dressed'), the character can be seen to foreground the unconscious weight of a culture that has made the homosexual synonymous with the well-groomed man in contemporary culture, based on the presupposition that an 'overt interest in clothing implie[s] a tendency towards unmanliness and effeminacy' (Breward 1995: 171). This man appears distraught when his new 'hard man' haircut is mistaken for a 'gay cut' (1:04 'Inferno') and both Geoff and Patrick look inconsolable when they realise that a threesome could possibly involve two men (2:05 'Jane and the Truth Snake'). From this estimation, *Coupling*, like the long-running *Friends* is committed to presenting intimate and nurturing male friendships, while presenting 'a clear dividing line . . . separating homosocial (platonic) bonding and male homosexual relationships' (Tropiano 2002: 194).

Although 'straight' sitcoms such as *Friends* and *Coupling* can be seen to depict potentially positive representations of male relations and intimate male friendships, these shows have not actually scripted a central gay protagonist into the programme and therefore have not been seen to depict representations of homosociality between gay male characters. Furthermore, if one considers that the ways in which representations of gay men on television can and do 'impact on personal and social perceptions' of homosexuality (Cowan and Valentine 2006: 15), then it is important to look at the representation of masculinity and male friendship in those contemporary texts with gay male friendships at the core of the narrative. With this in mind, this chapter will now look at the ways in which the long-running *Will & Grace* represented gay male friendships to a majority straight audience.

WILL & GRACE: HOMOSOCIALITY IN THE GAYCOM

Television has tended to represent gay men as limp-wristed sissies or confused and unhappy protagonists, so that their presence on screen is greeted with either 'horror, laughter, pity or disgust from a mainstream heterosexual audience' (Gwenllian Jones 2002: 109). Throughout the 1960s and 1970s 'jokes and derogatory comments about gay men were encouraged as "appropriate" and "entertaining" forms of content' (Hart 2004: 243). However, since the 1980s (due to a heightened awareness of homosexuality following the AIDS epidemic and a recognition of the controversial appeal of gay protagonists) British and

American television has witnessed broader and more positive representations of homosexuality on the small screen, culminating in the success of the gaycom *Will & Grace* (Gwenllian Jones 2002: 109–12).

Will & Grace follows the lives of four close friends loving and occasionally working in sophisticated Manhattan, namely, Grace Adler/Debra Messing, the straight self-employed interior designer; Karen Walker/Megan Mullally, the wealthy married socialite and alcoholic who works for Adler Designs; Will Truman/Eric McCormack, a successful gay male attorney and Jack McFarlane/Sean Hayes, the flamboyantly gay yet routinely unemployed actor/dancer/choreographer. When *Will & Grace* was first aired in the late 1990s, the programme was seen to break new ground due to the fact that it offered the first gay male leads on American broadcast television and because it dared to comment on such social and political issues as anti-gay bullying, civil partnership ceremonies and gay celebrity culture. However, although many television theorists are currently examining the representation of homosociality and homosexuality in the programme, there is little agreement on how the central male protagonists should be read.

Loren Jarvier, a spokesperson for GLAAD (Gay and Lesbian Alliance Against Defamation) has applauded shows such as *Will & Grace*, commenting that 'it's great because television is finally saying "We're not a sideshow. We're just like you. We're your friends and your family. We go to school with you" ' (Jarvier cited in Becker 2004: 397). The point here is that homosexuality is finally visible on our television screens, and such increased visibility can be seen to stand for society's growing acceptance of the gay community (Svetkey 2000: 26). However, while Jarvier and Svetkey read greater visibility as greater social acceptance, it is worth noting that several critics are currently arguing that the 'visibility of gay men and lesbians in the mainstream media is not unproblematic' (Shugart 2003: 69).

Will & Grace makes homosexuality safe for its mainstream audience by presenting such standard sitcom scenarios as 'quirky behaviours, silly misunderstandings [and] embarrassing peccadilloes' (Shugart 2003: 71). Moreover, the programme reinforces existing gay stereotypes due to the fact that it positions gayness in opposition to masculinity. For example, although Will is uninterested in stereotypically heterosexual sporting activities (Battles and Hilton-Morrow 2002: 91) he appears overly concerned with his surface appearance and attractiveness (ibid.: 90). We are told that the programme desexualises Will by routinely failing to present him in romantic encounters or sexual situations, and that those few romantic relationships that are presented in the show are safely situated within the conventions of heterosexual male bonding (ibid.: 91). Likewise, we are informed that the two gay leads spend little time on screen together, and that 'much is made of the fact that Jack and Will find each other repulsive insofar as potential romantic prospects' are concerned (Shugart 2003: 77). Indeed, the character of Jack further reinforces the longstanding and negative link between the gay man and camp performance, with critics reading the character as nothing more than the 'narcissistic, witty, flitty fag next door' (Walters 2001: 108).

However, before critiquing the representation of homosexuality as either asexual or hypersexual in the series, it is worth reminding ourselves of the ways in which the sitcom genre can make potentially controversial issues appealing to the mainstream audience. Therefore, rather than apologise for the fact that *Will & Grace* presents standard sitcom scenarios, it is precisely these situations which allow the programme to present potentially subversive and challenging images of homosexuality. Although the programme is accused of presenting stereotypical images of gay men, it is worth remembering that the show has actually been praised by gay and lesbian groups precisely for its depiction of two different, yet likable gay characters (GLAAD 1998: online). In fact Susan Bordo has gone as far as to suggest that these gay men offer a 'fresh image . . . a glamorous new image of manliness, from the "margins" of masculinity' (Bordo 1999: 26). Although the show has been charged with skirting the 'realities and implications of homosexuality by desexualizing the characters . . . by almost never depicting them in romantic or sexual situations' (Shugart 2003: 69) with 'straitlaced Will as a cop-out, so blandly gay as to seem almost asexual' (Svetkey 2000: 28), it must be remembered that Jack is presented as a sexual omnivore (3:20 'The Young and the Tactless') and Will settles down in a loving, sexual and committed relationship towards the end of the final series (8:23, 8:24 'The Finale'). And although the show is critiqued for the fact that the two leading men do not spend any time together, I would argue that the presentation of male friendship is potentially empowering in the show due to the fact that Will and Jack are not scared to reveal their inner emotions and confide their vulnerabilities to one another. These men are seen to disclose much more freely with one another than they ever do with the female protagonists in the series (Good, Porter and Dillon 2002: 423).

We see Jack help Will to find the courage to come out of the closet (3:08 'Lows in the Mid Eighties, Part 2'), to help him to overcome his fear of school bullies (3:02 'Past and Presents') and to reassure his friend about his future as a parent (3:03 'Husbands and Trophy Wives'). Likewise, we see Will offer Jack accommodation (1:02 'A New Lease of Life'), help him to face up to (and then pay) his debts to the IRS (1:08 'Where There's a Will There's No Way') and reassure him on that rare occasion when he is facing relationship insecurities (8:17 'Cowboys and Iranians'). Furthermore, these two men are seen to talk about the importance of their long friendship (8:07 'Birds of a Feather') which extends beyond any sexual attraction between the pair (1:01 'Pilot'). And although the two men can be seen to make ostensibly cruel jokes about one another throughout the series (7:21 'It's a Dad, Dad, Dad, Dad World'), the fact that they provide emotional and financial support for one another 'means that the humour, within the diegesis, lacks bite' (Mills 2005: 97).

The point here is simply that *Will and Grace* presents gentle and emotional men who connect meaningfully with one another. The programme never resorts to presenting homosexuality and gay life as a temporary interruption in the flow of heterosexual life (Gross 2001: 74). Therefore, by presenting two gay men who are not only comfortable with, but proud of, their sexuality as the central leading protagonists of a prime-time sitcom must be seen as a positive representation. However, that said, positive visibility is not the same as political progress, and the fact that 'more than half of all socially active gays and lesbians have experienced some sort of anti-lesbian and anti-gay violence' is testament to that fact (Dow 2001: 136).

Conclusion

This chapter has briefly outlined the ways in which the situation comedy can be seen to respond to wider sexual and political changes in society, paying particular attention to the representation of male friendships within both the straight sitcom and what has been termed the gaycom. Although I have pointed to the ways in which contemporary American and British sitcoms exploit dominant cultural ideologies regarding male friendship, it is worth noting the ways in which they also depict potentially empowering representations of male bonding and homosociality for the mainstream audience. That said, the fact that the sitcom deals with such standard fare as the politics of the home, the workplace and the family means that the genre rarely 'explores either macro social structures or the relationship between the individual and society as a whole' (Mills 2005: 45). With this in mind, one must acknowledge that the sitcom has routinely reflected rather than actually intervened in implementing social change.

4. ANIMATION: MASCULINITY IN THE NUCLEAR FAMILY

INTRODUCTION

INTRODUCTION

Cartoons can challenge the dominant conventions of mainstream television programming, and as such, the animated sitcom is in an ideal position to present alternative and even subversive representations of family, friendship and masculinity on the small screen. After all, while the traditional domestic sitcom is said to be 'largely limited to projecting a tame, normative, and uncontroversial version of family life' (Palmer-Mehta 2006: 183) 'animation seems to have given television comedy the appropriate mode in which a subversive view of [the] family . . . could be presented' (Tueth 2003: 140). Therefore, this chapter will outline the history of film and television animation before looking at a range of cartoon masculinities in the prime-time cartoon sitcom, paying particular attention to the ways in which contemporary programmes such as *The Simpsons*, *King of the Hill* and *Family Guy* can be seen to confirm or challenge traditional and patriarchal representations of masculinity, paternity and the male role in society.

HISTORY OF THE GENRE

Cartoons such as *Mickey Mouse* (1928–) and *Felix the Cat* (1919–36) were popular with both adult and adolescent cinemagoers in the 1920s, and this seemingly universal appeal continued throughout the 1930s and 1940s when animated shorts were screened alongside major studio film releases. However, after the Paramount Decision in 1948 led to the collapse of the vertically integrated studio system (by demanding that film studios divorce themselves from their movie theatres) film studios were seen to sell off their cartoon libraries to television. And when this new medium decided to show their newly acquired programmes on weekday afternoons (safe in the knowledge that they could entertain large numbers of children returning home from school) animation came to be seen as a children's genre (Felperin 1999: 1... cated cartoon channels such as Cartoon Network and ... established to appeal to this particular demographic, a... genres status as children's television. In fact, it was not unti... development of prime-time (the time-slot between 8.00pm an... 'families' are assumed to be watching television together) ani... toons would once again be viewed as a universal rather tha... medium, and with this in mind, it is worth noting the import... *Flintstones* (1960–6) here.

Prime-time animation began in the early 1960s with *The Flintstones*, a cartoon about modern suburban life set in the Stone Age. The programme challenged the standard codes and conventions of animated programming by drawing on the situation comedy format 'complete with single half-hour narrative episodes, suburban setting, domestic plots, and even a laugh track' (Mittell 2003: 45). Moreover, *The Flintstones'* popularity with the universal, or what has been termed the 'kidult' audience (ibid.: 43) spawned a range of prime-time imitators including *Top Cat* (1961–2), *The Jetsons* (1962–88) and *Jonny Quest* (1964–5). Therefore, rather than continue to position these texts as children's television, it is clear that such shows appealed to a rather more diverse age group. Indeed, while children would tune in for the simplistic humour to be found in the silly images and lurid colours, adults were kept entertained by the more sophisticated verbal jokes that were said to dominate such texts (Farley 2003: 151). Jason Mittell says it best when he comments that the goal of reaching the mixed-age audience was achieved 'not through creating unified cartoons with universal appeals, but by specifically aiming the visuals and "wacky" sound-effects at the "moppets" and the dialogue at adults . . . creating children's visual shows and adult audio shows' (Mittell 2003: 43).

However, after *The Flintstones* came off the air in the mid-1960s (to be sold into syndication and scheduled as children's fare in some eighty-seven countries thereafter), cartoons in general, and the animated sitcom in particular, were not to appear in prime-time schedules until the late 1980s with the premiere of *The Simpsons* on *The Tracey Ullman Show* (1987–90). Even though there is more than two decades separating the two programmes, *The Simpsons* is happy to acknowledge its debt to its prehistoric predecessor in a range of Flintstone-inspired scenarios and Stone Age-inspired sequences (4:01 'Kamp Krusty'; 4:12 'Marge vs. the Monorail'). The success of this particular show led to a resurgence of prime-time animation, with the 1990s witnessing a proliferation of successful television cartoons aimed at the adult audience, or rather what Kevin Donnelly has referred to as 'the juvenile in adults' (Donnelly 2002: 73) such as *King of the Hill, Family Guy, Futurama* (1999–) and *South Park* (1997–).

While shows such as *The Flintstones* 'tossed in sophisticated little rewards for parents who paid attention' to the text (Richmond 1996: 40), programmes such as *The Simpsons* have taken 'the humor of these shows to a new level' (Hilton-Morrow and McMahan 2003: 87) by presenting deliberately adult in the animated text. Therefore, although the prominent producer eph Barbera once commented that animation is a children's medium and that it is 'wrong to introduce adult themes' into the genre (Felperin 1999: 16), it is worth noting that more adults watched the first season of *The Simpsons* than children, 'with viewers aged above 18 constituting nearly 60 percent of the audience' (Hilton-Morrow and McMahan 2003: 81). Due to the genre's risqué and politically incorrect adult humour and the fact that the baby boomers are now seated in prominent network positions, critics and commentators are predicting the continued success of prime-time animation. After all, Eileen Katz, senior vice president of programming for Comedy Central comments that 'the adult audience that was weaned on cartoons and is comfortable with animation is telling us they want a product that just isn't aimed at their kids, and TV is responding' (Richmond 1996: 40).

Therefore, programmes such as *The Simpsons* must be understood as adult entertainment (although the show never fails to please children with its bright colours, comical characters and slapstick antics) due to their biting and often sophisticated satire on contemporary society in general and on popular culture in particular, and it is the animation of such texts that enables them to be more bold and brazen than their live action counterparts. Paul Wells makes this point when he comments that animation 'offers a greater opportunity for film-makers to be more imaginative and less conservative' (Wells 1998a: 6). Likewise, Kevin Sandler finds that 'the animated form, more than live-action, was a safer way to push the envelope of acceptable television fare' (Sandler 2003: 90). And push the envelope they did, as programmes such as *The Simpsons*, *King of the Hill* and *Family Guy* exploited such controversial topics as sex education, corporate capitalism, pop psychology, the health-care system, modern child-rearing, globalisation, commercialism, consumerism, racism, religious intolerance, alcoholism, drug abuse, nuclear power safety, environmentalism, vegetarianism, immigration, violence in children's entertainment, media effects, campaign finance reform, sexism, show business, homophobia, education and changing gender roles. Even though earlier shows such as *The Flintstones* and *The Jetsons* were seen to comment on job pressures for the male breadwinner, poke fun at the institution of marriage and point to the hypocrisies faced by employees in the workplace 'the critical insights on these programs were never as pointed or expository' as those seen in contemporary animation (Mullen 2004: 82).

THE SIMPSONS

The Simpsons began life in the late 1980s as a series of short segments that bridged the commercial breaks on *The Tracey Ullman Show*. Today, *The Simpsons* is not only the longest-running prime-time animated series on American television (beating *The Flintstones'* earlier record back in 1997 on its 167th episode), but also the longest-running situation comedy ever aired. After all, first and foremost, the show is a domestic sitcom that focuses on the trials and tribulations of a working-class nuclear family, or perhaps more accurately, the show is actually a leftist satire upon those idealised images of family life (dependent on the dominant father, submissive mother, obedient children and compulsive heterosexuality) that were routinely depicted in the 'glowingly optimistic and artificial' post-war American sitcom (Gray 2006: 49).

However, while 1950s sitcoms such as *The Adventures of Ozzie and Harriet* (1952–66), *Father Knows Best* (1954–62) and *Leave it to Beaver* (1957–63) were keen to focus on the privileged middle-class nuclear family unit, with the father being presented as 'knowing, correct, and superior to his wife and children' (Henry 2003: 265), those shows that dominated the 1980s were rather more interested in depicting the lives and loves of the working classes. Both *Married . . . with Children* and *Roseanne* depict a fall from grace for the white American patriarch wherein the 'male heads of house were consistently portrayed as dumb but loveable, i.e. they cared about their families but were bumbling, incompetent and often immature, not figures of respect' (Butsch 2003: 21). With this in mind then, it is clear that *The Simpsons*, like *The Flintstones* before it, continues (and potentially transcends) the live-action working-class sitcom format.

In 1997 *The Simpsons* won a Peabody Award (an honour routinely awarded to news journalists and documentary filmmakers) due to the show's 'exceptional animation and stinging social satire, both commodities which are in extremely short supply in television today' (Peabody Committee cited in Turner 2005: 41). The show is so significant to American popular culture that during a 1992 election campaign centred on promoting traditional family values George Bush declared 'we're going to keep on trying to strengthen the American family. To make them more like the Waltons and less like the Simpsons' (Bush cited in Donnelly 2002: 74). Less like *The Simpsons* indeed, a family headed by Homer J. Simpson/Dan Castellaneta, a 36-year-old husband and father-of-three who works as a safety inspector at the Springfield nuclear power plant, Marge/Julie Kavner, the put-upon wife and mother who stays at home to look after her family, son Bart/Nancy Cartwright, the destructive troublemaker and proud underachiever whose mother routinely frisks him for weapons before they leave for church, eldest daughter Lisa/Yeardley Smith, the overachiever who functions as the social conscience of the family and baby Margaret, better known as Maggie.

THE INEFFECTUAL HUSBAND AND FATHER

Homer is a completely incompetent nuclear safety manager at the power plant and a danger to his local community, a man who fakes his own death to get out of working litter duty on a Saturday, a man who happily engorges himself to obese proportions in order to work from home, a man who takes a bucket of fried chicken to church, a man who complains about taking his children out on a Saturday afternoon and misses his son's little league games because he finds them dull. In short, Homer is 'a gluttonous, lazy oaf who puts butter in his coffee, and whose aspiration in life is to be a "pin monkey" at the local bowling alley' (Gray 2006: 57), a man who 'stays up an entire night to work his way methodically through 64 slices of American cheese. A man who knowingly scarfs down expired ham and month-old rotting hoagies, and who installs a children's lightbulb oven in his car for muffins on the go' (Turner 2005: 88).

Countless episodes focus on Homer's lack of understanding of and appreciation for his wife and his deep failings as a father. For example, when Marge and Homer go away to a couples' retreat to work on their rocky marriage, Reverend Lovejoy tells Marge 'as a trained marriage counsellor this is the first instance where I've ever told one partner that they were 100 per cent right. It is all his fault. I'm willing to put that on a certificate you can frame' (2:20 'War of the Simpsons'). When Homer's children are taken into care he tells his wife that he is a 'terrible parent, the boy bugs the hell out of me and I can't help Lisa with her homework' before concluding that 'I'm not going to win father of the year . . . in fact I'm probably the last guy in the world who should have kids' (7:04 'Home Sweet Home Diddly-Dum-Doodily'). In fact, a classic sequence shows Homer in Moe's seedy bar, telling his friend that 'Oh well you're closing, it's getting late, my kids are probably wondering where their daddy is . . . there's got to be some other place we can go, think Moe, think' (7:12 'Team Homer'). Although he admits 'I don't know jack about my boy' (3:09 'Saturdays of Thunder') and cannot bond with his eldest daughter due to her superior intellect, the appalling state of his relationship with his youngest daughter is also a long-running joke in the series. When Homer babysits for the infant he forgets the very fact of her existence, and when reminded of her status in the family he asks 'who the heck is Margaret Simpson?' (7:08 'Mother Simpson').

Even when Homer actually makes a conscious effort to transform himself into a model father after attending a lecture at the National Fatherhood Institute, the man still lacks (or misunderstands) basic parenting skills. For example, we see him trying to teach Bart to ride a bike even though the boy is already capable, encouraging Lisa to play on a dirty, greasy tyre-swing and allowing Maggie to both drink beer and play with an electric drill. Moreover, his rare fatherly advice to Bart and Lisa consists of such maxims as 'if something goes wrong . . . blame the guy who can't speak English' (4:07 'Marge Gets a Job'). The programme makes it clear that Homer cannot and must not be viewed as an upstanding role model of masculinity, fatherhood or parenting more generally. After all, Bart and Lisa show little respect for their oafish father, routinely commenting on his 'half-assed under-parenting' (3:09 'Saturdays of Thunder'). In fact, Bart has so little respect for this man that he refuses to call him dad. Bart, Lisa and one might even suggest Maggie, are more intelligent and worldly-wise than their ineffectual father, after all, 'second-grader Lisa betters her dad at Scrabble; Bart consistently beats him in a boxing video game [and] both better him in arguments, with him resorting to shouting at the kids' (Butsch 2003: 25).

It is not just Homer's parenting skills that are called into question, but also his ability to provide for his family. The Simpsons cannot afford a new television when their beloved set is in need of repair, nor can they pay for family holidays or specialist schooling for the gifted Lisa. Indeed, the children's college fund only amounts to $88.50. Homer is clearly an ineffectual breadwinner, but more surprisingly in relation to the traditional sitcom format, the man is an unwilling one, routinely trying to shirk his financial responsibilities and family obligations. For example, on a rare occasion when we see the Simpson adults considering the idea of Marge re-entering paid employment, Homer's immediate reaction is not about the welfare of his children or the extra financial security for his family, but rather a fantastical and childlike response concerning his dream to 'live in the woods and keep a journal of my thoughts' (4:07 'Marge Gets a Job'). Valerie Weilunn Chow makes this point when she comments that 'the implication of Homer's fantasy is that with Marge . . . filling in as the breadwinner, he can be not only unemployed, but also living away from his family' (Chow 2004: 121).

Sincere affections and good intentions

Although Homer appears to be an inconsiderate husband and inattentive father, it is necessary to acknowledge this character as something more than a one-dimensional stereotype of white working-class masculinity in the sitcom tradition. After all 'for every moment of overt stupidity or appalling childishness . . . there is a display of tenderness, or selflessness, or profound love' for his dysfunctional family (Turner 2005: 105). The point here is that behind Homer's incompetent parenting there is always 'an underlying sense of commitment and caring that does not appear artificial or prefabricated; ultimately, the affection here is sincere' (Henry 2003: 269–70). Therefore, seeing Homer and his children trying to develop their relationship, by whatever means necessary, can be taken as a sign of a father's deep love for his children, and hearing this seemingly uncaring man tell Marg that 'you work yourself stupid for this family' (7:04 'Home Sweet Home Diddly-Dum-Doodily') does demonstrate (at least on occasion) his gratitude and respect for his wife. Robert Sloane makes this point when he notes that 'at its heart, the show is about family, and no matter how much the portrayal of the Simpsons satirizes or critiques the institution of the American family, the program continually comes back to reaffirm the bond between these people' (Sloane 2004: 140).

For example, when Homer steals the Christmas fund to buy (and then subsequently crash) a new car, we hear him comment 'what a family . . . my wife and kids stood by me' (9:10 'Miracle on Evergreen Terrace') and at this point the programme presents the sitcoms somewhat predictable family-affirming moment for the audience. And yet, before condemning the programme for adhering to unrealistic images of familial harmony and happy-ever-afters, it is necessary to note that such endings are routinely undermined in the animated text. In this case we hear Homer continue 'what a family . . . my wife and kids stood by me . . . on the way home I realised how little that meant to me' (9:10 'Miracle on Evergreen Terrace'). However, although family-affirming endings are routinely challenged, they are not denied altogether in the show. After all, according to Jonathan Gray's work on television, parody and intertextuality 'in offering a sweet ending, then a sarcastic, parodic pull of the rug, as is their common technique, *The Simpsons* still gives us that sweet ending, if in modified form' (Gray 2006: 59). Therefore, although on the surface of the text *The Simpsons* can be read as an attack on the traditional nuclear family in line with the working-class sitcom, like its live action predecessors the show is by no means anti-family. Rather, the programme simply aims to destabilise and ridicule 'the traditional American family sitcom's solitary and peculiar *version* of the way a family should look' (ibid.: 61). In fact, the programme's commitment to the loving and committed family is so ingrained in contemporary popular culture that both the Archbishop of Canterbury and Tony Blair have applauded the 'pro-family' stance of *The Simpsons* (ibid.: 61).

King of the Hill

More recently we have seen the creation of *King of the Hill*, an animated comedy featuring the Hill family in suburban Arlen, Texas. Like *The Simpsons* before it, *King of the Hill* is a domestic situation comedy that focuses on both the trials and tribulations of a working-class nuclear family. Hank Hill/Mike Judge is the 40-year-old lower-middle-class primary breadwinner who works in the propane industry, Peggy/Kathy Najimy is a housewife, substitute teacher and erstwhile writer and artist, Bobby/Pamela Segall is the 12–13-year-old chubby son and Luanne/Brittany Murphy the caring but wild niece.

The iteration of masculinity

King of the Hill is said to be 'producing some of the subtlest insights into the construction of American masculinity in television history' (Alberti 2004: xxx), and the show manages to do this by presenting the audience with three very different (although all potentially dysfunctional) generations of Hill men, and examining the sometimes struggling relationships between them. These relationships are routinely tried and tested due to the fact that each generation has its own idea about 'the appropriate iteration of masculinity' (Palmer-Meha 2006: 194). Anthony Clare makes this point when he comments that today's fathers cannot help but be affected by their own experiences of being fathered, pointing out that these men sometimes struggle to combine their own recollections of being fathered with their own ideas of what a parent should be (Clare 2001: 169). The very fact that the programme provides a range of competing and often contradictory masculinities goes some way towards challenging the myth of the hegemonic male.

World War II veteran Cotton Hill/Toby Huss presents the archetypal image of hegemonic masculinity in that he places all his professional and public responsibilities before his family; he represses genuine emotions and considers all women (including his own young girlfriend Didi/Ashley Gardner) as nothing more than unpaid sexual and domestic labour. Alternatively, Hank is a keen sports fan and former high-school football hero who seeks to treat his own wife with the care, consideration and respect that his own father failed to show to his mother, while Bobby is the overweight pre-teen who has no interest in or aptitude for sports or physical violence.

In flashbacks we see Cotton and a young Hank at a shooting range, however, rather than witness a touching moment of father and son bonding we see Cotton barking orders at a nervous Hank, with the patriarch belittling his son's masculinity as he derides his shooting skills. Cotton's parenting style resembles that 'of a drill sergeant' (Palmer-Meha 2006: 193) as he shouts 'you're never gonna be a war hero like me if you shoot like that' (2:01 'How to Fire a Rifle without Really Trying'). However, while Cotton sees war and violence as important vehicles through which 'young men are taught to embody power and dominance in society' (ibid.: 183), Hank challenges his father's commitment to such activities in favour of sport.

Therefore, while Cotton sees the battleground as a way to enact a socially acceptable version of masculinity, Hank sees sporting prowess as the correct way to express physical power, control and hence hegemonic masculinity. Thus, in the same way that we see Cotton despair at Hank's shooting skills, so too, we witness Hank's total frustration at Bobby's lack of sporting prowess, hearing him tell his wife that 'I never get to bond with Bobby on account of he's not much good at stuff' (2:01 'How to Fire a Rifle without Really Trying'). *King of the Hill* shows Hank encouraging his son to participate in a range of sporting activities such as baseball, football, wrestling and fishing when Bobby would much rather be having a bubble bath, gardening or watching PBS with his mother. Moreover, when we hear Hank mutter 'that boy ain't right' during such disastrous sporting sessions, it clearly signals Hanks irritation at his son's inability to perform what he sees as the appropriate display of masculinity. However, *King of the Hill* negotiates what Hank sees as appropriate masculinity when he discovers that the gentle Bobby has an amazing natural shooting ability that he himself cannot compete with, one that Cotton himself would be proud of. Indeed, it is when we hear the usually quiet Bobby on a shooting range ask his dad 'what's wrong with you . . . how can you hit anything the way you're holding it?' (2:01 'How to Fire a Rifle without Really Trying') that the 'the production and normalization of masculinity are highlighted and rendered absurd' (Palmer-Mehta 2006: 193).

In her seminal research on the representation of masculinities in *King of the Hill*, Valerie Palmer-Mehta draws on Michael Kimmel's work on the sociology of masculinity in order to explain Cotton's tough treatment of Hank and Hank's disappointment in Bobby. We are told that fathers socialise their sons in line with hegemonic masculinity in the knowledge that a range of male eyes (be they teachers, coaches, bosses, peers, friends or workmates) will watch and then judge them (Palmer-Mehta 2006: 193). Therefore, if we consider that, 'our society . . . stratifies men according to physical strength and athletic ability in the early years' (Pleck 2004: 62), then we can begin to understand Hank's desire to raise his son in line with patriarchal rule. However, although Palmer-Mehta's work is convincing, one might also want to consider the ways in which both Cotton and Hank are keen to position their sons as strong and powerful young men so that they themselves continue to be judged as the dominant male, and therefore positioned quite literally as the patriarchal father. What I mean by this is that if men's real fear is a fear of 'being ashamed or humiliated in front of other men' (Leverenz 1986: 451) then a father may be judged and found wanting if his son fails to conform to the stereotypical image of hegemonic masculinity. Therefore, when Bobby is heard asking his dad 'why are you trying to turn me into you, why can't you just accept me for who I am?' (2:06 'Husky Bobby') we hear Hank mockingly reply 'yeah yeah we both saw that after-school special' (2:06 'Husky Bobby') rather than actually consider the fact that he is trying to transform his son into an athletic sporting hero in his own image based precisely on his own masculine insecurities. In this way, one might suggest that Hank is desperately trying to position himself as Bobby's 'role model' (2:03 'The Arrowhead') rather than looking to reconcile his version of acceptable masculinity with the more sensitive image of the white American male that is being presented here.

Although Hank is clearly carrying what psychologist Zick Rubin refers to as a 'father-hunger' into his adult life (Rubin cited in Messner 1992: 27), perhaps due in part to the fact that in the early 1970s, during Hank's formative years 'fathers were spending an average of thirty-seven seconds a day with infants' and leaving childcare and domestic labour to women (Messner 1992: 27), the show makes it clear that the relationship between Hank and Bobby is set apart from that between Cotton and Hank. The programme suggests that although Hank doesn't always understand Bobby and tends to find himself frustrated at his son's 'inability to iterate his masculinity properly' (Palmer-Mehta 2006: 182), Hank is nothing if not a loving and devoted father. The man really does try to respect and appreciate his son for who he is growing up to be, even if this is not the son that Hank would have hoped for. After all, he openly admits that 'I just want to spend Halloween with my son [because] it's just no fun without you' (2:04 'Hilloween') and looks to find activities that 'a father and son can do together' (2:01 'How to Fire a Rifle without Really Trying') and, on occasion, actually declares his love for his family (2:02 'Texas City Twister').

Therefore, although Peggy informs us that 'Hanks priorities are propane first, family second and friends third . . . in that order' (2:12 'Snow Job') it is clear that this man is a proud blue-collar American who considers it his role and responsibility to provide for his family, and therefore Hank's 'pride, responsibility and feverish enthusiasm' (2:19 'Junkie Business') for the propane industry can simply be understood as a sign of his love, commitment and dedication to his family. After all, the social researcher Daniel Yankelovich has suggested that about 80 per cent of America's male workers view their jobs as worthless and tiring, but rather than dwell on the intrinsically meaninglessness of such employment, these men 'prid[e] themselves on the hard work and personal sacrifice they are making to be breadwinners for their families. Accepting these hardships reaffirms their role as family providers and therefore as true men' (Pleck 2004: 65). After all, until recently, a man's ability to provide for his family had been seen as a significant part of his masculine identity with 'no other conception of what it means to be a real man' such as virility, physical power, authority, decisiveness, rationality, calmness, discipline, resourcefulness or strength of character coming close (Yankelovich cited in Clare 2001: 134). Mike Messner makes this point when he tells us that 'most men never learn to express love to their children directly. More often, men show their love indirectly and symbolically, through actions such as working to support the family and teaching athletic skills to sons' (Messner cited in West 1996: online).

However, although Hank is both hard-working and committed to his public role, when his boss, Buck Strickland/Stephen Root, suffers a heart-attack and puts a young business-school graduate in charge of the company over and above the reliable, responsible and loyal Hank (2:12 'Snow Job'), this desertion by his employer can be seen in relation to wider debates about the much-touted 'crisis of masculinity' in which the modern man is said to be angry, discontent, constantly disappointed and betrayed by the workings of society (Faludi 2000: 27). Therefore, while the contemporary male seeks 'a promise of loyalty, a guarantee . . . that his company would never fire him, his wife would never leave him, and the team he rooted for would never pull up stakes' (ibid.: 27), Hank too seeks such reassurance about his role and relationships in society. However, rather than offer such reassurances to the head of the household, the series continues to question the role and responsibilities of the American white male.

FAMILY GUY

. Since the continued success of both *The Simpsons* and *King of the Hill*, we have seen the arrival of *Family Guy*, another animated series firmly situated within the working-class situation comedy tradition. The show depicts the mundane day to day existence of the Griffin Family, with 42-year-old Peter Griffin/Seth MacFarlane, an overweight, routinely unemployed, obnoxious and irresponsible father-of-three who seems to do little but watch television, avoid work and reserve his Sundays for browsing internet porn (4:20 'Patriot Games'), Lois/Alex Borstein, the long-suffering stay-at-home wife and part-time piano teacher; Chris/Seth Green, the overweight and underachieving eldest son; Meg/Mila Kunis, the unpopular nerdy daughter and one-year-old baby Stewie/Seth MacFarlane who is hell-bent on world domination.

Like its animated sitcom predecessors, *Family Guy* presents an outrageously irreverent commentary on all aspects of contemporary American culture, with particular emphasis on changing gender roles and the role of organised religion. With this in mind, Peter, like Homer and (to a lesser extent) Hank before him, is seen ridiculing his children and disregarding his wife. For example, in the same way that Homer refuses to attend Bart's little league games because he finds them boring, so too, Peter is uninterested in his daughter's school play because 'Meg sucks, everything she does is so freaking terrible and depressing' (4:14 'PTV'). When this man is left (begrudgingly) in charge of his infant son, he leaves him sweating like an animal in the family car while he entertains exotic dancers in a sleazy strip club. After telling Lois that he and Stewie were at a ball game (the expectant form of bonding for the American male), his wife challenges him on the outing due to the fact that her son 'smells like sweat and beer' (4:16 'The Courtship of Stewie's Father'), and rather than admit to his reckless and irresponsible behaviour, Peter feigns anger at his wife's shocking allegations and announces that 'I think I know how to spend time with my own kid all right, the bond between a father and son is sacred' (4:16 'The Courtship of Stewie's Father'). However, in this instance the bond between father and son is less sacred and more an easily overlooked inconvenience for the male. It is not only Stewie that Peter lets down, but the whole Griffin clan; in fact this failed patriarch routinely takes his family to the verge of financial and social disaster, and seems surprisingly proud of the moments when he (usually unwittingly) saves the day. Lois makes this point herself when she comments 'Oh Peter I'm so proud of you, once again you brought our family to the edge of the abyss and at the very last minute you saved us all' (4:26 'Petergeist'). However, rather than question or challenge her husband's behaviour here, she simply gushes 'I love you, honey' (4:26 'Petergeist') rather than risk questioning his role as father, husband or provider.

Although the definition of mature masculinity has (until recently) been the male who protects and provides for his family, it is worth noting that medical evidence exists to suggest that such masculinity has been deemed 'a hazard to men's health' in the form of coronary heart disease (Ehrenreich 1984: 68). Therefore, one might suggest that those men who refuse to find gainful employment or take on the breadwinning role are simply aware of the danger of being diagnosed with coronary heart disease, or what the medical professions termed 'the burden of responsibility' (ibid.: 70). That said, although masculinity itself was being considered as a factor in coronary heart disease, so too are Peter's beloved fatty foods. If one considers the fact that 'the most vulnerable personality appeared to be the best adjusted, most respectable and clearly masculine' (ibid.: 81) male or what Business Week described as an 'aggressive, hard-driving, vigorously competitive' figure (Business Week cited in ibid.: 83) then we realise that Peter is not looking after his health but simply not looking after his family.

However, like Homer and Hank before him, Peter is not always presented as a one-dimensional sitcom buffoon. Although the programme acknowledges Peter's obvious shortcomings as a husband and father, it also (on occasion) takes time to present him as 'a genuine object of sympathy' during those moments when he 'attempts to cope with the failures of his life' (Booker 2006: 86). For example, when Peter sees his friends achieving perfect bowling scores and saving women's lives, we hear him tell his family that he is the only man he knows who has never done 'anything remotely memorable' (4:03 'Blind Ambition'). And although the format of the programme demands that Peter try and set a World Record for eating nickels and then go blind due to nickel poisoning, the fact that Peter does acknowledge his position in life as lacking respect, responsibility and reassurance remains, albeit satirised, with the audience.

INEFFECTUAL BUT NOT ABSENT

If one considers that the situation comedy 'has remarked upon almost every major development of postwar American history . . . to a greater degree than perhaps any other popular art' (Hamamoto 1989: 2) and that 'fatherhood is the commonest experience of adult men' (Clare 2001: 166) then it is clear that the genre in question (be it live action or animation) will present a commentary on the role and responsibilities of contemporary fatherhood. Moreover, at a time when 'nine out of ten fathers involved in divorce leave the family home to become non-resident' (Clare 2001: 135) and 'approximately 8 per cent of all birth certificates in Britain . . . do not reveal the identity of the father' (Clare 2001: 166), the very fact that the patriarch of prime-time animated sitcom is resident in the family home cannot help but situate these men as heroic images of the white male. Kenneth MacKinnon makes this point when he tells us that 'the fundamental requirement of approved fatherhood is that the father is physically present and, in that particular but limited sense, supportive' (MacKinnon 2003: 47). Therefore, even though these men may be, at times, ineffective and disinterested in their families, the very fact that they remain in the family home with the mother of their children sets them apart from those men who refuse to take on the responsibilities of fatherhood. However, that said, it is clear from the work of authors such as Susan Faludi that being a father should mean that you are not merely in the home, but actually showing your son 'how the world worked' (Faludi 2000: 596) and how a young man is supposed to find his place in it. After all, the patriarch needs to be more than a good shooter or sportsman, he has to acknowledge his role and responsibility in educating his son about both the public realm of work and the private realm of family responsibility (ibid.: 596).

CONCLUSION

This chapter has offered a brief introduction to film and television animation, drawing attention to the history of the animated sitcom on the small screen. The chapter then went on to outline the ways in which the prime-time animated sitcom can be seen to respond to wider debates about family roles and relationships in contemporary society, paying particular attention to the representation of present but often problematic fathers and father–son relations. However, although the depiction of dysfunctional family life in general and fatherhood in particular were once considered satirical and even occasionally shocking in such prime-time animated sitcoms as *The Simpsons, King of the Hill* and more recently *Family Guy*, it is worth noting that since *The Simpsons* originally aired in the late 1980s, what was once seen as an innovative representation of the American working-class family has since become formulaic (Tueth 2003: 140). And as such, it is those animated programmes that are removed from the sitcom frame such as *South Park* that are heralding some of the most satirical representations of sex and gender roles in contemporary society, however, with the exception of that programme, those prime-time cartoons that dare to deviate from the classic sitcom format struggle to find an audience.

5. TEEN PROGRAMMING: ISOLATION, ALIENATION AND EMERGING MANHOOD

Introduction

Television has routinely featured teenagers and the teen experience in a range of talent shows, variety programmes, soap operas and sitcoms, with such programming culminating in the teen television drama of the early to mid-1990s. These texts do not merely reflect adolescent interests and anxieties, but rather, they play a significant role in managing and shaping the teen experience. However, even though the small screen appears saturated by the trials and tribulations of teen life and a varied spectrum of adolescent concerns, this youth demographic has little or no control over such representations. After all, if one considers that the depictions of teen life that inundate our screens are planned and produced by dominant adult society, then one might conclude that those images are deemed appropriate by, and of use to, the wider adult agenda. Therefore, it is interesting to examine the representation of boyhood and the adolescent male in contemporary teen programming and consider the ways in which such depictions can be seen to educate young men about male behaviour and appropriate gender roles in society. With this in mind, this chapter will look at the history of teen programming from the 1950s to the present day, before examining the representation of adolescence in the supernatural teen text. The chapter will pay particular attention to the ways in which American programmes such as *Roswell* and *Smallville* highlight the problems and confusions that are associated with teenage masculinity, using the teen alien as a motif through which to explore those issues of difference and otherness that are encountered by the average teen. Both shows have proved popular with an adolescent British audience, and as such, they go some way to provide evidence of the fact that, in televisual terms at least, 'the teenager remains profoundly American' (Moseley 2002: 43).

The restrictions and responsibilities of teen life

The image of the teenager that we see today emerged in the Western world in the 1950s, and since that time the teenager has been seen to struggle with both a burgeoning sense of freedom and a set of limitations that are routinely put on adolescent life (Davis and Dickinson 2004: 3). After all, although teenagers are encouraged to show independence and autonomy in their daily lives in their schoolwork, extra-curricular activities, health, time keeping and relationships, they also face distinct adult controls surrounding these selfsame activities. Glyn Davis and Kay Dickinson make this point when they comment that teen life 'straddles a huge and often incommensurate set of situations – the inability to vote, to access the welfare state independently, to earn little more than the minimum wage . . . at the same time as offering increased rights, mobility and . . . consumerism' (ibid.: 11). Moreover, the ways in which teenagers can be seen to try and find their own social, sexual, political and sartorial voice by watching popular television, listening to alternative music or socialising with friends, simply reminds us of 'just how conformist teenagers can be' (ibid.: 3). After all, although adolescents put much time and energy in to projecting what they may see as a distinct cultural identity, be it the preppy type, goth, jock, nerd, fashion queen or cheerleader, little room exists for difference or deviation in such presentations. What I mean by this is simply that what adolescents wear, watch, listen to and show interest in tends to be motivated more by a desire to fit in with other teens than by any real development of the self or presentation of citizenship.

History of the genre

Television has long been interested in presenting teenagers and addressing the teen experience. For example, in the 1950s and 1960s teenagers on both sides of the Atlantic were able to tune in to a range of youth-inspired popular music programmes such as *Six-Five Special* (1957–9), *Oh Boy!* (1958–9) and *The Monkees* (1966–8). The late 1960s and early 1970s then witnessed the presentation of the teen experience in the situation comedy genre in such family themed shows as *The Brady Bunch* (1969–74) and *The Partridge Family* (1970–4) while soap operas such as *Brookside* (1982–2003) and *EastEnders* increasingly highlighted the trials and tribulations of teenage life in their depiction of family and community conflicts throughout the 1980s. Since that time, television has continued to appeal to the teen audience by developing such genres with the youth demographic in mind, therefore the *Six-Five Special* paved the way for *Popworld* (2001–) and *The Monkees* paved the way for the *S Club 7* series (1999–2003). Although the sitcom and soap opera genres have routinely featured the teen experience as part of their family-orientated programming, these genres have recently been seen to present texts that are deliberately and decisively about the lives, loves, trials and tribulations of the youthful protagonist. In this way, *The*

Brady Bunch has led the way to such teenage fare as *California Dreams* (1992–7) and the adult world of *Brookside* has led the way to more adolescent-fuelled programmes such as *Hollyoaks* (1995–).

However, it was only in the mid- to late 1990s that 'the quality teen television drama series appeared, developed and flourished' (Moseley 2002: 41) with the emergence of shows such as *Beverly Hills 90210* (1990–2000), *Party of Five* (1994–2000), *My So-Called Life* (1994–5) and *Dawson's Creek* (1998–2003), and these shows have since led to the success of more recent series such as *The OC* (2003–), *One Tree Hill* (2003–) and *Skins* (2007–). These programmes can all be considered teen television due to the fact that they tend to focus on a recurring set of themes that are said to be of interest to the teen experience, including anxieties about love, sex, alienation, rebellion, impending adulthood, concerns over family relations and issues surrounding one's place in the world. Such texts tend to focus on a group of teenagers who feel as if they do not belong at home, at school or in the wider society more generally, who feel 'caught somewhere between childhood and being an adult in an intense emotional landscape' (Turnbull 2006: 14). And what is particularly significantly here is the fact that such programming actually 'invites us to consider how the world looks' from this teenage point of view (ibid.: 14).

These texts all employ actors who are embodied teenagers, and have these performers converse in an intelligent, knowing and emotional manner. Deidre Dolan says it best when she comments that the teen protagonist 'can express every single one of the ten feelings they're having [and] don't appear to have an unconscious moment' (Dolan 1999: online), and this is said to be of interest to a teenage audience who are 'hyper aware of their [own] feelings, but less prone to the loud and constant analysis' that is presented in these shows (ibid.). Therefore, we are informed that 'young people don't watch teen series to learn, they watch them to experiment with new feelings' (Pasquier 1996: 356). However, if one considers that these teen texts are created by adults with an arguably adult agenda, it is relevant to note that although 'plot lines might deal with passion, jealousy or deception . . . they all lead to the same message: it is within the couple, with the one regular partner, that happiness can be found' (ibid.: 355). Therefore, even though these shows draw on a range of teen experiences, foreground a variety of adolescent emotions, draw on youth-inspired popular cultural reference points, play themselves out to a prominent pop music soundtrack and strive to find plausible ways in which to keep the central teen protagonists in school, at home or simply within the confines of the teen experience, the aim of such programming is always to tame, contain and mould teen life in line with the dominant interests of adult society. These shows present teen life as a way of educating young people about their future role and responsibilities in both the home and the workplace, drawing on resourceful and respectful adolescents to act as role models for future generations of young people, and presenting the downward spiral of problematic and promiscuous teens to act as a warning to that demographic.

ALIENATION AND OTHERNESS IN THE SUPERNATURAL TEEN TEXT

Although all teen television drama interrogates those issues of otherness and disenfranchisement that are said to be of interest to the teen experience, and therefore of interest to the teenage audience, there exists a particular strand of teen drama that uses supernatural powers as a motif through which to explore such questions of difference, otherness and alienation. The very fact that a number of teen texts are situated within the science fiction and fantasy genre is relevant due to the fact that such programming is culturally constituted as a youth product due to its 'status as spectacle' and due to the genres ability to celebrate 'the pleasures of possibility' (Rutherford 2004: 29).

Beyond this rather simplistic notion of science fiction and fantasy as teen fare, it is necessary to note that programmes such as *Sabrina the Teenage Witch* (1996–2003), *Buffy: The Vampire Slayer* (1997–2003) and *Charmed* (1998–2006) can all be seen to present teenagers as both alienated teen and extraterrestrial, after all, Sabrina and the *Charmed* sisters discover that they have inherited the power of witchcraft; the eponymous Buffy Summers discovers that she is the all-powerful slayer and four of the main characters in this vampire text are presented as part-alien. Indeed, the challenges faced by having superhuman powers are seen to be intensified examples of those love trials and social tribulations experienced by the average teen and therefore, these texts make it clear that to be a teenager is to be 'not quite human' (Moseley 2002: 43). The point here is simply that these programmes are as much about feminine adolescence as they are about monsters (Johnson 2002: 42). Glyn Davis and Kay Dickinson make this point when they argue that 'the alienation teenagers may experience in their lives becomes metaphorically mapped onto the representation of extraterrestrials and monsters in these series' (Davis and Dickinson 2004: 7). Therefore, teen television drama makes a point of celebrating difference and championing otherness in its narrative, asking audiences to sympathise with the respectful and morally upstanding high school nerds and social misfits rather than the more ostensibly popular teen stereotypes. In fact, such programmes only encourage the audience to empathise with the beautiful cheerleader or the prom queen when 'these characters are themselves insecure in these highly fabricated and difficult to maintain social roles' (ibid.: 7).

ALIENS, OTHERNESS AND EMERGING MANHOOD

While shows such as *Sabrina*, *Buffy* and *Charmed* can all be seen to draw on supernatural motifs in order to treat feminine adolescence, questions of social alienation and sexual angst seriously, programmes such as *Roswell* and *Smallville* 'blend . . . science fiction, action-adventure, young romance and melodrama' (Banks 2004: 17) in order to treat masculine adolescence with this selfsame sincerity. Both *Roswell* and *Smallville* 'deal with questions of difference, otherness [and] increased power' (Moseley 2002: 43) in relation to the central male teens, focusing on the ways in which the superhuman abilities of these organic outsiders can be seen to impact on and speak for their social, sexual and familial relationships. However, before presenting shows such as *Roswell* and *Smallville* as examples of the ways in which contemporary teen programming can present adolescent difficulties symbolically, it is worth briefly noting that representations of the other and the outsider have a long history in the science fiction and fantasy genre. For example, Harvey Greenberg's work on *Star Trek* (1966–9) suggests that Spock's half-vulcan body reflected the physical changes that the adolescent male sensed taking place in himself (Greenberg 1984: 52–65).

Roswell, Smallville and the adolescent outsider

Roswell follows the teen anxieties and extraterrestrial tribulations of three adolescent aliens who crash-landed in the infamous Roswell, New Mexico; Max Evans/Jason Behr, his sister Isabel Evans/Katherine Heigl and best friend Michael Guerin/Brendan Fehr. The teens in question face anxieties concerning love, sex, alienation, family relations and impending adulthood. For example, during the first series of the show in question, Michael is scared to open himself up to an emotional relationship with Maria DeLuca/Majandra Delfino out of fear for his and therefore the couple's unknown future, Max (who is privileged by the text through on screen time, storylines and narrative perspective here) is concerned about both the emotional and physical implications of a relationship with his earthly classmate Liz Parker/Shiri Appleby, Isabel is terrified of social alienation, while all three struggle with having to hide their supernatural powers from their adoptive parents and the wider outside world. Although these characters are scared of never finding their place in this world, they are even more anxious of knowing their position as saviours of their home planet.

In this same way, *Smallville* begins with a meteor shower that brings a young Clark Kent/Tom Welling to his adoptive parents in Smallville, Kansas. The show goes on to follow the teen anxieties and extraterrestrial tribulations of the adolescent Superman as he tries to decipher the meaning of his life both on Krypton and here on earth. Like Max before him, Clark can be seen to struggle with both his own superhuman abilities and the more mundane teenage anxieties concerning sex, love and family relations. And again, like Max, Clark is seen to develop his superhuman skills, discover his other-worldly origins and decipher his future destiny, which enables the drama to speak to the adolescent audience about the teen experience and their place in this world. Clark is so concerned about how his superhuman powers will affect those around him that he does not play sports at school and chooses not to have a physical relationship with his then girlfriend Lana Lang/Kristin Kreuk. In fact, the only time we see him experience life as a normal teenager is when he temporarily loses his powers. Therefore, although the audience is fully aware that both Max and Clark are destined to save the world and take their rightful position as rulers on their home planets, the fact that these programmes focus on these characters as 16-year-old boys during their awkward teenage years is appealing to the adolescent audience because if Superman was once shy around women, awkward in social situations and bookish, then there is the hope that they themselves will grow out of their awkward teenage years to become a physically strong, emotionally open and socially confident male.

THE ADOLESCENT MALE AS HERO AND MARTYR

Miranda Banks' seminal work on the representation of masculinities in teen television outlines the importance of both *Roswell* and *Smallville* in producing what she sees as a new image of American heroism on the small screen (Banks 2004: 17–28). We are told that Max and Clark are handsome, intelligent and considerate young men who are nonetheless still somewhat innocent in matters ranging from schoolwork and surveillance to sex and seduction. Indeed 'while still boyish and innocent, these orphaned other-worldly teenagers each seem to possess a superlative emotional sensitivity and a deep desire to do good in the world' (ibid.: 17). Both Max and Clark routinely look to help out friends, family and neighbours rather than use their powers to improve their own schoolwork, social skills, domestic chores or financial status. It is because both young men have lost their biological parents that they can 'justifiably experience life with an emotional intensity and . . . an eloquence about their situation not typical of the average television teen male' (ibid.: 22).

Therefore, while the contemporary young male may feel paralysed by his emotions, unable to either form or vocalise his innermost thoughts and feelings, these extraterrestrials are presented as 'emotionally capable, thoughtful young men' (Banks 2004: 20) for the teenage audience to admire and aspire to. Although Clark is told that his emotions are his weakness because 'each time you let human emotions guide you, you put the fate of the entire planet at risk' (5:01 'Arrival'), the audience is aware that it is in fact Max and Clark's ability to 'emote without losing control that sets them apart as a new type of hero' (ibid.: 22). In fact both protagonists are seen to be entirely comfortable with their emotional, thoughtful and considerate feminine side. After all, these boys are seen as sensitive figures whose strength lies in their ability to care for others (Pasquier 1996: 360), boys who are 'much more likely to tend to the emotional needs of the women around them than to act out with anger or violence' (Banks 2004: 26).

Miranda Banks makes it clear that Max and Clark are aware of and comfortable with both their masculine and feminine sides, and I would agree that this new male hero is comfortable talking about his human and alien emotions (with those who share their supernatural secret) and equally happy to turn to their physical powers when necessary. Banks makes it clear that this new hero 'can be sweet and gentle, but he is also comfortable with his masculinity' (Banks 2004: 26), and as such, she is positioning these young men as what Sue Turnbull has elsewhere termed the 'emotional androgyne' (Turnbull 2006: 5). In other words these boys are capable of 'combining feminine sensitivity and tenderness with masculine aggression and violence' (ibid.: 5). However, it is worth noting, as Turnbull herself does, that talking about masculinity as aggressive and femininity as sensitive in this way is actually engaging in a 'false dichotomy since most people are capable of the entire range of emotions' (ibid.: 5). Therefore what is important in the representation of these protagonists is not simply that they are capable of both emotional expressiveness and physical aggression, but that they draw on their physical, emotional and moral strength to safeguard and protect friends, family and the wider community. Therefore, although these men have extraordinary powers that could position them as the very zenith of strong, aggressive and forceful masculinity, these young men make it clear that they are seeking to defend rather than dominate their surroundings, and as such, these teenagers have little interest in encouraging or upholding rigid images of the hegemonic male.

We are told that these young men are both heroes and martyrs because they routinely risk exposing their superhuman secret when they try and save others from earthly and extraterrestrial dangers, and as such, they have been understood as examples of the melodramatic male teen hero. After all, while the mother must make sacrifice after painful sacrifice in order to maintain the family unit within the classic female melodrama, it is now the young adolescent male who is seen to be self-sacrificing here. With this in mind, Miranda Banks informs us that this new melodramatic hero 'offers himself up each week for physical as well as emotional torture. And because of his alien status, which allows him to spontaneously heal himself, this suffering hero can return each episode anew' (Banks 2004: 20). On those rare occasions when these young men realise that they must protect their extraterrestrial secret over saving a human life, they are tortured with guilt and grief over such a decision. In fact, on one such occasion when Max is simply unable to risk saving a dying man because doing so will ultimately and without doubt reveal his secret he is so totally overwhelmed by guilt that he tries to compensate for what he sees as his selfish act by healing an entire children's hospital cancer ward. The point here then according to Banks is simply that 'these leading boys are innately good; episode after episode, they are forever the self-sacrificing heroes of the melodrama' (ibid.: 25).

Although Max and Clark are situated in loving and supportive families, they are missing the biological parents who can help to explain and nurture their growing powers. Therefore, the protection and affection offered to these boys from their adoptive parents may be understood as a metaphor for the well-meaning but rather unhelpful advice proffered by parents and guardians to the average teen regarding sex, sexuality and impending manhood. These boys are seen to look outside their adoptive family for relevant advice concerning their socialisation into adulthood and appropriate gender roles, and it is clear that 'the peer group plays an ever important part in th[is] initiation process' (Pasquier

1996: 355). With this in mind, the supernatural teen series can be seen to pick up on wider social patterns as they 'show us adolescents learning how to become men and women *together*: the initiation is made by the peer group and within the peer group' (ibid.: 355) with parents simply being 'superfluous to the drama' here (Banks 2004: 21).

For example, we see Clark trying to come to terms with his growing powers as he talks to Chloe Sullivan/Alison Mack about his superhuman abilities, and after he informs her that 'I wasn't born anywhere near Smallville, in fact I wasn't born anywhere near this galaxy' (5:01 'Arrival') we find out that not only did Chloe already have her suspicions after all 'the quick exits, the miraculous recoveries and bad excuses' (5:01 'Arrival') but that she respected the friendship enough to allow Clark to tell her when he felt comfortable enough to reveal his secret. Moreover, when Clark seems concerned that Chloe is about to throw scorn or pity on him since discovering his alien identity, he tries to explain that 'I'm still the same person' (5:01 'Arrival') irrespective of his powers. However, whereas a range of adults in the programme either want to use, abuse or destroy the young man in question because of his abilities, Chloe makes it clear that she not only loves and supports her friend but that she thinks he is 'so amazing', telling him that 'you save peoples lives and take zero credit for it, to me you're . . . a superhero' (5:01 'Arrival'). Chloe draws parallels between Clark's alien status and the identity issues of the average teenager when she comments that 'every single one of us has gone through some sort of an identity crisis at one point or another, it's like a rite of passage in Smallville' (5:16 'Hypnotic'). In this way these superhuman teens and their earthly counterparts can be seen to develop emotionally and find their sense of self within their close-knit peer groups, and as such, any differences between them becomes blurred here.

Roswell and *Smallville* present a sense of 'community based on generation' (Davis and Dickinson 2004: 1) due to the fact that these alien adolescents request and receive limited advice or assistance from earlier generations of either humans or aliens. Instead, these young men choose to learn about themselves, their growing powers and their vulnerabilities from their interaction with other adolescents, be they alien or earthly. In fact *Roswell* goes as far as to present adoption as a metaphor for the alien experience as we hear a guidance counsellor tell the other-worldly teens that 'some adopted kids go through tough times around this age, you know identity issues, things like that' (1:03 'Monsters'). Therefore, although Max is not struggling with superhuman skills, his origins or his future destiny due to his earthly adoption, the same feelings of otherness and disenfranchisement could be seen to apply here.

Alternatively, the character of Michael in *Roswell* offers an interesting point of departure because he is suffering an identity crisis at the hands of his adoptive father, and as such, struggles to come to terms with and hence control his superhuman powers. After all, while Max and Clark are placed in loving homes and are given the full support of their adoptive parents to grow and develop as individuated males, Michael is placed in a filthy trailer with the unemployed and brutal Hank Whitmore/Robert F. Lyons. Throughout his time in that home Michael is either ignored or abused, and his fear and hatred of his adoptive father can be seen to extend to the wider adult population as we hear the character comment that 'adults are the enemy' (1:11 'Toy House'). Therefore, although adoptive parents cannot help these alien teens with the practicalities of discovering their origins or developing their powers, the fact that they can help them grow and develop as strong, upstanding and moral citizens is clearly linked to their alien abilities. The character of Clark makes this point himself when he says that he feels lucky to have such loving, affectionate and protective parents because 'every time I ever woke up and had a new ability you helped me adjust' (5:01 'Arrival'). The point here then is quite simply that a young man raised to uphold strength, morality and intelligence will be able to tame and contain his other-worldly abilities whereas a young man without adult affection, protection or discipline simply 'doesn't know how to control his powers' (1:02 'The Morning After'), and the same could be said about the earthly teen trying to tame and contain his raging hormones. Therefore, we are reminded of the fact that these teen protagonists are presented as role models for a teen demographic and therefore that teen television has a significant input from dominant adult society. After all, the message in these programmes is that adolescents should feel a moral obligation to both serve and protect the social good, and that teenagers should both appreciate and respect parental rulings, irrespective of whether the adult actually understands the teen concern in question. However, that said, the programme does make it clear that adults must be responsible for their children's welfare, because when Hanks physical and verbal abuse forces Michael to quite literally destroy the power of the patriarch, we are asked to sympathise with the young man in question for his lack of security and safety rather than punish him for his lack of control or restraint here.

EARTH TEENS, EXTRATERRESTRIALS AND THE DESIRE TO BE NORMAL

Although the characters of Max and Clark share an aptitude for schoolwork, self-sacrifice, an emotional understanding of themselves and those closest to them and those non-threatening teen idol good looks that demand youth, smoothness and sad puppy-dog eyes (Sweeney 1994: 51), what these two have most in common is their desire to fit in at school, at home and in their respective communities (Banks 2004: 17). Indeed, the characters in *Roswell* themselves tell us that 'Roswell is not the sort of town you can be unique in' (1:05 'Missing') and that 'there's nothing wrong with wanting to be normal' (1:03 'Monsters'). Likewise, Smallville's Clark tells us that 'all I ever wanted was to be normal' (5:01 'Arrival') and his friend supports his desire, telling us that 'I know how much you've dreamed of having a bland, generic life' (5:03 'Hidden').

Sue Turnbull comments that 'these bulked up beautiful boys are inevitably outsiders because of their alien status' (Turnbull 2006: 3). In fact, both characters find themselves quite literally alienated from potential friends and partners due to the fact that they have to keep their powers a secret from the outside world, and in both cases we see the boys turn down social and sexual invitations for fear of revealing their secret to the outside world. And it is this quite literal alienation from the community that leads to a sense of angst and frustration for these teen protagonists, after all, 'group exclusion is the worst thing' that could happen to an adolescent (Pasquier 1996: 360). The characters are so anxious about accidentally revealing their powers that they are constantly monitoring the ways in which they are being viewed by the outside world, be it by friends, colleagues or the police authorities. In this way, the effort that these young men put in to being viewed as 'normal' and their desire to live a 'normal' life might be understood as an extreme take on the teen experience, and act as a further reminder of the teens desire to conform and belong. Miranda Banks makes this point when she comments that both Max and Clark 'are constantly concerned with how they are viewed by others; as teenage aliens, their deep desire to be seen as "normal" is more than typically magnified' (Banks 2004: 26).

Max and Isabel hint at the comparison between their literal alienation and the more expectant sense of teen alienation when they ask a trusted friend if he has 'ever felt different from everybody else, like if you tried to reveal your true self to someone they would never understand' (1:10 'The Balance'). The point here, of course, is that the human teen has experienced such alienation and otherness because to be an adolescent in contemporary society means being neither fully child nor adult, but somewhere in between. Max is so aware of the social implications of his alien status that he tells Liz that he 'prefers the term not of this earth' (1:01 'Pilot'). Moreover, we can see the pain and torment on his face when, during a history class, the teacher comments 'everybody has their secrets, there isn't a person alive today who is what they appear to be, exposing these secrets is the job of the historian' (1:06 '285 South'), especially when the class are then asked to uncover the 'extraordinary qualities' of one another in an oral history report (1:06 '285 South').

Although Max and Clark struggle to keep their secret safe from the outside world in a desperate bid to ward off social exclusion and scientific experiments, these young men are also seen to struggle with the physical responsibility and emotional insecurity that comes with their growing powers. In this way, 'Max and Clark's transformations are like alien puberty: they often feel uncomfortable at first with their growing abilities, and sometimes letting people know about how their bodies are changing makes them more vulnerable' (Banks 2004: 24). After all, even though 'the powers of both characters are constantly developing . . . these boys are still not entirely in control of what is happening to their bodies' (ibid.: 24). Clark himself make this point when he tells Chloe that 'there are a lot of things about me that even I don't understand' (5:03 'Arrival'). The point here then is quite simply that these other-worldly teenagers make puberty and growing up seem exciting and stimulating rather than simply painful and awkward. This is not to say that Max and Clark's physical growth is not uncomfortable or clumsy, but simply that 'alien puberty . . . seems a bit cooler to audiences than the real, human version' (ibid.: 24). Developing x-ray vision is far more exciting than the earthly male equivalent. However, the programmes do seem to suggest that earthly teenage puberty is more physically and emotionally demanding than its alien equivalent when Clark's mum comments 'its just that you're so much more vulnerable now' (5:03 'Hidden') after her son has lost his superhuman abilities.

CONCLUSION

This chapter has offered a brief introduction to the representation of the teenager and the teen experience on the small screen from the 1950s to the present day, drawing attention to the ways in which such depictions are controlled by the interests of and investment in dominant adult society. The chapter then went on to argue that quality teen television and the supernatural teen drama appeals to the adolescent audience due to the genre's focus on themes such as love, sex, impending adulthood, concerns over family relations and issues surrounding one's place in the world that are said to be of interest to the average teen. We looked at the ways in which programmes such as *Roswell* and *Smallville* depict alien life as an extension of the teen experience in general and as a metaphor for male puberty in particular, concluding that these shows reward physical restraint and emotional connectedness in the next generation of the heroic American male and the everyman respectively. With this in mind, it is also worth noting that teen television appeals to a broader audience than the much-coveted 13–19-year-old demographic. After all, due to the society's increased accessibility to higher education, the social pressure to stay younger for longer and the decay of the notion of the job-for-life as a marker of adult maturity, the current cultural understanding of the youth market can 'be seen to welcome anyone from pre-teens to people in their forties' (Davis and Dickinson 2004: 11).

6. SCIENCE FICTION AND FANTASY TELEVISION: CHALLENGING DOMINANT GENDER ROLES

INTRODUCTION

Although telefantasy covers a wide and diverse range of science fiction and fantasy texts (Johnson 2005: 2), this seemingly loose genre can be distinguished by a number of key codes and conventions that include interplanetary travel, encounters with aliens, advanced technology and visions of the future. Moreover, telefantasy routinely draws on different times and distant planets in order to reflect contemporary social, cultural and political concerns. Because telefantasy is not confined to either naturalistic or realistic conventions, this genre is in a position to offer alternative representations of sexuality and gender on the small screen. Although early examples tended to be unsophisticated space operas whereby handsome American heroes fight against evil, the genre's current representations of masculinity are rather less stable. Therefore, this chapter will look at the history of telefantasy before examining the ways in which contemporary American texts such as *Farscape* and *Firefly* can be seen to both challenge and confirm common sense assumptions about hegemonic masculinity and the male role in society. The focus is primarily on American productions due to the fact that British science fiction and fantasy fare 'have failed to have the cultural impact of their US counterparts' (ibid.: 12). Although a number of contemporary British programmes such as *Neverwhere* (1996), *Ultraviolet* (1998) and *Invasion Earth* (1998) hoped to follow the success of *The X Files* (1993–2002) in the UK, all of the aforementioned texts failed to find an audience. Johnson makes this point when she talks about the export of telefantasy programmes, commenting that the 'export of US programmes to the UK and vice versa, is not an equal exchange, with US television programmes making up a far more significant part of the British schedules than UK programmes do in the US' (ibid.: 14).

HISTORY OF THE GENRE

Telefantasy began on American television in the late 1940s and early 1950s with rudimentary space operas such as *Captain Video and His Video Rangers* (1949–55), *Tom Corbett, Space Cadet* (1950–5) and *Space Patrol* (1950–5) establishing science fiction as a central television genre. These juvenile programmes presented self-righteous and square-jawed heroes championing conformity and conservatism through a range of clear-cut morality tales (Bould 2003: 88). However, although these early shows were popular with young audiences, they were critically derided as a low-cultural form that eschewed any real understanding or explanation of scientific discovery. In fact, it was not until programmes such as *Man in Space* (1955) *Man and the Moon* (1955) and *Mars and Beyond* (1957) examined the realities of space exploration in the mid-1950s that the genre received more serious critical treatment, with *The Twilight Zone* (1959–64) firmly establishing science fiction as 'thoughtful, adult-orientated programming' (Booker 2004: 6).

Since the mid-1950s science fiction has used the 'cloak' of fantasy to address a range of social, moral, ethical, political and philosophical themes that are relevant to society such as racism, economic and political colonialism, ecological disasters, changing class and gender identities, fears about over population, anxieties over the globalisation of communications and counter cultural concerns about nuclear weapons (Casey *et al.* 2002b: 209). Therefore, while programmes such as *The Quatermass Experiment* (1953) reflected the post-war anxieties of 1950s Britain by representing sinister alien threats to humanity, shows such as *Captain Scarlet and the Mysterons* (1967–8) exploited the fears of 1960s America by presenting civil disobedience and the potentially negative impact of new technologies. Likewise, shows such as *Battlestar Galactica* (1978–9) can be seen to foreground a range of international rivalries relating to the cold war while comedic shows such as *Third Rock from the Sun* (1996–2001) were seen to explore a range of sex and gender concerns for a contemporary audience. More recently, *The X Files* has been seen to examine a range of modern day anxieties including 'environmental issues, the role of medicine, the threat of scientific experimentation and most overtly, the duplicity of the US government' (Johnson 2005: 100).

Although much science fiction and fantasy programming has a history of exploring a range of socio-cultural concerns, it is necessary to point to the significance of the long-running *Star Trek* franchise in this regard. After all, *Star Trek* 'presents an entire "parallel universe" with its own political, economic and social system, a symbolic landscape in which a great many contemporary concerns . . . can be explored' (Gregory 2000: 21) such as racial discrimination (*Star Trek*, 3:10 'Plato's Stepchildren'), homosexuality (*Star Trek: The Next Generation*, 5:17 'The Outcast'), genetic engineering (*Star Trek: The Next Generation*, 5:13 'The Masterpiece Society'), arranged marriage (*Star Trek: The Next Generation*, 5:21 'The Perfect Mate'), disability (*Star Trek: Deep*

Space Nine, 2:06 'Melora'), euthanasia and medical ethics (*Star Trek: Voyager*, 1:09 'Emanations') and the nuclear stand-off of the Cold War (*Star Trek*, 1:03 'A Taste of Armageddon'). And although theorists have on occasion critiqued the early *Star Trek* series for its sexism, misogyny and female subjugation due to the fact that 'seventeen women died for the love of Kirk' (Lewis and Stempel 1999: 324), more recently, *Star Trek: The Next Generation* (1987–94) has been championed for 'removing women from the domestic sphere' (Helford 2000: 3) and portraying 'a female head of security, a female chief medical officer, and a female counselor' (ibid.: 4) which encourages the audience to view women as 'more than receptionists in this brave new era of *Trek's* high-tech militarized future' (ibid.: 4). In fact, we are told sexism is a thing of the past (Gregory 2000: 18) in federation society and that 'sexual differences and all forms of biologi-cal diversity [are] seen as positive elements to be celebrated' (ibid.: 18) in this parallel universe.

REPRESENTATIONS OF WOMEN: ROBOTS, ALIENS AND ADVENTURERS

Telefantasy has 'always provided a narrative space that allows the reader to consider alternative ways of living' (Moody 2002: 51) through a wide range of 'ethical issues and fundamental human dilemmas' (Gregory 2000: 11). However, it soon becomes clear that science fiction and fantasy television has a keen interest in exploring representations of sex and gender in society. For example, Helen Merrick informs us that science fiction has 'functioned as an enormously fertile environment for the exploration of sociocultural under-standings of gender' (Merrick 2003: 241). Likewise, Wendy Pearson comments that the genre is 'ideal for the examination of alternative sexualities' (Pearson 2003: 149). After all, while the codes of telefantasy such as 'robots, aliens, psychic powers [and] death rays' (Attebery 2002: 6) can be understood as gender markers in alternative realms, the representation of the female djinn, witch, space adventurer, ruler, mother and superhero can be used to display female strength, power and control whilst presenting a challenge to patriarchal authority (Helford 2000: 4). While Adam Roberts comments that 'the stock conventions of science fiction – time travel, alternate worlds, entropy, rela-tivism, the search for a unified field theory – can be used metaphorically and metonymically as powerful ways of exploring the construction of woman' (Lefanu cited in Roberts 2000: 91), Robin Roberts argues that 'contemporary women writers use the tropes of science fiction to depict worlds that are non-sexist, non-hierarchical, and centred on androgynous values shaped by feminist concerns' (Roberts 1993: 92). In fact, the representation of gender is so crucial to the genre as a whole that 'it is virtually impossible for [an author of the genre] to take gender for granted any more' (Attebery 2002: 6) and therefore 'if a writer wishes to portray unchanged sex roles in the future or in an alien society, that fact has to be explained somehow' (ibid.: 6), be it the result of 'biological imperatives, for instance, or reactionary social pressures' (ibid.: 6).

However, while a range of theorists such as Linda Badley (2000), Rhonda Wilcox (2000), Sharon Ney and Elaine Sciog-Lazarov (2000) are considering the representation of women's bodies, feminine roles and female responsibilities in programmes such as *The X Files, Lois & Clark: The New Adventures of Superman* (1993–7) and *Babylon 5* (1994–8), little work exists on the representation of male bodies, masculine roles and men's responsibilities in telefantasy. My point here is simply that extant literature on gender in the telefantasy genre is actually a consideration of women in science fiction and fantasy television. Therefore, while feminist theorists are presenting the female body as a site of visual scrutiny and social control in telefantasy, these same critics are 'allowing the male body to become invisible' in the genre (Matthews and Mendlesohn 2000: 52). Even when programmes such as *Star Trek* are dedicated to the 'comings and goings and heroic adventures of a band of (essentially male) space travellers, a group of functional orphans without family or ties save their intense loyalty to one another' (Bick 1996: 193), feminist theorists continue to overlook the construction, circulation and interrogation of masculinity, male roles and male friendships in the text. With this in mind, it is necessary to readdress this balance by focusing on those representations of masculinity, machismo and the male role that dominate contemporary telefantasy.

REPRESENTATIONS OF MEN: THE PATRIARCH, PHILANDERER AND POST-FEMINIST

Feminist theorists tend to present *Star Trek*'s Captain James T. Kirk/William Shatner as a one-dimensional bounder and cad who 'can rarely keep his hands off the nubile human and humanoid women he encounters' (Tetreault 1984: 121). However, Elyce Rae Helford's seminal work looks beyond such predictable readings of the Captain as the epitome of sexist masculinity or the personification of misogyny in order to examine the multiple masculinities that make up the character in question. Helford argues that Kirk is routinely transformed from body to body (*Star Trek*, 3:24 'Turnabout Intruder') or divided against himself (*Star Trek*, 1:05 'The Enemy Within'), and as such, the man can be seen to draw on a set of both masculine and feminine characteristics, which in turn challenges any assumed or supposedly innate link between sex and gender in society (Helford 1996: 11–31). Helford's work makes it clear that the fantastic nature of telefantasy can be used to comment on real world experiences of sex, gender and social conventions. Likewise, Catherine Johnson comments that 'by disrupting socio-cultural and generic verisimilitude through their representation of the fantastic, these series invite the viewer to question, not the fantastic aspects themselves, but the normative conventions of the everyday' (Johnson 2005: 7). Therefore, this chapter will now look to more contemporary examples of masculinities in telefantasy in order to examine representations of manhood, the male body and male responsibilities beyond the surface image of the interstellar superhero, paying particular attention to the ways in which *Firefly* and *Farscape* can be seen to challenge the status of hegemonic masculinity in society.

FIREFLY

Shows such as *Star Trek* have been termed space operas due to the way in which their larger-than-life characters and vast intergalactic backdrops are clearly based on the western genre, or what Robson terms 'the romantic frontier horse operas of old' (Robson 2005: 5). However, because *Firefly*'s naturalistic future setting was modelled on the traditional Hollywood Western, the programme can be understood quite literally as 'a horse opera in space, replete with frontier towns and livestock' (ibid.: 5). However, although the backdrop for the outer-space adventure may appear unusual for the contemporary telefantasy genre, *Firefly* can be seen to conform to the codes and conventions of science fiction in terms of its tone, narrative and characterisations. After all, the series is set 500 years in the future after humans have arrived at a new star system, and the programme follows the trials and tribulations of a renegade group who bond while on board the Firefly-class spaceship, Serenity. The core crew members are Malcolm Reynolds/Nathan Fillion, the taciturn Captain; Zoe Washburne/Gina Torres, the tough second-in-command; Hoban Washburne/ Alan Tudyk, Zoe's husband and pilot; Jayne Cobb/Adam Baldwin, the hired muscle of the crew and Kaylee Frye/Jewel Staite, the mechanic. These core crew members are joined on board by Inara Serra/Morena Baccarin, the highly respected companion (courtesan); Shepherd Book/Ron Glass, the equally respected Shepherd (priest); Simon Tam/ Sean Maher, the young medical researcher and trauma surgeon and River Tam/ Summer Glau, Simon's younger sister and child prodigy. Although the crew members are simply seeking carrier employment, they find themselves routinely 'doing battle against the oppressive forces of official authority in a dystopian intergalactic future' (Booker 2004: 175). And although the crew are not confronted by alien nations in the year 2517, they do find themselves in a range of hostile and chaotic environments.

EQUALITY ON SERENITY: FROM CAPTAIN TO COMPANION

Firefly draws on the codes and conventions of science fiction and fantasy programming in order to examine a range of contemporary socio-cultural issues such as the potentially negative impact of new medical technologies (1:12 'Serenity Part 2'), and, like much telefantasy before it, the programme raises some interesting questions regarding femininity, feminism and a woman's role. For example, we are introduced to the character of the companion (1:01 'The Train Job'), a female-run brothel (1:13 'Heart of Gold'), and a maiden house where woman are married off for trade (1:03 'Our Mrs Reynolds'). However, although *Firefly* is clearly not presenting a post-patriarchal society or any contemporary 'ideals of gender equity and awareness' (Badley 2000:

64), it is relevant to note that Malcolm believes in equality for women, be they whore, wife, mechanic or soldier. After all, while he has fallen in love with a companion and happily offered a job to a female mechanic, he has been heard telling Jayne that women are 'not to be bought, or bartered or borrowed or lent' when the hired muscle tries to swap his most loved gun for an attractive girl (1:03 'Our Mrs Reynolds'). Malcolm leans on his female second-in-command for fire-power and physical strength, either distracting the villains so that Zoe can throw a punch (1:01 'The Train Job'), asking her to kill his torturer when he cannot find the strength (1:09 'War Stories') or disguising himself in order to keep her physical force as the upper hand in battle (1:03 'Our Mrs Reynolds').

That said, Malcolm is not the sort of man who would choose to talk through a problem, negotiate with the enemy or show compassion in line with the 'feminine' role, but rather, he looks to brute force and aggression at each and every turn, even when it might be considered unnecessary by his own crew members. For example, he seeks out an alliance bar for a fight on unification day, telling Simon that 'they tell you to never hit a man with a closed fist, but on occasion it's hilarious' (1:01 'The Train Job'). When he is telling a seemingly victimised young woman to demand respect and equality from men, what he actually says is 'you've got the rights same as anyone to live and try to kill people' (1:03 'Our Mrs Reynolds'). When he is duelling to protect Inara's honour he cannot help but tease his opponent with his sword when the man is already down on the ground, stating that it is 'just funny' to wound him (1:06 'Shindig'). Furthermore, rather than applaud his sensitivity, caring or other supposedly feminine character traits, his comrades are actually heard commenting that 'he makes everybody cry', 'he's a monster' and an 'evil lecherous hump' (1:03 'Our Mrs Reynolds'). And yet, he is understood to be loyal to his crew members, so that 'if you turn on my crew, you turn on me' (1:08 'Ariel'), and when he has a chance to save them at the risk of his own life, he happily takes that risk (1:05 'Out of Gas'). The Captain's proudest moment in the short series seems to be when he tells an opponent that 'I've got people with me, people who trust each other, who do for each other and ain't always looking for the advantage' (1:03 'Our Mrs Reynolds').

In this way, Malcolm Reynolds appears to represent a new kind of traditional masculinity. After all, while he relies on brute force and values loyalty, he also believes in fluid gender positions in a future where women are respected as lovers, mothers, mechanics and soldiers. However, although one might look to position this man as a new (and potentially positive) version of old masculinity and applaud him for his treatment of other men, women and children, it is worth noting that the character remains reserved and taciturn at every stage of the narrative, unable to express himself or articulate his inner emotions. Therefore, this chapter will now turn to the character of John Crichton/Ben Browder and consider the ways in which *Farscape* represents the American action hero, paying particular attention to the ways in which the character can be seen to challenge assumptions about hegemonic masculinity, the male hard body and men's talk in contemporary society. After all, existing literature routinely comments that this particular programme 'is committed to presenting us with fascinating and perverse models of masculinity' (Battis 2007: 65), and the central male protagonist makes a point of distancing himself from earlier versions of the hard-bodied and heroic science fiction hero by telling us that 'I am not Kirk, Spock, Luke, Buck, Flash or Arthur frelling Dent' (4:11 'Unrealized Reality').

FARSCAPE

Farscape focuses on the trials and tribulations of John Crichton, an American scientist and astronaut with the International Aeronautics and Space Administration after he is accidentally sucked through a wormhole to a distant part of the galaxy. And although this is an ensemble show, the man 'remains a sort of anchor point for audiences, given that he is a contemporary earthling from the same culture as the viewers' (Booker 2004: 163). In the opening episode of the show, John's Farscape shuttle is taken on board a biomechanoid Leviathan ship named Moya, where our hero finds himself in the company of aliens, namely the Delvian Priestess, Pa'u Zotoh Zhaan/Virginia Hey, a Luxan warrior Ka D'Argo/Anthony Simcoe, the exiled Hynerian Dominar Rygel XVI/Jonathan Hardy, a Peacekeeper officer named Aeryn Sun/Claudia Black and Moya's guide Pilot/Lani John Tupu. Ka D'Argo, Rygel and Zhaan are prisoners who have taken control of Moya and are escaping from the militaristic Peacekeepers, while the pursuing Peacekeeper Aeryn finds herself taken aboard the living ship during starburst. The point here is that *Farscape* follows the travels of 'seven odd mates . . . every one . . . from a different species' (Robson 2005: 6) in an unknown ship rather than loyal crew members aboard a comforting and civilised craft. Therefore, 'this is not a tame, friendly universe; these characters are not calm, competent professionals' (Cavelos 2005: 32). With this in mind, *Farscape* positions John in a hostile and chaotic world, paying particular attention to the ways in which this man adapts to an unknown environment and to the other members on board the living ship, all of whom are 'united by their loathing of and need to escape from the Peacekeepers' (Robson 2005: 6).

Farscape, like the aforementioned telefantasy shows, has had 'a reasonably good whack at some heavyweight moral and philosophical subjects' (Robson 2005: 7) such as drug-induced slavery (1:06 'Thank God it's Friday Again') and anti-terrorism (4:13 'Terra Firma'). In fact, '*Farscape* is as much a show about cultural convergence, racial tension, and colonial expansion, as it is a show about astronauts, wormholes, and impressive explosions' (Battis 2007: 4). Even though the programme had all the hallmarks of poor, predictable and pedestrian telefantasy in the form of an 'American hero, obviously human "aliens" in squiffy Nazi uniforms running another version of the ancient and banal *Star Wars* Empire' (Robson 2005: 2), the series was routinely praised by fans and theorists alike for its potentially progressive representations of sex and gender. For example, Caitlin Kiernan applauds *Farscape* for its 'willingness to deal openly, honestly, erotically, and often very humorously with sex' at a time when 'sexuality and sensuality are subjects traditionally deemed taboo by the producers' of science fiction and fantasy television (Kiernan 2002: online). In this same way, Renny Christopher congratulates the programme for its ability to challenge 'how we understand women, men, gender roles and sexuality' (Christopher 2004: 258). After all the show 'is set in a universe . . . of experimental, alternative sex and gender roles that appeal to viewers who like their men to be women, their women to be men, their chicks to be tough, and their guys to be soft' (ibid.: 277).

Farscape has been championed by feminist theorists for its presentation of Aeryn Sun as a strong, powerful woman and for its presentation of a post-patriarchal Peacekeeper 'culture that practices no gender differentiation' (Christopher 2004: 257). The programme makes it clear that both men and women train to be Peacekeeper soldiers and that a soldier's rank has nothing to do with gender:

> in traditional human terms, it is a masculinist culture, but women get to play too, on not only equal but undifferentiated terms . . . not only is there gender equality between male and female Peacekeepers but there is no gender difference between them.
>
> (Christopher 2005: 262)

If one considers the ways in which contemporary society continues to question a woman's role in the armed forces based on 'rationales of the rights of decency and privacy as well as concerns regarding women's lack of physical strength and the aggressive instincts required for combat' (Moody 2002: 59), then it may come as no surprise to find that the representation of a female soldier who 'can not only hold [her] own, but prevail in combat' (Spicuzza cited in Christopher 2004: 261) would appeal to the feminist theorist here. However, rather than focus on the post-patriarchal Peacekeepers or the masculinised Aeryn Sun, it is relevant to focus on the feminisation of American astronaut John Crichton and the ways in which the programme depicts 'various deconstructions of the type of heroic masculinity that normally drives fantasy narratives' (Battis 2007: 5).

The American hero becomes smaller, slower and weaker

When we first see John board the alien spaceship in the pilot episode, the man is weak, menaced, lost, scared, spat on, penetrated by translator microbes, knocked unconscious by another crew member, stripped and imprisoned (1:01 'Premiere'), or to put it another way, when we first see John board the alien spaceship, the man is 'placed in a "feminized" position' (Christopher 2004: 266). However, my point is not simply that John takes on this 'feminised' position at the outset of the series, but rather that he continues to embody this space throughout the shows history. After all, although this is a man 'in excellent physical condition' (Butcher 2005: 68), he is neither the superior pilot nor the strongest fighter on Moya. John is a man who 'operates through brain, not brawn' (Christopher 2004: 266), a man who would rather protect his crew members than kill the enemy, a man who demands emotional commitment over sex, a man who wants to be a father to his child and more crucially a man who has flaws, is seen to live in torment and who makes mistakes.

Therefore, one might suggest that John is able to present a new image of contemporary masculinity by combining such supposedly feminine traits as emotionality, sensitivity and openness with those supposedly masculine qualities of power, strength and bravery. After all, over the course of the show's history, John repeatedly proves himself in battle and presents himself as 'a ruthless fighter when his own life or anyone else's was at risk' (Wells 2005: 77). Moreover, he 'is always the one best able to use his head and to employ [feminine] cunning . . . to discover a way out of dangerous situations' (Christopher 2004: 267). For example, in the opening episode of the show he escapes from his Peacekeeper captors by distracting them with a puzzle ring before working out how to save their ship from attack through an experimental gravity-sling manoeuvre. The point here then is that he can take up arms, employ feminine ingenuity or write down equations as and when necessary. In short, John can be seen to be both 'aggressor and pursued, rescuer and rescued', 'tough without being brutal . . . brave and strong without being devoid of emotion' (ibid.: 269, 272). Indeed, when our hero is compromised, it is not unusual to hear him pray quietly to Aeryn for rescue like a damsel in distress (1:07 'PK Tech Girl'), and yet, he is just as convincing when he provides fire-power and useful cover to his physically superior crew members in battle (5:02 'The Peacekeeper Wars Part 2').

With this in mind, John is 'simultaneously an action hero in the traditional sense (he shoots bad guys, flies spaceships, and performs other heroic feats) and a character who embraces his "femininity" in that he values sensitivity, emotionality, and connectedness' (Christopher 2004: 273). In fact, it is not unusual to see him try and talk through a problem with an alien race while Aeryn and Ka D'Argo turn to violence (2: 09 'Out of Their Minds'), and it is often his combination of physical strength, compassion and self sacrifice that saves the crew from certain death (2:10 'My Three Crichtons'). While the action hero of popular film and television routinely fights in battle to prove himself as powerful, controlling and masterful (Neale 1995: 12), our hero seems uncomfortable with such struggles of will and strength, victory and defeat. Therefore, although Aeryn and Ka D'Argo treat each and every situation on Moya as a personal challenge, John appears frustrated with such macho posturing, telling Pa'u Zotoh Zhaan that 'it's like everything's a test . . . It's like I'm in some neverending frat hazing at Alien U' (1:03 'Exodus from Genesis').

John foregrounds his own model of mature masculinity when he informs his newborn son that 'Crichtons don't cry . . . often' (5:02 'The Peacekeeper Wars

Part 2'), and as such, it is clear that our central male protagonist can be understood as an emotionally and physically vulnerable take on the science fiction hero. At a time when men are said to be afraid to reveal their insecurities to other men, the astronaut seems happy to share his inner anxieties and deepest emotions with his 'most intensely vulnerable moments [occurring] in the company of other men' (Battis 2007: 66). One might go as far as to suggest that John is answering the call for male liberation by freeing himself of traditional sex role stereotypes (Sawyer 2004: 25). After all, those supposedly masculine traits such as logic, discipline, control, rationality and aggression that were once understood as the signifiers of male maturity 'are now seen as the stigma of deviance' and those traditionally feminine characteristics such as emotion, spontaneity, intuition and compassion 'are increasingly being seen as the markers of maturity and health' for the male (Clare 2001: 68). From this perspective, John can be seen to represent the height of male maturity in contemporary society because

> today's rough-looking heroes must conceal beneath an unruly exterior a soft heart . . . their exterior must figure forth their robust personality . . . but within the butch clothing . . . they must be new men, reconstructed men, able to express and articulate their feelings.
>
> (Church-Gibson 2005: 72)

John can be seen to challenge existing images of the space adventurer or action hero through his commitment to emotion, intellect, bravery and scientific calculations over and above muscular yet emotionless bravado. In fact, the programme goes further to destabilise the status of the masculine hero as the show quite literally toys with John's mind and physical form. For example, in one episode we see John embody Aeryn's body (2:09 'Out of Their Minds') while in another we are presented with three alternative versions of the astronaut (2:10 'My Three Crichtons'). We see the villainous Scorpius take over John's psyche in the second season (2:18 'A Clockwork Nebari') and spend much of the third watching two separate yet identical Johns taking on different story arcs (3:06 'Eat Me'). Therefore, while Helford's work on Captain James T. Kirk suggests that the *Star Trek* hero draws on both masculine and feminine characteristics because he is transformed from body to body and divided against himself (Helford 1996: 11–31), likewise, John can be read in this selfsame way.

MASCULINITY, MUSCULARITY AND BODILY DISPLAY

Before concluding that John represents an empowering new image of contemporary masculinity, it is worth considering the ways in which his body is presented to the viewer. After all, while numerous film, television and comic book masculinities present the contemporary action hero as a hard body with 'clenched fists . . . bulging muscles [and] hardened jaws', a body who is always taut, forever tightened and born ready for action (Dyer 1992: 136–7, 129), *Farscape* does little to challenge the notion of the tight male body as defensive armour against the outside world (Yeates 2001: online). After all, John is routinely viewed as 'pleasantly built' (Robson 2005: 10), a 'handsome young American astronaut' (Booker 2004: 163) with 'a butt that looks great encased in leather' (Elrod 2005: 187), a 'dishy hetero-dreamboat with a chiseled physique' and 'probably one of the most attractive astronauts ever to supervise an EVA mission' (Battis 2007: 66–7, 24), and as such, one may suggest that he is simply a modern-day incarnation of those square-jawed heroes who dominated 1950s science fiction. When we see him naked (1:01 'Premiere') his body adheres to the 'dominant ideal of male desirability' (Church-Gibson 2005: 63) with its pumped-up pecs, strong jaw-line and flat stomach (Edwards 1997: 130), and when we see him clothed he is routinely wearing a tight T-shirt and fitted leather trousers. The point here then is that the T-shirt has a long history of 'eroticising the male torso' (Bruzzi 2005: 48), whereas the tight leather trousers not only show his taut body off to great effect, but actually make a point of signalling the strength of the man underneath because his muscularity can 'only be kept in check by the toughest clothing available' (Robson 2005: 11).

However, rather than read John's muscularity as a sign of natural power in the unknown *Farscape* universe, or as a signal of strength and dominance over his comrades on board Moya, what his hard body actually signifies is his own fear and terror. After all, if one considers that the hypermasculine body is achieved rather than natural then this image must be read as a hysterical construction and a fascist performance rather than a powerful or dominant figure of the male. Indeed, the image of hypermasculinity can be seen to expose rather than alleviate anxieties about gendered identity because 'the emphatic masculinity of these bodies "protests too much"' (Jancovich 2004: 95). Roger Horrocks makes this point when he states that the macho male 'is not simply an over-the top assertion of male white might' but a 'roar of despair, hysteria and panic' (Horrocks 1995: 52). In this same way we are told that, 'there is an increasing focus on masculinity as troubled and unsure of itself – never more unsure than when it is shouting its self-confidence via exaggeratedly muscular heroes toting modern weaponry' (MacKinnon 2003: 63).

Therefore, rather than critique *Farscape* for presenting a stereotypical image of hard, taut hypermasculinity, the show might be applauded for challenging existing images of the dominant male. John may well look like the overconfident, all-powerful American hero, but in a post-patriarchal science fiction universe where numerous species are trained to fly military craft, use firearms and fight in hand-to-hand combat, John's hard body merely signifies fear, anxiety and loss of control. After all, while hypermasculinity acts as a 'means of dominating both women and other men who are in the competition for the spoils of the earth' (Dyer 1992: 132), in the *Farscape* universe John is seen as 'weak, fragile [and] half blind' (Butcher 2005: 68). Thus, *Farscape* cleverly draws on the codes and conventions of science fiction to comment on the status of masculinity in society, pointing to the ways in which the hegemonic male is a carefully constructed image that is presented as a 'manly front' to signal strength, stamina and potency in the face of fear and anxiety over changing sex and gender roles in society.

Conclusion

This chapter has outlined the ways in which telefantasy can be seen to examine a wide range of social, cultural and political concerns that are of importance to society, paying particular attention to the ways in which the genre has been applauded by feminist critics for its empowering representations of feminism, femininity and a woman's role. However, while much work on the representation of sex and gender in science fiction and fantasy television focuses on the representation of woman, this chapter has examined the presentation of masculinity, musculinity and a man's role in alternative space and time dimensions, concluding that contemporary texts seek to present an alternative action hero who can combine the supposedly feminine traits of emotionality, sensitivity and connectedness with those traditionally masculine qualities of bravery, strength and dominance. Therefore, telefantasy can be seen to explore the possibilities of social change, with shows such as *Firefly* and *Farscape* being seen to examine the very real notion of a culture beyond gender differentiation and sex role stereotyping.

7. HOSPITAL DRAMA: REASSURANCE, ANXIETY AND THE DOCTOR-HERO

INTRODUCTION

Although the 1950s hospital drama was home to morally principled and caring male doctors, more recently, this image of infallible masculinity has been replaced by less exalted representations of the male. In fact, today's audiences are exposed to a large number of doctors who are not only tortured and tormented in their personal and professional lives, but who are actually culpable for the deaths of their patients. Therefore, this chapter will document the history of the feminine nurse, the female practitioner and the male doctor-hero on the small screen, from the 1950s to the present day, paying detailed attention to both the private and public lives of these medical professionals. By looking at the representation of the male doctor in shows such as *ER* and *House* this chapter will examine the ways in which the contemporary hospital drama challenges the saintly image of the doctor-hero and consider the ways in which such depictions negotiate traditional images of masculinity and the male sex role in society.

HISTORY OF THE GENRE

The 1950s saw large increases in healthcare spending and major advances in biomedicine in both Britain and America, and as such, early medical dramas such as *Medic* (1954–6) and *Emergency-Ward 10* (1957–67) were extremely 'respectful of the growing power and authority of the medical institutions' (Jacobs 2003: 4). Indeed, the medical associations were so keen to 'augment public trust in the medical profession' (ibid.: 4) that they actually supplied advisors to such shows, making sure that scripts and storylines were accurate and reassuring to the public. The medical advisors had a clear agenda here as they were seen to 'make sure that the doctors were shown in the best light possible so that the public wouldn't lose their faith in medicine' (Emrys-Roberts cited in Jacobs 2003: 4–5). In fact, the medical advisors were so concerned about the representation of their profession that they complained when doctors in *Medic* were seen drinking coffee while discussing patient care because they suggested that it showed a lack of concentration, consideration and professionalism, and as a result of their complaint, 'the coffee was dropped from the scene' (Turow 1989: 38). Moreover, it was rare for these infallible television doctors to lose a patient because 'that would not have sat too well downtown at the Medical Association' (ibid.: 39), and although these early hospital dramas 'almost always' cured the sick and saved the dying, on those rare occasions when a patient did pass away, the death was always 'confined to off-screen space' so that the programmes did not alienate the Medical Association or offend the television audience of the period (Jacobs 2003: 15).

Both *Medic* and *Emergency-Ward 10* reassured audiences about the professionalism of medical staff and the advances in medical technology through the central and capable figure of the male doctor-hero who was 'at the centre of authority in the hospital or practice' (Jacobs 2003: 5). The depiction of the doctor-hero was so reassuring during this period that he came to be seen as 'the most trusted and respected figure on television' (Philips 2000: 50–1). After all, he was 'god-like' (Hallam 1998: 26), a 'matinee idol . . . with a great bedside manner' (Spadoni 2006: online), 'a handsome paragon of masculine virtue' (Hallam 1998: 32), 'an emblematic figure for the brave new post-war world' (Philips 2000: 51) and the personification of a benevolent, kind and caring healthcare system (Karpf 1998: 182). In fact, these shows were so keen to present low mortality rates and high standards of professionalism that they routinely ignored 'the day-to-day political and economic concerns that shaped and limited healthcare' in both British and American society (Turow 1989: 78). John Turow does well to summarise these early programmes when he comments that 'the driving assumption behind TV's premier doctor series was that the physician was the unquestioned king of health care in a society where medicine was an infinitely expandable commodity' (ibid.: 78).

Although the 1960s continued to value the high professional standards, low mortality rates and matinee-idol good looks of the television doctor, programmes such as *Dr Kildare* (1961–6) and *Ben Casey* (1961–6) did make one significant change to the hospital drama. After all, while programmes from the 1950s focused on the towering and infallible doctor-hero, shows from the 1960s presented the working relationship between a young junior doctor and his more experienced teacher and mentor. Julia Hallam makes this point when she says that the doctor is 'envisioned as a handsome young man whose idealism and hot-headed enthusiasm is tempered by the knowledge and wisdom of an older, wiser figure, his mentor and boss, who treats his young protégé like a son' (Hallam 1998: 32). In this way, these programmes continued to reassure audiences about the professionalism of medical staff and the advances in medical technology because 'the education of a young idealistic doctor was both instructional for the viewer and a way of showing how the eternal values of medical care and wisdom were reproduced in action' (Jacobs 2003: 5). *Dr Kildare* and *Ben Casey*, like *Medic* and *Emergency-Ward 10* before them, were keen to protect their 'idealised image of the doctor' (Philips 2000: 52) and present the 'stamp of quality' provided by the medical authorities (Jacobs 2002: 24). Because these programmes encouraged the American Medical Association to review each script and storyline for medical and professional authenticity, both shows were given 'a permanent seal of AMA approval' (Turow 1989: 62). Furthermore, the American Medical Association was heard commending *Dr Kildare* for giving 'the public an accurate picture of the long, tough struggle to become a practicing physician' (Hoffman cited ibid.: 71), and in 1964 it presented an award to the show for 'furthering public understanding of the medical profession and the practice of medicine' (Turow 1989: 72).

However, although the American Medical Association was heard praising the show for its 'accurate' picture of the medical profession, it is worth noting that the programme was in fact very heavily censored so as not to shock or disturb the viewing audience. After all, the programme could not 'mention the word "cancer" in its dialogue because of a cigarette sponsor' and it was advised not to use words such as 'urine . . . pregnant . . . venereal disease [and] breast' in order to maintain television's 'boundaries of propriety' (Turow 1989: 64). Because the programme 'vetoed any story line suggesting anything other than the most respectable of diseases' (Philips 2000: 52) and 'disallowed the exposure of sensitive body parts and the showing of blood or the body cavity during operations' (Turow 1989: 64), one might suggest that these programmes were unable and unwilling to present an authentic image of the medical profession or a realistic image of the doctor-hero. And therefore, while the American Medical Association was heard praising the hospital dramas for 'doing precisely what they hoped they would do to boost their profession's image' (Turow 1989: 77), individual physicians could be heard criticising the 'unrealistic' nature of the texts in question.

After all, not only were these programmes quick to show doctors diagnosing chronic medical problems and curing serious illnesses, but they also showed them happily counselling their patients, taking the time to make house calls and even sitting with them through the night when they were scared, lonely or at risk (Turow 1989: 129). The point here is simply that 'millions of Americans were becoming resentful of their physicians for not living up to the image of the wise and caring physician' (ibid.: 129) that is depicted by the television doctor of the period, because while *Dr Kildare* may be seen to make house calls and spend long periods of time with a single patient, this was simply not the reality of the medical profession at this or any other time. Indeed, the representation of the heroic doctor has been understood as 'a factor contributing to the rise in malpractice suits against doctors' (Karpf 1988: 189) because audiences watch *Dr Kildare* for example 'and then expect miracles' of their real life medical counterparts (ibid.: 189).

While these early medical dramas were keen to present an impeccable medical profession and deliberately avoided acknowledging 'the sociopolitical changes that were beginning to reshape the medical system' (Turow 1989: 155), shows from the 1970s sought to present a less capable image of the doctor-hero and a more realistic portrayal of the wider medical environment. For example, in the late 1960s and 1970s, programmes such as *The Bold Ones: The New Doctors* (1969), *Medical Center* (1969–76) and *Angels* (1975–83) were dealing with a range of social problems such as abortion, rape, drug addiction, artificial insemination and venereal disease while openly acknowledging that healthcare providers had limited resources. Therefore, these shows could be seen to challenge post-war optimism in science and medicine in favour of a more cynical presentation of the medical industry in general and the doctor-hero in particular. After all, although the British and American healthcare context differ (with the former dependent on the National Health Service and the latter more dependent on Health Maintenance Organizations and private insurance), both 'had to face the various critiques of medical science and practice from the 1970s onwards' (Jacobs 2003: 43) such as funding, waiting lists, hospital closures, bed shortages, staff shortages, medical litigation, debates about the hours worked by junior doctors and the issue of care in the community. These programmes presented a shift from the paternalistic junior–senior doctor relationship to a more ensemble-based drama, perhaps suggesting that a patient 'could no longer be credibly healed by one infallible figure' or by a dynamic medical pairing (Jacobs 2002: 25). After all, 'the single doctor treating the hospitalized patient with all but total independence was gradually becoming an anachronism in the face of hospital bureaucratization, medical specialization, increased patient distrust of specialists, and impending government involvement' (Turow 1989: 49). Therefore, the 1970s medical drama can be seen to challenge not only the financial limitations of healthcare provision, but also the omnipotent image of the capable doctor-hero.

The 1980s hospital drama, as exemplified by programmes such as *Casualty* (1986–) and *St Elsewhere* (1982–8), could be seen to present a wide range of medico-political concerns such as AIDS, homosexuality, organ donation and euthanasia; point to societies loss of 'confidence in medical institutions, medical science and doctors' (Jacobs 2002: 25) and draw attention to the personal and professional lives of an overworked and underpaid medical team. However, although *Casualty* is most often acknowledged for its critique of welfare cuts on the NHS and for foregrounding 'the stupidity of introducing free market principles into a healthcare system' (Jacobs 2003: 23), it is the programme's depiction of the medical profession that could be seen as most groundbreaking here. Both *Casualty* and *St Elsewhere* made a conscious effort to present a medical team who are suffering from a range of personal and professional problems such as divorce, depression, harassment and bullying, problems which meant that the once infallible doctor-hero was now fragile, vulnerable and making mistakes (Karpf 1988: 193). And yet, rather than condemn these programmes for presenting a damning image of the medical doctor, it is worth noting that such portrayals were simply exploiting a wider social discourse. After all, it would be difficult to 'fill dramas with flawless, unfailingly empathetic doctors while the documentaries and news programmes were busy featuring malpractice suits, allegations of medical greed, and examples of the peremptory treatment of patients' (ibid.: 193). In short, the comforting image of the confident and capable medical elite was replaced 'by team work and a crisis environment' (Hallam 1998: 34), and as such, audiences have had to 'accept heroes who were less godlike' (Turow 1989: 163) than their heroic medical predecessors.

Although programmes such as *Casualty* span 'the period of transition when new medical dramas began to assert themselves in the 1990s', it is actually the fast paced *ER* that 'constituted a distinctive development in the medical drama' (Jacobs 2003: 10, 1). After all, this programme focused on both the working and personal lives of its medical staff, depicted explicit images of emergency treatment and high-tech equipment, used fast-paced camera work and even faster medical jargon and presented an unremittingly cynical tone regarding the 'medical failures as well as the larger failures of American society' (Cassidy and Taylor 1997: 6). Therefore, this contemporary hospital setting cannot be viewed as a quiet safe haven or peaceful refuge where patients could be cured and cared for, but rather a stressful, tense environment with little control, confidence or certainty. This fictional emergency room has been understood as a 'war zone' (Jacobs 2003: 1) due to the fact that 'the disorder and irrationality of the city keeps intruding upon the hospital' (West-Burnham and Roberts 1998: 258). Such disorders can be seen quite literally when a helicopter crashed onto the roof of the building (10:08 'Freefall') or a gunman takes a nurse hostage (12:22 '21 Guns'), or more figuratively when a doctor is abused and beaten up by a sick patient (6:13 'Be Still My Heart'). While the early medical dramas presented 'dashing young interns magicking away rare diseases while their impeccably white gowns stay pristine' (Karpf 1988: 180), *ER* routinely presents the diagnosis and misdiagnosis of rare diseases, bloodied gowns, overworked doctors and neglected patients. Moreover, while it was rare for the early dramas to lose a patient, *ER* shows the audience that doctors are, on occasion, actually responsible for their deaths, be it through 'mistakes or negligence or simply circumstance' (Jacobs 2003: 125). In this way, the programme has been said to be as much about disillusionment as it is about miracle surgery (Cassidy and Taylor 1997: 6).

REPRESENTATIONS OF WOMEN: WIVES, NURSES AND PATIENTS

Since the emergence of *Medic* and *Emergency-Ward 10* in the 1950s, the male doctor has been presented as the heroic central protagonist, relegating women to the nurturing roles of wife, girlfriend, patient and nurse (Philips 2000: 50). In the 1950s and 1960s the medical drama was in fact known for its 'female guest stars playing patients, not physicians' (Turow 1989: 175). While *Dr Kildare* was especially famous for its 'procession of dying beauties who fell into the arms of their solicitous, handsome healer' (ibid.: 175), *Emergency-Ward 10* was renowned for its 'marked absence of . . . women doctors' (Karpf 1988: 183). The doctor-hero was 'supported by a revolving cast of female nurses . . . whose function was to allow for the display of his medical expertise' (Philips 2000: 52), and as such, it was routinely the handsome male doctor who was in the position of legitimacy, respect and authority in the drama.

Although one might assume that the new hospital drama would be presenting powerful and empowering female physicians due to the fact that a growing number of women are applying to medical school, and indeed because a growing number of women can already be seen in the medical profession, the contemporary hospital drama continues to focus on 'male actors at the centre of the action' (Hallam 1998: 45). It seems that it is 'men who are at the cutting edge of medical technology' (Philips 2000: 60) with central protagonists such as Dr Gregory House/Hugh Laurie, Dr Preston Burke/Isaiah Washington and Dr Luka Kovac/Goran Visnjic in *House, Grey's Anatomy* (2005–) and *ER* respectively. On those rare occasions when a mainstream hospital drama such as *The Bold Ones: The New Doctors* or *Medical Center* did 'place female guest stars in physician roles' (Turow 1989: 177) audiences routinely saw the physician have to make a hard choice between hospital work or a successful home life, with the desire for a relationship taking precedence time and again. Furthermore, when medical dramas such as *The Nurses* (1962–5); *Julie Farr, M.D.* (1978–9) and *Women in White* (1979) sought to present a female nurse or physician as a central or continuing character, the failure of such shows merely confirmed that a successful medical drama 'had to revolve around male physicians' because 'men were turned off by women as leads' in the genre (Turow 1989: 105, 175).

The medical drama continued to feel awkward about situating women as doctors due to the fact that 'a doctor is professionally required to demonstrate qualities of decisiveness and authority' whereas the nurse is asked to demonstrate qualities such as 'patience and tenderness' (Philips 2000: 53), with the former being understood as masculine and the latter as feminine here. Therefore, the contemporary medical drama continues to situate women as nurses with care in the community being presented as 'woman's work' (ibid.: 60). On those rare occasions where women are presented as qualified doctors, they are shown as problematic figures who are 'literally or metaphorically incapacitated' (ibid.: 59), 'depicted as crippled, dependent and sexualised' (Hallam 1998: 45) in relation to their supposedly authoritative and competent male counterparts. However, while theorists such as Julia Hallam and Deborah Philips are examining the representation of the female doctor in the medical drama, little work to date considers the representation of the male doctor beyond the matinee-idol surface appearance and God-like medical substance. Therefore, this chapter will now consider the representation of the male doctor in *ER* and *House*, paying particular attention to the crisis of confidence both within and beyond the hospital that seems to befall these medical professionals.

ER

The fast-paced *ER* focuses on both the personal and professional role of the medic at the cash-strapped County General Hospital in Chicago, with particular attention paid to the doctors running the crowded emergency room. We are informed that 'the hospital scenes in *ER* occur on an elaborately realistic set where the medical team encounters emergency medicine cases ranging from drug overdoses and rape victims to motor vehicle crashes and gunshot wounds' (O'Connor 1998: 854), with multiple plots, fast pacing and emotional crises being used to depict the traumatic environment of the emergency ward. Commentators suggest that the programmes 'greatness lies in its deviation from the Hollywood format. The good guys do not often save the day, and there's no evidence of that CIA–syndicated "God Bless America, we'll put the world to rights" message' (Cassidy and Taylor 1997: 6). Rather, we are informed that the programme 'keeps us hooked with a team that continued to develop realistically and gratifying as flawed human beings' (ibid.: 6)

Although the long-running programme has seen several cast changes, the programme continues to present the male doctor-hero at the centre of the narrative. At the time of writing, the cast includes Dr Tony Gates/John Stamos, the paramedic-turned-medical-doctor who continues to rebel against his male superiors; Dr Ray Barnett/Shane West, the musician who wanted to tour with his band rather than commit to the medical profession; Dr Archie Morris/Scott Grimes, the ambitious resident who would rather be a medical advisor in front of a news camera than an overworked doctor in a busy emergency room; Dr Greg Pratt/Mekhi Phifer, a doctor who is being investigated for his role in supplying medication to a local church clinic and struggling to come to terms with his brother's homosexuality; and Dr Luka Kovac/Goran Visnjic the chief of emergency medicine who has lost his wife and children, suffered a nervous breakdown and been charged with malpractice. Therefore, these doctors have not only 'come down from their pedestals and revealed their humanity' (Hallam 1998: 43) but they been positioned as vain, vacuous and vulnerable images of the male.

Jason Jacobs has looked at early episodes of *ER* to suggest that the programme 'enacts a process of mourning for the white male . . . in decline' (Jacobs 2003: 151), and one might suggest that later episodes continue to reinforce this notion of masculinity in crisis. After all, although early seasons could be seen to follow Dr Mark Greene/Anthony Edwards' 'disintegration from happy husband and parent in series one to lonely, alienated, divorced absent father; from idealistic doctor to embittered recluse, as a consequence of being personally assaulted and attacked' (West-Burnham and Roberts 1998: 256), more recent episodes have followed the equally tortured story arc of Dr Luka Kovac, the longest-residing doctor at County General Hospital.

ER: TORTURE, TORMENT AND THE CONTEMPORARY DOCTOR-HERO

Dr Kovac trained as a medical doctor, served in the Croatian Army and lost his wife and children in the Croatian War of Independence before coming to County General Hospital to work as an attending physician, and although the doctor came to America in a bid to put the torment of war-torn Croatia behind him, the character seems unable to escape the grief of losing his family. His sexual encounters with a string of prostitutes, medical students and nurses has only left the man feeling more tortured as one date ended in the brutal beating and subsequent death of a man who tried to assault him (7:04 'Benton Backwards'), and another in a serious car accident that left his date shocked and terrified (9:10 'Hindsight'). Unsurprisingly then, Dr Kovac suffered a nervous breakdown, took sabbatical leave from the hospital and reconsidered his role in the medical profession, and as such, he can be understood as the personification of the new hospital drama that depicts a 'hostile outside world' and 'foregrounds nihilism, self-destruction and despair' (Jacobs 2003: 25, 147).

However, although Dr Kovac's torturous story arc demonstrates the fragility and lack of potency in the contemporary male, it continues to present the man as a committed and approachable doctor who is content to work long hours in the ER, dedicate time and energy to his patients and offer his medical services to the 'Doctors Without Borders' programme. In this way, *ER* continues to present the 'saintly demeanour, high moral character, and good looks of the archetypal television doctor', taking time to depict the character as a morally principled and caring man 'who placed the interests of humanity above profit motive . . . who placed public good and self-sacrifice above personal financial gain' (Hallam 1998: 26, 32). Therefore, although 'the medical world today has changed fundamentally from the way it was when Dr. Kildare first walked prime-time hospital corridors' (Turow 1989: xix), one might suggest that *ER*'s doctor-hero is simply an extension of 'the saintly image of the doctor as a handsome paragon of masculine virtue' (Hallam 1998: 32), that encapsulated the early hospital drama. After all, although *ER* can be seen to present a tortured and tormented doctor-hero, it is worth noting that 'no matter how bleakly it represented medical practice and bureaucracy . . . the good doctor, repository of all the hopes we invest in medicine and the ideals we hold dear' endured (Karpf 1988: 201). In short, the upstanding doctor-hero 'remains an invariable component of even the most abrasive medical fiction' (ibid.: 201). Therefore, although the *ER* doctors routinely reveal their personal and professional flaws, it is worth considering the ways in which 'this humanisation is generally conducted through a focus on the ethics and responsibilities of maintaining the medical ideal' (Hallam 1998: 43), with that ideal being the image of the sincere doctor-hero.

If one considers the ways in which *ER* is 'able to balance its often-unbearable assertions of despair and hopelessness with the promise of potential, if short-lived, rewards of collegiality, friendship and romance' (Jacobs 2003: 11) then it is worth noting that Dr Kovac has, on occasion, appeared content, and even happy in both his personal and professional life, most recently by becoming chief of emergency medicine, committing to Dr Abby Lockhart/Maura Tierney and having a new baby. However, perhaps unsurprisingly, due to the fact that *ER* does tend to be 'unremittingly despairing' (Jacobs 2002: 24), it is not long before the man in question is being injured in a hospital shootout (12:22 '21 Guns'), defending himself against a malpractice suit (13:05 'Ames v. Kovac') and fighting through physical and mental torture (13:14 'Murmurs of the Heart').

Although this list of personal troubles and professional tribulations seems so long that it might actually threaten to alienate the viewing public, it is actually these trials that continue to attract the audience. After all, unrealistic images of 'a confident, god-like medical elite who have everything ordered, organised and under control' (Hallam 1998: 34) can actually estrange rather than comfort the viewing public. Hannah Shearer, co-producer of *Emergency!* (1972–9) made this point when she commented that the representation of medical professionals in the hospital drama have to be made 'as vulnerable as possible in their normal lives' (Shearer cited in Turow 1989: 169) because otherwise the viewing public may resent them for 'performing heroic deeds as part of their everyday life [while] they're sitting at home in front of the TV set not doing that' (ibid.: 168). With this image of a troubled doctor in mind then, the chapter will now turn to *House* and consider the ways in which this drama continues to both challenge and conform to the saintly image of the doctor-hero.

House

House focuses on the professional role of Dr Gregory House and his small, hand-picked team of medical experts, Dr Eric Foreman/Omar Epps, Dr Robert Chase/Jesse Spencer and Dr Allison Cameron/Jennifer Morrison, in the state-of-the-art Princeton-Plainsboro Teaching Hospital. *House* tends to focus more on the trials and tribulations of the small diagnostic team as they are seen working on challenging medical cases than it does on the sexual chemistry and interpersonal relationships between the central characters of the show. Indeed, the success of the series has been put down to the fact that the programme depicts 'virtually all work and no play' for the doctors in question (Spadoni 2006: online) as they struggle to diagnose everything from seizures and African sleeping sickness to breast cancer and rabbit fever.

DR HOUSE: INACCESSIBLE AND UNPROFESSIONAL

Dr House is a sarcastic, abrupt and anti-social diagnostician with a dual speciality in infectious disease and nephrology, a diagnostician who has to take pain medication and walk with a cane after an operation on his upper leg left him crippled. Unlike previous representations of the medical doctor, Dr House dislikes patients, despises their families and disagrees with hospital administrators. The man is inaccessible to patients, authoritarian to his own team and he can, on occasion, be unprofessional; be it by playing on his Game Boy when on duty (1:03 'Occam's Razor'), ignoring other doctors so that he can watch *General Hospital* (1963–) (1:01 'Pilot'), sharing painkillers with patients (1:02 'Paternity'), running paternity bets (1:02 'Paternity') and turning a diagnostic session into a cruel game (3:08 'Whac-A-Mole'). In fact, Edward Vogler/Chi McBride, one of the hospital board members makes this point when he tells his colleagues that Dr House recently 'violated a DNR and was charged with assault, he brought a termite into the OR and spat on a surgeon [and] accepted a Corvette from a patient who was a known member of the New Jersey mafia', concluding that the doctor in question 'has personally had more complaints filed against him than any other department in this hospital' (1:18 'Babies and Bathwater'). Patients routinely tell Dr House that he is 'not a very nice doctor' (1:03 'Occam's Razor'), refer to him as an 'arrogant jerk' (1:07 'Fidelity') or go as far as charging him with criminal assault and battery (1:09 'DNR') and even his closest friend Dr James Wilson/Robert Sean Leonard comments that he is 'cold, uncaring [and] distant' (1:21 'Three Stories'). When one of his own diagnostic team asks Dr House 'isn't treating patients why we became doctors?', he comments 'no . . . treating illnesses is why we became doctors, treating patients is what makes most doctors miserable' (1:01 'Pilot'). Furthermore, in order to avoid his weekly clinic duties he has been seen to make bets with senior doctors (1:11 'Detox'), hide from patients (1:02 'Paternity') and scare them into demanding to see a different physician (1:03 'Occam's Razor'). For example, when he is faced with an overly populated waiting room, instead of looking at the patients alongside the other doctors on duty, Dr House introduces himself to the potential patients by telling them his name and his specialisms before commenting that he is bored, at the clinic against his will, stoned and addicted to vicodin (1:03 'Occam's Razor').

Dr House: rudely reassuring

However, before critiquing or condemning the character for disillusioning audiences or augmenting panic about the medical profession, it is worth noting that *House* continues to exploit the more reassuring codes and respectable conventions of earlier hospital dramas. Therefore, although the doctor refuses to wear a white jacket or work on his bedside manner, he rarely loses a patient. And likewise, although he can appear bored by clinic duties and abrupt with patients, he refuses to be interrupted when he is working on a medical case. Therefore, like Dr Kildare and Dr Casey before him, Dr House 'works at the most languid pace, seeing one or at most two patients per episode' (Karpf 1988: 185). Although Dr House has 'all the bedside manner of a rude waiter you would refuse to tip . . . he would be the man you would want if no other doctor could figure out what was wrong with you' (Spadoni 2006: online). Dr Wilson makes this point when he comments that Dr House 'should probably re-read the ethics code . . . but he has saved hundreds of lives' (1:17 'Role Model'). Moreover, he refuses to kowtow to hospital administrators, would rather lose his job than endorse a drug he does not believe in, and only ever takes professional risks in the interest of his patients. Therefore, while Dr House can be seen to present an inaccessible, unorthodox and inconsiderate image of the doctor-hero, he 'still sh[i]ne[s] with integrity' and the medical system continues to be 'portrayed as ultimately sound and caring' (Karpf 1988: 195). Dr Cameron confirms this point when she is heard telling Dr House that 'you are abrasive and rude, but I figured everything you do, you do it to help people . . . because it's right' (1:17 'Role Model').

While much trauma television examines the male doctor and his 'increasing loss of confidence' in his ability to make life and death decisions (Jacobs 2003: 125), one might suggest that *House* presents us with an exceedingly confident and capable doctor-hero, a hero who will stop at nothing to diagnose a patient and find the appropriate cure or course of action. After all, while it has been suggested that the 'new hospital dramas sought to . . . demystify the idea of the male doctor as God-like and all-powerful in the face of injury and disease' (Jacobs 2003: 105), *House* presents a rather different view of the doctor-hero here. In fact, Dr House, much like Dr Kildare and Dr Casey before him, is presented as a seemingly infallible doctor, who can be heard telling a patient that 'you've got a better shot believing in me' than believing in God (1:05 'Damned If You Do'), telling Dr Lisa Cuddy/Lisa Edelstein that 'I take risks, sometimes patients die, but not taking risks causes more patients to die' (1:11 'Detox') and when Dr Wilson tells Dr House that 'I want you to accept that sometimes patients die against all reason and sometimes they get better against all reason' (1:05 'Damned If You Do') he refuses to accept this explanation of illness and injury. Dr House might be accused of 'playing God' with patient care, which is condemned as an 'expression of unqualified arrogance and overconfidence' in the doctor-hero (Jacobs 2003: 126). That said, it seems to be precisely his unqualified arrogance and overconfidence that make him a capable doctor. After all, this is a man who 'proved a case based on no medical evidence whatsoever' (3:02 'Cane and Able'), has a flip chart keeping score between himself and God (2:19 'House vs. God') and when told that he has a God complex, simply growls that 'God doesn't limp' (3:02 'Cane and Able'). Therefore, although one may suggest that those physicians such as Dr House who aspire to not only play God, but challenge him for power 'are typically coded as a toxic presence in the medical community' (ibid.: 126) it does not mean that such figures are not respected by other professionals or reassuring to the viewing public.

And yet, *House*, like much contemporary medical drama, can be seen to 'incorporate the growing criticism of masculinity that was emerging in cultural studies, criminology and psychology during the 1990s' by presenting 'a suspicious view of confident masculinity' (Jacobs 2003: 106, 105). After all, the originally dogged and infallible Dr House has more recently been seen to suffer both physically and professionally, not simply because the husband of a former patient shoots him, but because the side effects of the shooting leave him questioning his own professional abilities (2:24 'No Reason'). Dr House's increasing reliance on prescription drugs finds him facing trial for forging prescriptions (3:11 'Words and Deeds') and in jail after resisting arrest on such charges (3:06 'Que Será Será'), and as such, the earlier reading of the doctor as an infallible capable hero with a sarcastic tone and a crude bedside manner is perhaps replaced with a more problematic image of contemporary masculinity.

Conclusion

This chapter has outlined the ways in which the hospital drama has presented the medical profession from the 1950s to the present day, paying particular attention to the role of female nurses, feminine physicians and the male doctor-hero. The work has introduced the image of the infallible individual doctor in *Medic* and *Emergency-Ward 10*, the paternalistic junior–senior doctor relationship in *Dr Kildare* and *Ben Casey* and the harassed medical team in *Casualty* and *St Elsewhere*, before examining the tortured and tormented image of the doctor-hero in such new hospital dramas as *ER* and *House*. However, although the pace of the shows may have changed, the level of cynicism and despair increased and the image of the organised doctor challenged, the sincerity and integrity of the doctor-hero in the hospital drama remains.

8. POLICE AND CRIME DRAMA: INVESTIGATING MALE AUTHORITY

INTRODUCTION

The police and crime drama can be understood as one of the most masculine of television genres due to the fact that it tends to focus on the public sphere, professional roles and the male world of work (MacKinnon 2003: 69). Moreover, if one considers that the genre relies rather heavily on a rather simple formula of 'crime, pursuit and capture' (Sparks 1992: 5), then one might assume that the cop show is responsible for some of the most tired and passé representations of hegemonic masculinity on the small screen. However, irrespective of the simplicity of the formula and the success of the officers, the genre has produced some of the most tormented and troubled images of the male on contemporary television. Indeed, the cop show has witnessed a dramatic change in the representation of the police from the safety of the citizen in uniform to the more ambiguous image of the undercover field agent in recent years. Therefore, this chapter will examine the depiction of the television cop from the 1950s constable to the present day counter-terrorist officer, paying particular attention to the ways in which the structuring hero of shows such as *24* and *Spooks* negotiates success in the private realm for victory in the professional sphere. The chapter will examine a range of British and American cop shows although it is worth noting that there is little to distinguish the key themes, narrative arcs or central characters here. After all, when we consider the idealised portrait of the police in a British drama such as *Dixon of Dock Green* (1955–76), one could also be talking about the American *Dragnet* (1951–9), in this same way, when the aggression and violence of Britain's *The Sweeney* (1975–8) is under consideration, one could also look to America's *Starsky and Hutch* (1975–9) or *The Rockford Files* (1974–80) for further examples. Likewise, when considering the anxiousness and ambiguity of the new police and crime drama one could consider Britain's *The Cops* (1998–2000) alongside alternative titles such as America's more recent *The Wire* (2002–).

HISTORY OF THE GENRE

Dixon of Dock Green showed the police having to deal with lost dogs, stolen bicycles and the occasional anti-social elements of British society such as post office robberies or small-scale burglaries. The programme presented the 'bobby-on-the-beat' as courageous, dedicated and hard-working men who were committed to 'reason; simplicity; attention to due process; respect for tradition . . . justice and fairness' (Cashmore 1994: 160). These men were seen to uphold standards of honesty, decency and humanity in both their public and private lives, providing 'a constant good example' to the wider viewing public (Clarke 1992: 240). The show presented the eponymous George Dixon/Jack Warner as an upstanding and honest policeman who could cope with both public and domestic tribulations, who knew his neighbours and who could protect his local community (McQueen 1998: 81). Alan Clarke makes the point that George Dixon was a 'man of integrity who would not have devalued himself or the force he was serving by bringing the possibility of dishonour to the uniform' (Clarke 1992: 241). In this way the show was very keen to present 'a clear and severe division between good and evil' (Cashmore 1994: 160) and make the point that officers such as Dixon were working for the common good of society. However, while *Dixon of Dock Green* was busy presenting a 'cosy and rosy' (Delaney 2007: online) view of British society, it was soon evident that this representation was actually at odds with the reality of that period. It has been noted that George Dixon 'seemed horribly out of place in the 1960s and, by the 1970s, the whole series had become tiresome and irrelevant' (Cashmore 1994: 156). After all, although crime rates in Britain had increased in the 1950s, it was assumed that this was simply a passing problem brought on by the disruption of the war years, and that as society retuned once again to an orderly routine, so too, crime rates would return to a more acceptable level (Clarke 1992: 238). However, crime rates did not decrease and the *Dixon of Dock Green* tradition of community policing was being challenged by more aggressive and depersonalised modes of law enforcement both on and off screen (Cooke 2002: 19–21). Therefore, while officers from the 1950s were keen to highlight restraint, reason and respect for the police force, the 1960s saw 'more and more police . . . being trained in crowd and riot control [with] joint operations between the police and the army [being] organized' (Clarke 1992: 239).

Z-Cars (1962–78) offered a clean break from the conservatism of *Dixon of Dock Green* by seeking to represent both the changes and challenges to British policing that were taking place in the early 1960s. The programme focused on the trials and tribulations of uniformed constables including PC Smith/Brian Blessed, PC Weir/Joseph Brady, PC Lynch/James Ellis and PC Steele/Jeremy Kemp, as they were assigned to crime patrol duties in a fictional north-west town in Britain. The programme took its name from the Ford Zephyrs that had been introduced into British policing at that time. *Z-Cars* was seen to present a more frank and often less flattering portrait of police work than audiences were used to seeing on *Dixon of Dock Green*. Unlike the earlier programme, *Z-Cars* made a conscious effort to depict the police as 'flawed, bad tempered, even violent . . . and aggressive' men (Delaney 2007: online). However, although the programme seemed committed to presenting the police force as a group of men who would drink, gamble and abuse their wives, it was always careful to show that despite their brutish behaviour the police 'were essentially good men who cared about the lives and crimes they were involved in' (McQueen 1998: 81). In this way, *Z-Cars*, much like *Dixon of Dock Green*, made it clear that the police were working for the good of the community and that however flawed their personal characteristics, their commitment to justice was paramount.

The 1970s saw further changes to both policing practices and the representation of masculinity within the police and crime drama. As British crime rates continued to rise, the police opted for specialisations within the force (Cooke 2003: 114), and likewise, the police in America were 'transferring vice control, traffic regulation, crime prevention and a range of routine tasks from ordinary patrolmen to organized squads' (Cobley 2001: 58). This change in policing was soon acknowledged on the small screen as programmes such as *Fraud Squad* (1969–70), *Special Branch* (1969–74) and *The Sweeney* were seen to focus on the harsh, combative hero in such specialist units. The representation of these services could be seen to reflect the social reality of the 1970s, with rising crime rates and the presentation of aggressive heroes using more extreme and unorthodox measures of violence, aggression and rule-breaking in the performance of their duty (Cooke 2002: 22).

The Sweeney is based on the exploits of two members of an elite group of detectives in the London Metropolitan Police, known as the Flying Squad. Jack Regan/John Thaw and his partner George Carter/Dennis Waterman, and although there are many differences between this and earlier shows in the genre, one of the key distinctions is in the programme's representation of crime and criminality. Whereas both *Dixon of Dock Green* and *Z-Cars* were keen to consider the 'underlying causes of the action, the criminal's individual problems as well as the police response which was deemed to be most appropriate' *The Sweeney* makes it clear that the police barely have enough time to chase and arrest criminals, without the luxury of introspection or contemplation (Clarke 1992: 236, 237). The other marked distinction is in the representation and reception of the police officer. After all, George Dixon was a friend of the community, the patrolling Z-Cars were a welcome sight in their fictional northern location and yet Regan and Carter were presented as outsiders in their own London community (ibid.: 237).

Even though Regan uses weapons and breaks into buildings without the proper warrant, consorts with criminals for information and intimidates suspects in interrogation, his unorthodox and occasionally illegal methods seem justified as he routinely catches the villain of the piece in what was seen to be an increasingly lawless society. Although this rather hard presentation of crime, society and the police force appears far removed from that of earlier dramas, the programme can actually be seen to present the same powerful 'moral certainties' that were evident in the earlier conservative texts (ibid.: 248). After all, Regan may have been presented as a pathologically rude protagonist, but the very fact that he stands for honesty, incorruptibility and fairness harks back to the core values of those earlier productions (ibid.: 243). In this way, one might suggest that the programme wanted to update the aesthetics of the show but retain the moral compass of previous police and crime dramas. Therefore, the message of this seemingly hard-hitting and brutish show is that crime does not and must not pay, which is of course a message that 'would not be out of place in the 1950s' (Delaney 2007: online).

It was not until the 1990s that the police and crime drama was seen to challenge the moral certainty of the police force and question the clear divisions between good and evil. It became more and more difficult for the genre to show honest policemen and a successful police force when 'even a cursory glance at a daily newspaper tells the reader that this is a hopelessly inaccurate reflection of what really happens' (Cashmore 1994: 155). The contemporary news media are keen to inform society that police and villains both lie, that criminals do not always get caught and that justice is not always served (ibid.: 154), and as such, programmes such as *The Cops* picks up on such coverage as they focus on uncompromising images of police brutality, corruption and charges of institutionalised racism, making it difficult for audiences to distinguish between 'perpetrators and victims, heroes and villains' (Bignell 2004: 121). Existing work tells us that 'in the past, criminals were obviously "bad" and police invariably "good" [whereas] in recent times the definition of the moral and legal has become clouded by the representation of "bent cops" and sympathetic "villains" ' (Casey *et al.* 2002a: 44). *The Cops* makes it clear that serious crime is committed by the police more often than it is by members of society, and presents officers of the law exploiting their institutional authority in order to pursue vendettas against members of the public, to victimise suspects and to secure 'unsafe' convictions (MacMurraugh-Kavanagh 2000: 48). In this way, the contemporary police and crime drama can be seen to have shifted the image of the British police from a site of heroic assurance to one of hazardous anxiety.

REPRESENTATIONS OF WOMEN: FLESH, SEXISM AND FRUSTRATED PROMOTIONS

Ellis Cashmore makes the point that police and crime dramas 'are not equal opportunity employers' (Cashmore 1994: 164) because the genre has continued to present the police as a white, male, heterosexual domain. Indeed, on those rare occasions where we are introduced to a female officer in an effort to 'challenge the masculine hegemony' of the genre (Cooke 2002: 22), the character is either asked to bare her flesh from week to week (*Police Woman*, 1974–8), to investigate gendered crimes and domestic concerns such as sexual abuse and rape (*Cagney and Lacey*, 1982–8), to examine women's issues such as sexism, misogyny and frustrated promotion or to play out the pressures of police work on personal relationships (*Prime Suspect*, 1991–2006). All in all 'the characters hang on to familiar aspects of their feminine world, not least in the programme's interweaving of public workspace and private lives' (Casey *et al.* 2002a: 47). David McQueen makes an enlightening observation when he comments that 'the masculinity of male characters . . . is an integral part of the characterization but is seldom explored as an issue, whereas in police dramas which have women as their central characters such gender issues are frequently central and explicit' (McQueen 1998: 84).

SACRIFICING THE FAMILY

McQueen notes that those police dramas with women in the central role can be seen to examine the pressures of police work on personal relationships, whereas male-driven cop shows fail to examine masculinity as an issue in the text (McQueen 1998: 84). From this perspective, it is necessary to consider the ways in which the genre can be seen to present the masculine hero both within and beyond the world of work. What is important here is that police and crime dramas routinely show male police constables, detectives and special branch officers ignoring the needs of their family in favour of the force, sacrificing their personal life for the good of the wider society. In short, their success in the public sphere seems to demand a sacrifice in the private realm. For example, in *The Sweeney* Regan is routinely seen to ignore, overlook or disappoint his ex-wife, daughter and girlfriend. He argues with his spouse, fails to turn up for arranged meetings with his child and treats his partner like a disposable plaything, bedsit and laundrette respectively, all with the excuse that 'I'm on an important case' (Clarke 1992: 246).

When the newly married Carter worries that his working late will upset his wife and put pressure on his marriage, Regan makes it clear that the job should come first, telling him that 'you're not a nine to five man. Over there sitting behind a desk, swigging tea all day and waiting to get home to the roses. You're like me, you're a copper' (Clarke 1992: 246). While Regan 'never had any time for his wife or family, his work always had to come first' (Clarke 1986: 229), more recently the central male protagonist in a wide range of police and crime dramas ranging from *Taggart* (1983–), *Between the Lines* (1992–4) *Cracker* (1993–6) and *The Cops* have all been seen to put their professional commitments before their personal ones. One might go as far as to suggest that it was only George Dixon's status as a widower that allowed him to perform so successfully in the wider community. Making a sacrifice in the private sphere for the good of the professional role appears to be a structuring theme in the police and crime genre, and it is a theme that is clearly exploited in contemporary texts such as *24* and *Spooks* wherein the central male protagonist seems hell bent on destroying his marriage and straining his family to breaking point all in the name of the public good.

24

24 focuses on the working lives of the Los Angeles Counter Terrorist Unit as they try to safeguard America from a range of threats including assassination plots, nuclear bombs and bio-terrorist attacks. The programme is presented in real time so that each season depicts a twenty-four-hour period in the life of the CTU agents and accompanying government officials, paying particular attention to the elite field agent Jack Bauer/Kiefer Sutherland. At the outset of the show Jack is married to Teri/Leslie Hope, he is father to Kim/Elisha Cuthbert and he works alongside his ex-mistress Nina Myers/Sarah Clarke. And although the man is soon widowed, estranged from his daughter and living under a pseudonym, the programme continues to position him in a range of personal and professional relationships throughout each new series.

24 can be seen to hark back to earlier police and crime dramas because although the programme is set in the counter-terrorist unit and our central protagonist is a CTU field agent, the issues of good and evil and the central narrative of crime, chase and arrest are in evidence here. Indeed, one might compare the programme to *Dixon of Dock Green* due to the fact that Jack remains a figure of integrity working for the good of the public. Alternatively, one might consider it in line with *The Sweeney* because this man is seen to live a troubled private life and can, on occasion, be seen to bend if not actually break the rules of law and order (even going so far as killing a material witness) in order to serve and protect society. The programme can also be seen to exploit *The Cops* as it blurs the lines between hero and villain through the presentation of double agents and sympathetic criminals.

PUBLIC GOOD OVER THE PRIVATE SPHERE

The very fact that the programme is aired in real time over a period of twenty-four hour-long episodes makes it clear from the outset that Jack's life is dedicated to the public sphere, to his work and to the good of society. The way in which Jack is routinely seen to work such long and gruelling days without comment or complaint makes it clear that this man will prioritise his working life over his domestic arrangements. Even after we learn that Jack is trying to make an effort to spend more quality time with his wife and take a more active role in bringing up his teenage daughter, he is soon heard making apologetic phone calls from the office and making excuses for not being in the family home. When Teri rings Jack to suggest counselling for their wayward daughter he simply dismisses the idea with 'we can talk about this when I get home' (1:01 '12.00–01.00') and then later in the same episode with 'look, I can't really talk right now, let me call you back' (1:01 '12.00–01.00'). And later, when Teri starts to worry about Kim's whereabouts and asks her husband to come home to keep her company during this stressful period, Jack makes the by now predictable excuse that 'I can't right now, look I don't have time to explain but some very bad things are happening tonight' to which Teri firmly replies that 'our daughter is missing, I think that's pretty bad' before signing off (1:02 '01.00–02.00'). The programme seems to suggest that Jack is professionally compromised by his involvement in the domestic sphere as Kim is kidnapped (1:01 '12.00–01.00'), Teri is later killed (1:24 '23.00–24.00') and Nina is discovered to be a traitor (1:23 '22.00–23.00'). Therefore, irrespective of whether the women in his life turn out to be passive victims or treacherous turncoats, 24 makes it clear that they are either unnecessary or unwelcome in the world of work. Masculine genres have been said to foreground the status of hegemonic masculinity by 'exclud[ing] women or else represent[ing] men's importance as far exceeding that of women' (MacKinnon 2003: 68), and the police and crime drama is no exception here.

FINDING TIME FOR THE FAMILY

On several occasions throughout the shows history Kim asks her father for help, and very rarely does she contact him at work unless it is quite literally a matter of life and death, and yet, even in such desperate situations he is often seen to ignore her calls, rebuff her requests or occasionally ask another agent to help his daughter. On one occasion when she has been wrongfully charged with kidnap and murder she speaks to her father, desperately pleading 'oh my God dad, help me . . . I need you here now' (2:08 '15.00–16.00'). And yet, once again, Jack is in the middle of a dangerous and treacherous mission so he cannot be by her side, and so he tells her 'CTU is going to send someone over, they're going to get you out of there now' (2:08 '15.00–16.00') and when she cries 'I want you to come and help me, can you do that?' (2:08 '15.00–16.00') he asks her to 'hold on . . . hold on' rather than confess that he cannot take the time away from his public role to be with her (2:08 '15.00–16.00').

One of the few times that we see Jack voice any real emotion for his daughter is after he has volunteered to pilot a plane on a suicide mission in order to protect the nation from a bomb that is on the aircraft (2:15 '22.00–23.00'). We hear Jack speak to Kim, revealing his love, respect and devotion to her before explaining that he will not be coming home after this particular flight, and yet, after a series of plot twists has enabled him to escape unharmed from the aircraft, he goes back on field duty without informing his daughter of his survival. In fact, it is only hours later when Kim asks another member of the counter-terrorist team for assistance that she is eventually told of her father's safety. When she asks to speak to him after finding out about his rescue she is simply told that 'he's not available right now . . . not for a while . . . he's in the field' (2:16 '01.00–02.00').

Although the series regularly positions Jack as a hero and martyr and praises the man for his selflessness and bravery and for putting the needs of society and public safety before his own concerns, it is worth considering the ways in which this character might be read as an emotional coward. After all, although Jack volunteered without hesitation for the suicide mission, it was made clear that they were looking for a member of the team without a family or children. When his colleague George Mason/Xander Berkeley volunteers to take over the mission in the knowledge that he himself only has a few hours to live, Jack still appears reluctant to leave the cockpit. Rather than view this as a brave and heroic stance, George sees through Jack's bravado, commenting that:

> Jack, you've had a death wish ever since Teri died, the ways things have been going for you the past year and a half this doesn't look like such a bad idea, you get to go out in a blaze of glory, one of the greatest heros of all time, leave your troubles behind, this could be the easy way out.
>
> (2:15 '22.00–23.00')

The point here is simply that after being separated from his wife, reuniting, then being faced with her murder at the hands of a double agent in the counter-terrorist team, Jack may actually find it more comforting to face death than to have to deal with the emotional aftermath of these traumatic events. When he is ordered to leave the aircraft George makes it clear that staying with the plane is not a sign of heroism but of weakness, telling his colleague that:

> If you want to be a real hero, here's what you do, you go back down there and put the pieces together, find a way to forgive yourself for what happened to your wife, you make things right with your daughter and go on serving your country, that would take some real guts.
>
> (2:15 '22.00–23.00')

We are told in no uncertain terms that it would be harder and therefore more heroic for Jack to rekindle a relationship with his daughter and continue the fight against terrorism than it would be for him to go down with the plane. In this way Jack is accused of taking the one-way mission in order to face a heroic death and to escape his emotional torment, and as such, the man is being charged with emotional weakness rather than professional valour here. Furthermore, even though we hear Jack tell his daughter that 'I love you more than anything in the world and I will always be with you' (2:15 '22.00–23.00') it is worth considering the age-old adage that actions speak louder than words because even though his language appears emotionally charged, this man volunteered for the mission. Even though he told his daughter that 'we needed someone to fly the plane over the desert so when the bomb exploded nobody would get killed . . . that someone turned out to be me . . . sweetheart, I didn't have any other choice' (2:15 '22.00–23.00'), Jack had every choice, but still insisted on positioning himself as the hero and martyr here.

As part of his longer-term plan to protect his daughter, Jack assigns Kim to a job in the counter-terrorist unit, in order to 'keep an eye on her, make sure she's safe' (3:02 '14.00–15.00'). However, even though Jack shares an office with her, he still struggles to make any time for his daughter. For example, when Kim rings him in a nearby office to talk to him about 'something personal' (3:02 '14.00–15.00'), Jack's response is 'not right now sweetheart, I'm in the middle of something' (3:01 '13.00–14.00') and then later 'sweetheart, now's not a good time . . . when I've got a few minutes I'll come down and talk to you' (3:02 '14.00–15.00'). Although Jack is refusing to see his daughter due to the fact that he is suffering withdrawal symptoms after becoming a heroin addict during a recent undercover operation, and because he cannot or will not explain the severity of the situation to his daughter, it appears as if he simply cannot or will not make time for her, or more importantly, cannot make time for their relationship. After a couple of hours Jack finally speaks to Kim in what appears to be a genuine and tender moment:

> I know you tried to come up to my office earlier today and talk to me about something that was really important to you . . . and I know I wasn't very supportive, I just need to tell you I'm sorry, I know that I'm overly protective of you, I've just watched so many things happen to you over the last few years and I don't want you to get hurt anymore . . . I love you so much.
>
> (3:04 '16.00–17.00')

However, before applauding Jack for his newfound ability to open up to his daughter and for attempting to rebuild their relationship, it is worth noting that this moving monologue ended with Jack asking her 'is the document done yet?' (3:04 '16.00–17.00'). Not only did Jack ring his daughter on a work-related matter but in the following episode we realise that he actually used and abused his paternal relationship in order to 'violate protocol' (3:05 '17.00–18.00'). Jack was unable to ask another member of the team to provide him with the required paperwork due to the fact that they would have questioned his next move in a way that his daughter would not, and therefore one soon starts to question how genuine Jack's loving comments were earlier in that phone conversation.

Professional secrets and personal sacrifices

It is clear that the reason why Jack finds it so difficult to talk to or commit to his family is due to the fact that his job demands a level of deception and detachment that extends into the domestic sphere. On several occasions Jack is heard telling his wife, daughter or both that 'I don't have time to explain' (1:02 '01.00–02.00') when what he tends to mean of course is that it is a matter of national security that he simply cannot reveal to them, and as such, both his marriage and family life are being quite literally destroyed by deception and shattered by secrecy. Likewise, we hear Jack comment that 'it took me a long time to understand that if you want to do this job well you have to stay detached' (3:24 '12.00–13.00'). Therefore, even though this elite field agent is literally surrounded by satellite phones, mobiles, tracking devices and all manner of communications technologies, this same man appears ironically unable to communicate with his family or make any 'real human contact' (Baker 2006: 60) with his daughter.

However, even though Jack is seen to sacrifice his friends, family and colleagues throughout the course of the show's long history, placing the public good above his private role, the very fact that he is doing it for the safety of the American public demands that we see the character as hard-working, disciplined, firm and fair rather than as an uncommunicative husband, distant father or rogue agent. Moreover, because Jack works tirelessly to stamp out threats to national security and protect the status quo we are asked to see a man of strength, bravery, integrity and honour rather than a damaged maverick or a suicidal loner. Indeed, President David Palmer/Dannie Haysbert makes it clear how we should read the field agent when he tells Jack that 'your courage and level of commitment humbles me' (3:24 '12.00–13.00'). The point here is that we are being asked to overlook this man's motives, his recklessness, his disregard for his family and his inability to face up to his personal responsibilities in favour of positioning him as a hard-boiled hero.

Jack does on occasion show real love and respect for his family, and on those occasions where he is unable to commit to them or stand beside them it is only ever because of a threat to national security. Because of the importance of his career and the seriousness of his public work, it is rather too easy for Jack to blame his profession rather than his personal choices for causing a strain on his private life. Jack is often heard commenting that 'my wife was killed because of my job' (3:08 '20.00–21.00') and is keen to tell Chase Edmunds/James Dale (a new field recruit who is dating his daughter) the same story. We hear Jack barking 'you've seen what this job can do to you, you've seen what it's done to me, it's ruined every relationship I've ever had' (3:02 '14.00–15.00'). However, rather than applaud Jack for his courage or commend him for his selflessness, Chase suggests that it is not the job, but rather, Jack who has sabotaged his personal relationships. And yet rather than examine any truth or meaning behind this charge, Jack immediately launches a verbal attack on the younger man, snarling that 'it's the job . . . my wife died because of this job . . . you cannot have a normal life and do this job at the same time' (3:02 '14.00–15.00').

Jack makes it perfectly clear that a field agent cannot hold down a relationship or commit to a family, and yet, the notion of leaving the job or stepping down from the field (as Chase himself does as a way to secure his relationship) never seems to be an option here. With this in mind, Jack knowingly puts his family in the background, consciously and deliberately making the personal sacrifice for the good of his professional work, and as such, it is evident that the private space is expendable in a way that the world of work is not. Jack is not only aware of the personal trade-off but continues to privilege the world of work, and therefore, the man can be seen to adhere to the hegemonic model of masculinity which demands strength and self-sufficiency above domestic harmony, and an appetite for danger and self-destruction above success in the private realm. In this way, Jack seems unable to comprehend the fact that those traditionally masculine strengths such as 'heroism, independence, courage, strength, rationality, will [and] backbone' have somehow morphed into masculine weaknesses such as 'aggression, coldness, emotional inarticulacy, detachment, isolation, an inability to be flexible, to communicate, to empathise, to be soft, supportive or live-affirming' (MacInnes 1998: 47).

Spooks

Spooks is often compared to 24 (Mackenzie 2005; Mavis 2007), and while 24 makes it clear from the title that Jack Bauer's life is dedicated to the public sphere, to his work and to the good of society, so too, Spooks (although 'spooks' is taken from a popular colloquialism for spies, the term has acquired pejorative racial connotations and as such the programme is aired on BBC America under the title of MI5) focuses on a team of professionals who must prioritise their public role. The show is advertised with the slogan 'MI5 not 9 to 5' (BBC 2007b: online), and as such, the brief strapline signals that the working life and professional commitments of the central protagonists take priority over any private relationships and the domestic arena.

Spooks is an intelligent action series that presents the challenging professional lives and complex office politics of a team of young counter-terrorist agents in MI5 as they fight against extremist anti-abortionists, race-riot ringleaders and Kurdish freedom fighters on the streets of London. The programme makes a point of examining the characters turbulent private lives as our intelligence officers are routinely forced to deceive their closest partners, friends and family members. The fearless espionage team is led by senior case officer Tom Quinn/Matthew MacFadyen, until his disillusionment with the job sees him being replaced by the dogged Adam Carter/Rupert Penry-Jones. Therefore, Spooks, much like 24, focuses on a key male protagonist who is jeopardising his personal relationships and rejecting his domestic responsibilities for success in the workplace and for the greater good of society.

Public deception and private destruction

Although Tom has been dating restaurateur Ellie Simm/Esther Hall for several months when the show opens, she only knows him as Matthew, a name he had taken on for a particular undercover operation. And when he has taken the wrong wallet, with his real identity rather than his pseudonym, out for a meal he has to accept his girlfriend's offer to pay rather than reveal his true identity to her (1:02). When Ellie becomes frustrated by Tom's quiet phone calls and urgent meetings she tells him 'I need to know who you are' to which the agent replies 'a man who loves you very much' (1:01). And rather than reveal his true identity and job description at this point he simply covers for his evasiveness with a tried and tested masculine cliché in that 'I'm not like you, I can't open up very well' (1:01). We see Tom routinely having to work unsociable hours including his own birthday and even having to leave in the middle of his girl-friend's social gathering when work demands his attention (1:03). And yet, when a colleague asks him why he was taking so long to reveal his true self to her, they soon surmise that it is because the officer actually 'likes the idea of a secret life' (1:01). When he is asked to consider why he became an intelligence officer, he answers that it was because of 'the urge to be secret, to give a false name, to live a false life' (3:02).

When Tom does eventually reveal his true self and his chosen profession to Ellie, she struggles to come to terms with the fact that he has lied to her about his name, identity and life history for so many months. However, rather than actually listen to or try to understand the strain that his deception has had on their relationship, like Jack before him, Tom simply barks 'I am what I do' (1:04) and 'I've told you I do a job serving my country, is that so bad?' (1:04). And when he does eventually try to explain the need for all the secrecy and deception he makes it clear that it is not his fault but that of the job because of 'vetting . . . it's routine when officers form liaisons' (1:04). Colleagues and criminals alike are heard commenting on the levels of secrecy and deception that are needed in the public sphere, telling Tom that 'you're a fraud, your whole life is a lie' (1:01) and 'we're all con men aren't we' (1:04). When a sci-entist asks him how he copes with the different guises, he simply pronounces that 'you have to put yourself in a box, and only when you come home do you open up the box', and when this man tells Tom that he is 'clinically insane' for willingly taking on such a role, the officer coldly responds with 'no, we're pro-fessionals' (3:02). Therefore, again like Jack before him, Tom finds it easier to blame secret service protocols than to question his own choices here. When an ex-girlfriend talks about leaving the intelligence services Tom cannot even com-prehend such a move, telling her in no uncertain terms that 'no one resigns from what we do . . . this job is us, it's second nature' (3:01).

In the same way that Jack never questioned his commitment to the counter-terrorist unit even as it put a strain on his relationships, so too, Tom fails to question his allegiance to MI5 or consider alternative employment even though his work is clearly putting tremendous pressure on his personal life. Even after watching the horrific torture and subsequent murder of several co-workers and the horrific death of his girlfriend at the hands of terrorists Tom does not waver in his duty. In fact, the only time that he is ever seen to question his public role and challenge his dedication to the service is when he is brought under scrutiny in a highly organised set-up that sees him accused of 'the assassination of the head of the British Armed Forces' (3:01). Therefore, the man only questions his public role when professional colleagues turn against him, and as such, the genre is once again suggesting that the private role and personal commitments are ephemeral, expendable and unnecessary here.

While Tom is struggling to clear his name we are introduced to another case officer, Adam Carter. Adam is married to Fiona Carter/Olga Sosnovska, one of MI6's most respected officers, and the couple have a young son in the series. However, even though secrets and deceit are not a cause for concern for this couple, they are still seen to struggle with the conflicts of marriage, parenting and espionage. After all, husband and wife both work undercover, they are unable to contact one another for long periods of time and they are unable to offer a routine home life to their infant child. Indeed, because these parents only know about their son's most recent likes and dislikes through the current babysitter they routinely question whether they were selfish to even have had a child in their line of work (4:01). However, whereas Jack and Tom seem unable to prioritise their private roles over their professional duties it is clear that beneath his professional veneer, Adam 'dreamt of sharing a stable home life with his wife and child' (BBC 2007c: online).

We often hear Adam complaining to his wife about the fact that her under-cover work intrudes on their family time, telling her that 'we haven't done any-thing with [their son] together in ages' (3:07). And when Adam tells his wife that he 'likes the idea of being there for [their son] in the flesh', she does not volunteer to stay at home for any period of time, but rather comments that 'at least he's got one of us looking out for him' (3:07). When Adam continues with 'oh come on, aren't you even curious to know what it would be like to live together like a real family?', his wife shrugs before stating 'that's not what we were made for was it, we need more', before pausing and asking 'don't we?' (3:07). However, although both parents love their son, Fiona made it clear that she would 'never leave the world of the spooks willingly' (BBC 2007d: online), and it was only when she is shot by her ex-husband, a Syrian spy, that she pri-oritises her son in her final dying words (4:07).

One might assume that Adam would reconsider his career and refocus his attentions on finding a more routine, nurturing and safe life with his son after the tragic death of his wife, however, after a short period of denial, the man is seen to throw himself even more aggressively into his working role. Adam sends the young boy to live with his grandparents, and as such, he pays even less attention to the child that he was previously worried about neglecting. Rather than commit to his domestic duties and his paternal role, we hear the man telling colleagues that he would be 'nothing' if he left the service (4:08), as if overlooking or ignoring his position as father, provider and role model. After he has been ordered to see a psychiatrist we hear him bemoan 'I don't need psyche talk, what's the thinking here, because my wife's died I'm going bonkers? . . . I need some real work, something to fill the day, fill my mind to give me a buzz' (4:08). And yet neither the psychiatrist nor his own co-workers question his commitment to the public sphere over his responsibilities to his young son, and as such, it again suggests that the world of work and the public good must come first for the male.

CONCLUSION

This chapter has outlined the ways in which the central male protagonist has been presented in the police and crime drama, paying particular attention to the respected 'bobby on the beat' in the 1950s, the more brutish image of the police officer in the 1970s and the ambiguous image of the law enforcement officer in the 1990s, before examining the troubled image of the counter-terrorist officer in contemporary shows such as *24* and *Spooks*. Indeed, like the doctor-hero, one might suggest that the police officer has to sacrifice domestic duties and family commitments for the greater good of society. However, whereas the medical professional can retain a sense of self and personal identity during a long training programme or at the end of a particularly gruelling shift, the officer, detective or field agent has to surround himself with secrecy within and beyond the public sphere, so that he is quite literally on duty and therefore committed to the public realm twenty-four hours a day. Therefore, although agents such as Jack Bauer and Adam Carter might be heralded as the epitome of hegemonic masculinity for their unwavering dedication to the professional realm, the sacrifices that these men make in their personal lives must be seen to negotiate the social standing of this image of the male and challenge its credibility as a standard of masculinity to which men are said to aspire.

9. SPORTS: MEDIA EVENTS AND MASCULINE DISCOURSE

INTRODUCTION

Sports television is a loose generic label that covers a wide range of different production practices including live sports coverage, magazine programmes, quiz shows, fictional dramas and chat shows all dedicated to the world of sport. However, although there are clear distinctions in the style, presentation and format of such texts, what they all have in common is a commitment to masculine discourses in general and the hierarchy of hegemonic masculinity in particular. Therefore, this chapter will offer a brief history of organised sports and examine the depiction of sports coverage on the small screen before considering the relationship between the sporting arena, sportswomen and the sporting male. I will suggest that even though games such as football and rugby have tended to present the aggressive, powerful, forceful and stoic player as the very zenith of contemporary masculinity, the emergence of sports stars such as Andre Agassi, David Beckham and Gavin Henson in international tennis, football and rugby union respectively goes some way towards challenging stereotypical images of the sportsman as physically powerful but emotionally stunted. In this way, the chapter aims to illustrate the ways in which stars such as David Beckham 'become the condensing point of broader social discourses about the way in which we should live, about how to be a man – in short, about morality and masculinity' (Whannel 2002: 127). Indeed, the representation of such stars cannot be underestimated because although only a small number of men ever actually play sport at an international level, those men who do reach the peak of their sporting profession are emulated by little boys and admired by grown men, and as such, these players come to stand not just for sporting masculinity, but for the ideal image of masculinity in society.

History of organised sports

Sports such as football emerged in mid-nineteenth century England in elite public schools such as Winchester and Eton, privileged universities including Oxford and Cambridge and a small number of private clubs, and as such, they were seen to support the values of the ruling classes by paying strict attention to rules, records and the concept of fair play (Kidd 1990: 34). Organised sports were said to be crucial to the development of young men, so much so in fact that certain public schools announced that they were actually more important than academic performance. For example, the headmaster of Harrow was heard commenting that 'learning, however excellent in itself, does not afford such necessary virtues as promptitude, resource, honour, cooperation and unselfishness; but these are the soul of English games' (Horrocks 1995: 149). Organised sports were seen to reinforce the privileged status of the upper-class white male because 'the social Darwinist belief that a natural hierarchy emerges out of a competitive, meritocratic system . . . provided ideological support for the existing class and gender privilege' of these men (Messner 1992: 19). Therefore, although unstructured, localised and working-class versions of games such as football existed prior to the mid-nineteenth century, the industrial revolution and the movement of the populace from the country to the cities meant that the once rural games were being relocated to the upper-class urban centres and re-appropriated by the ruling classes. In fact, the codified and organised games were soon understood as the exclusive preserve of those upper-class white males who wanted to 'measure themselves against each other and to "build character" in preparation for roles as leaders in business and industry' (Messner 1994: 132). While games such as football were deployed in order to 'civilise, discipline and order the dangerous masses at home', organised sports also helped to civilise the British Empire by giving a structure and order to previously uncivilised and undisciplined forms of recreation (Clarke and Clarke 1982: 80). However, in the twentieth century, as the working classes, ethnic minorities and colonised groups learned to play the games of the privileged white male, success in the sporting arena came to be read as a show of resistance by subordinated males and, 'struggles to achieve a public masculine status through sport became a key locus around and through which men of different backgrounds competed with each other' (Messner 1992: 19).

Power and play in televised sports

There is a long history of sports coverage on both British and American television. The BBC showed its first FA Cup final in 1939, while NBC started to air baseball and American football during that same year. However, because of the poor technical quality and crude cameras that were being used at the time, sports coverage in the 1940s and 1950s tended to favour small-scale individual sports such as wrestling and boxing rather than larger team games such as football or baseball (Whannel 1995: 167). These larger games only became popular with television audiences after the introduction of replay and slow motion, colour pictures and satellite relays in the 1960s (Whannel 2002: 34). Thus, although both golf and tennis proved popular with audiences of the period, 'the big success of the 1960s was the emergence of American football as the dominant American television sport' (Whannel 1995: 168). Televised football has since remained popular with audiences on both sides of the Atlantic, so much so in fact that it is considered to be one of the most popular sports in the world (Meân 2001: 789), with the English Premier League becoming 'the most popular weekly football attraction in the world' (Milligan 2004: 10).

Although there exists a long history of televised sports, it is not simply that the medium provides coverage of particular events, but rather, that it has a hand in the structure, timing and organisation of particular sports. Ellis Cashmore makes this point when he tells us that 'an entire sports industry has developed, principally around the demands of television' (Cashmore 2005: 417). For example, the Brooklyn Dodgers and the New York Giants made a point of moving to California in 1958 in order to secure more lucrative television deals in uncontested media markets (Whannel 2002: 95) and snooker was quite literally reinvented for television in the late 1960s and early 1970s (Boyle and Haynes 2000: 67). More recently 'what could be called Sky's effective takeover of Rugby League' can be seen as one of the clearest examples of televisions power over the sporting world (Arundel and Roche 1998: 76). After all, the takeover led to a restructuring of the clubs, a reorganisation of the competitions, a change in playing seasons and the introduction of video playback and a big-screen format (ibid.: 76–7). Moreover, Sky's acquisition of television rights to Premier League football has been said to have revolutionised the game. After all, Sky paid around £1 billion for exclusive rights to live television transmissions, and this money has

> produced unprecedented income flows into the top forty to fifty British soccer clubs [which has in turn led] to the creation of new stadia, the acquisition of large numbers of foreign 'star' players and the floatation of clubs as investment-worthy businesses on the London stock exchange.
> (Arundel and Roche 1998: 73)

In short, in the new millennium 'there is more sport, more hype, more money and more media coverage . . . than at any other time in recent memory [and as such] television exerts a stranglehold over sports' (Boyle and Haynes 2000: x).

Sexuality, triviality and familiarity: the representation of women in sports

Although organised sports can be seen as a site of contested national, class, and racial relations among men (Messner 1992: 17), critical feminist writings note that the games ethic was created by men and for men as a way to reinforce the culturally dominant image of the hegemonic male, to retain patriarchal control and to resuscitate 'the flagging ideology of male superiority' (Clayton and Harris 2004: 320). There are clear inequalities for women in sports in terms of the 'funding of programs, facilities and equipment, coaching, medical and training facilities . . . travel, number of sport activities provided, scholarships, and media coverage' (Theberge 1981: 343). There are few female anchors, presenters or commentators and only a small number of female 'representatives in senior administrative, coaching, media, and academic positions' (Cashmore 2005: 162). Those women who do find sporting success tend to be paid significantly less than their male counterparts. With this in mind, numerous commentators condemn sport as being at best conservative and at worst misogynist, charging television coverage with either ignoring female athletes or with perpetrating familiar stereotypes involving biological and physical differences between the sexes. Television coverage can be seen to overlook the activities and achievements of women in sports because while *SportsCenter* (1979–) devotes a mere 2.9 per cent of reporting to women in sports, a wide range of extreme sports shows give only 1 per cent of their programming to female athletes (Messner, Dunbar and Hunt 2000: 382, 383). More recent research makes it clear that male sports receive more than 80 per cent of media coverage, and that male presenters, anchors and commentators continue to dominate the sporting world (MacKinnon 2003: 102). Television routinely ignores female sporting achievements, and as such, it seems to be suggesting that female sports are somehow less legitimate, credible and even less entertaining than male sports. In short '"sport news" still means *men's* sport news' (Messner 1992: 165) and females are discouraged from participating in this last bastion of hegemonic masculinity.

Much existing research on women and sport tells us that the only acceptable female sports are those which foreground stereotypical images of women as graceful, stylish, attractive and hence feminine. Traditionally, we are informed that female appropriate sports eschew any teamwork, physical contact, violence or aggression, and as such, we begin to understand why the limited female sports coverage on television focuses on gymnastics, ice-skating and singles tennis more than say rugby, baseball or football (Brookes 2002: 129). We are told that 'women's cricket, rugby and boxing still cause surprise, humour or revulsion amongst men' (Horrocks 1995: 151). Furthermore, when television does present female sports, it tends to sexualise, infantilise, trivialise or familiarise the women in question in order to maintain patriarchal authority in the sporting arena and undermine a woman's sporting prowess. For example, images of women in sports are routinely sexualised, be it through the depiction of the sportswoman herself or through the 'beauty shots' of attractive female spectators that are presented during breaks in the action (Brookes 2002: 29). Sportswomen are then regularly infantilised by being referred to as 'girls' or being marked out by their first name (ibid.: 130). The common practice of referring to football when it is being played by men but referring to 'women's football' when the same game is played by women makes it clear that women's sport is unusual, different and indeed inferior (ibid.: 129). Any female sporting achievements tend to be presented as personal rather than professional or physical victories, while any further discussion of these women tends to focus on their private and domestic lives (ibid.: 130). And then, commentators can be heard casting aspersions on the femininity of female athletes, drawing attention to the ways in which they have sacrificed their very femininity through training, competition and achievement (Clarke and Clarke 1982: 67–8). Lastly, if a woman continues to prove successful in a particular sport she might find her very sex to be in question (Graydon 1983: 9).

Ellis Cashmore echoes these points when he tells us that women in televised sport are 'marginalized, sexualized, put down, or just plain left out of sports coverage [in order] to preserve sports as a vehicle for reproducing conceptions of manhood' (Cashmore 2005: 165). Although the recent expansion of cable television has offered a marked increase in the coverage of women's sports on television, 'the lower production quality [and] the gender-biased language of commentators – are likely to reinforce existing negative attitudes or ambivalences about women's sport and women athletes' (Messner 1992: 165). However, rather than blithely condemn television sports coverage for creating sexual imbalance in the sporting world it is worth considering the roles that government agencies, sports promoters and even the education system play in fostering 'sport as a male endeavour' (Graydon 1983: 8).

POWER, PERFORMANCE AND STUNTED EMOTIONS: THE REPRESENTATION OF MEN IN SPORTS

Ninety per cent of boys watch sport on television (MacKinnon 2003: 102) and many of them view professional sportsmen as the ideal image of adult masculinity (Swain 2000: 101), and as such, it is necessary to examine those representations of the male that are on offer in contemporary sports coverage. Popular sports such as football and rugby tend to promote a specific image of masculinity, an image that is based on strength, activity, stamina, aggression and competitiveness. As such, the men who play what Rod Brookes terms 'male-appropriate sports' (Brookes 2002: 129) are 'marked by the signs and codes of hegemonic masculinity' (Rowe 1995: 135). Even though existing research on the sociology of masculinity tells us that this image of the male is in crisis and that 'men's relationships to the icons of traditional masculinity have been transformed' (Sabo 1994: 210), the sporting arena continues to present the hegemonic model as the heroic ideal of modern manhood. Sports can be seen to play an important role in the construction of contemporary masculinity because while organised sports are seen to normalise the hegemonic male they are also seen to marginalise and problematise alternative images of masculinity. In this way, sports in general and televised sports in particular can be seen to create a hierarchy of masculinity with the forceful, powerful and competitive image of the male as the pinnacle of contemporary manhood.

The world of sports encourages us to view this aggressive image of masculinity as heroic due to the fact that many of our sportsmen are seen to either withstand pain or play injured. Those men who are seen to risk damaging their bodies for the good of the team are 'consistently framed as heroes' and those who use their pain and injury as a reason to sit on the sidelines are questioned about their very character, commitment and masculinity (Messner, Dunbar and Hunt 2000: 387). For example, when footballer John Terry captained England during the European Championship qualifiers while wearing a protective facial mask just seventy-two hours after having surgery on a fractured cheekbone, television commentators did not question his use of painkilling injections, his ability to play for his team, or the stress that he was putting on his body, but rather, applauded the heroism of the man who continued to play for his country, telling us that he was a 'brave brave fellow . . . the brave heart' (*UEFA* 02/10/ 2007: ITV). Likewise, when footballer Michael Owen played for Newcastle United in the Barclays Premier League just eight days after a double hernia operation that would normally demand over four weeks of recuperation, the commentators did not question his ability or his right to play, but simply established the physical and mental toughness of the player because they had 'no idea how he's doing that' (*Match of the Day 2* 07/10/07: BBC2).

The world of sport goes further to legitimise this particular version of forceful and powerful masculinity by drawing parallels between the world of sport and the world of war. After all, if the battleground is understood 'as a place of sanctioned violence' (Meân 2001: 790) in which strong and stoic men are applauded for their heroism, then it becomes clear why the sporting world seeks to find parallels between the two arenas. Sports commentary routinely exploits a range of war and weaponry reference points so that the sports field is positioned as a battleground, male bodies are presented as weapons and sporting action tends to be described by using martial metaphors (Messner, Dunbar and Hunt 2000: 388). For example, during the rugby world cup final commentators were heard talking about 'wounded bodies' and about how the international players were 'putting their bodies on the line' (*Rugby World Cup* 20/10/ 2007: ITV). We were told that 'there was no surrender from England', that the English side 'have the bulldog spirit in bucketloads' and that from the opposition's point of view the final 'was about dousing England's war spirit' (*Rugby World Cup* 20/10/2007: ITV). The point here is simply that the ways in which commentators foreground war, pain, suffering and bravery is just one more way in which televised sports coverage seeks to present the sportsman as the heroic ideal of hegemonic masculinity, with games such as football and rugby being understood as a specifically masculine 'form of non-hostile combat' (Clare 2001: 65).

However, rather than criticise sporting commentaries for championing stereotypical images of the forceful and unfeeling male, one might suggest that these voices are offering a positive message by drawing attention to values such as teamwork, trust and comradeship in their presentations. After all, teams are routinely presented as a metaphorical family who strive for a common goal over and above individual achievement. For example, during a range of post-match football commentaries, we hear manager Alex Ferguson applaud 'a good team effort' (*UEFA* 02/10/2007: ITV) while Steve McClaren tells us that 'you can't fault the players, they're playing for each other, the spirit in the team is excellent' (*Match of the Day* 17/10/2007: BBC1). Likewise, we hear players such as Robin van Persie boasting about 'a real team presence in which everyone worked really hard' (*UEFA* 02/10/2007: ITV) while Michael Owen tells us that his is a 'team that sticks together' (*Match of the Day* 17/10/2007: BBC1). Likewise DaMarcus Beasley informs us that 'it was a great team effort today, not one player stood out from another, we all played well, we all defended well and that's what's great about us, we are a team, we fight for each other and that's what we did today' (*UEFA* 02/10/2007: ITV). And yet, although managers, players and pundits alike are all regularly heard praising particular teams for their group spirit and applauding the unity of a particular squad for working together, the truth of the situation is that rivalry and competition exists within any team. After all, sporting sides consistently test and qualify one individual over another in order to decide who achieves a first place, who will be granted playing time and who will be presented as the 'star' of the squad (Messner 1992: 88). In this way, the team ethos appears as a front for a group of men who continue to compete and challenge one another even before going head to head against the opposition. Players must be aware that to single out an individual in the team could lead to 'exclusion, hierarchisation, marginalisation and symbolic annihilation' for themselves or for other players (Whannel 2002: 12). After all, 'sport is presented largely in terms of stars' (Whannel 1998: 23) and many of today's teams are aware of the fact that the development of a star player with a global media profile can allow the sport in question to 'create new spectators and viewers for the game' (Arundel and Roche 1998: 82).

The fact that these men must continue to push and prove themselves both within and beyond the confines of their own team reminds us that hegemonic masculinity is 'always in process and never finished' (Kennedy 2007: 23). The point here is that masculinity is always under threat on the sports field and can always be challenged or attacked. As such, these men can never finally prove themselves, but can merely hope to 'just keep the critics at bay for a while' (West 1996: online). In this way, sport can remind us of the fragility of hegemonic masculinity by playing on male insecurities regarding age, health and physical performance. After all, if sportsmen are told that 'you're only as good as your last game' (Messner, Dunbar and Hunt 2000: 390) and that they should 'never be satisfied with [their] performance' (Messner 1992: 51) then these men have to keep proving their very manhood. Although some sports stars tend to find work in sporting quiz shows and as presenters and pundits after retiring from the field, the vast majority of sportsmen retire in their thirties with little remaining access to the sporting arena. Indeed, extant literature tells us that when a sportsman retires he is immediately ignored and overlooked by his team, with all personal and professional ties being cut, so that 'when a guy got cut we'd say he died [because] he's a different person, not a part of the team any more. Not even a person. He almost ceases to exist' (Bouton cited in Messner 1992: 126). Thus, hegemonic masculinity must be understood as an unstable and untenable image of the male. After all, even though sports tend to demand a presentation of strong, powerful and dominant masculinity, that very manhood must be routinely tested, qualified and eventually found wanting.

Unsurprisingly then, feminist critics are concerned with the representation of masculinity in sport in general and televised sport in particular because it continues to privilege the representation of a specific form of manhood that is characterised by athleticism, muscularity, strength, power and fearless domination (Swain 2000: 101). Although the strength, stamina and aggression that is associated with hegemonic masculinity helps to create champion athletes and successful footballers, these men are said to disconnect their physical power from 'emotional understanding and the skills of emotional maintenance' (Kidd 1990: 40). We are led to believe that sport asks athletes to deny their feelings and to disparage interpersonal skills and 'to close [men] off from [their] own inner feelings and those of others' (ibid.: 40). Sue Evison makes this point when she tells us that many young footballers gained their skills at the expense of education and emotional maturity (Evison 1998: 2). Therefore, even though our sportsmen are trained to be athletic, assertive and aggressive, they have little societal or emotional education. In short, 'mental and physical competitiveness wins championships, but it also throws up enormous barriers to the development and maintenance of close relationships' (Kidd 1990: 41).

In addition, feminist critics and sporting commentators alike seem concerned about the ways in which sporting aggression can be seen to extend beyond the pitch and into the domestic sphere. After all, there have been numerous cases in recent years where athletic, physically dominant and assertive sportsmen have used and abused their muscularity outside of the sports arena in all manner of physical and sexual assaults. Donald Sabo makes this point when he tells us that 'in recent years, the public image of male athletes has been transformed from that of an idealized role model for youth to that of an irresponsible, selfish, and often violent sexual predator' (Messner and Sabo 1994: 33). Likewise, Sue Evison comments that 'the despicable fashion for bashing women appears to be growing at an alarming rate among soccer stars hero-worshiped by many' (Evison 1998: 2). While Sabo talks about Mike Tyson's rape conviction, the New England Patriot's locker-room harassment of reporter Lisa Olson and the alleged sexual assaults by the Portland Trailblazers pro basketball team, Evison refers to professional footballers Stan Collymore and Paul Gascoigne, although the list could continue according to Whannel's recent research on the relationship between sport and violence (Whannel 2002: 168–72).

Therefore, although the sporting arena is often constructed as a safe site of masculine aggression, the concern here is that sporting violence is not necessarily being contained on the playing field. And if we consider the ways in which 'sport influences our . . . concepts of heroes' (Creedon 1994: 4) then it is important to condemn those sportsmen who demonstrate an excessive predilection for violence and make it clear that there is no justification for such aggression in contemporary society. Although raw, brutal strength may have proved useful in an earlier period when men were labouring in the iron, steel and coal industries, in shipbuilding, lumberjacking and pre-mechanised farming, we are now living at a time 'when more people are employed making Indian curries than mining coal [and] when computerised robots and not sweating men assemble cars' (Clare 2001: 7), and as such, there are few legitimate uses for such physical masculine force.

However, rather than critique all sportsmen on the thuggish actions of this sporting minority, it is worth noting that many of today's high-profile sports stars offer a positive image of masculinity by separating their sporting prowess in the public sphere from sensitivity and sincerity in the private realm, with David Beckham as a case in point. Therefore, this chapter will now examine the ways in which this particular sporting figure is represented both on and beyond the small screen as a sporting hero, masculine role model and commercial brand respectively. After all, this is a man who is as well-known for his professional skills as he is for his private life, celebrity endorsements and fashion sense. Indeed, when Ellis Cashmore writes about Beckham he refers to the footballer as 'a demigod' (Cashmore 2004: 120) because he is 'the most instantly recognizable human being on the planet' (Cashmore 2004: 3), while Garry Whannel refers to the man as a barometer of contemporary social relations (Whannel 2002: 215).

DAVID BECKHAM: THE EMERGENCE OF THE SENSITIVE SPORTS STAR

David Beckham made his team debut for Manchester United in 1992 at the age of seventeen, and since that time he has played for Real Madrid and today he plays for Major League Soccer's Los Angeles Galaxy. He was captain of the English football team from 2000 to 2006 and today he continues to play for the national side. The footballer married 'Spice Girl' Victoria Adams back in 1999 in a star-studded ceremony and the couple have three young sons, and even though there have been a number of allegations surrounding Beckham's fidelity since that time, little evidence exists to suggest that he is anything other than a doting husband and father. The footballer appears to show little interest in the 'belligerent macho behaviour. Drunken binges, wife-beating and serial model dating [that] are normal fare for players' (Cashmore 2004: 47). With this in mind, it is interesting that Beckham can be seen to challenge existing stereotypes of the sporting male without alienating audiences. After all, even though the man is understood to have 'violated every known norm associated with testosterone-pumped, homophobic, macho footballers', he continues to captivate 'a global audience that includes young females who have no obvious interest in sport, gay men [and] working class kids who proclaim their nationalism through their champion and countless other groups who have become enamoured by him' (Cashmore 2004: viii, 6). Therefore, at a time when many young footballers 'seem to believe a role model is something to do with a bedroom conquest, not good manners and dignified behaviour' (Evison 1998: 2), Beckham stands apart as a more positive image of sporting masculinity that manages to be both forceful and disciplined, respectable and rough, hard and controlled. Ellis Cashmore summarises the point succinctly when he writes 'here's the headline: "BECKHAM ATTACKS FOOTBALL'S ALPHA MALE" ' (Cashmore 2004: 155).

It is not simply that Beckham stands apart as a powerful and positive image of sensitive masculinity that is of interest here, but rather the way in which this image of the male is seen to appeal to a wide spectrum of society. For example, recent research on celebrity culture informs us that Beckham has emerged as the most influential man in Britain, informing us that he 'is making the world a better place by single-handedly transforming men's attitudes towards sex, love, babies, nights out with the lads and even homosexuality' (Campbell 2003: online). We are told that it is his relationship with his wife, his children, art and fashion that is currently altering society's perception of appropriate manhood. After all 'the player's combination of traditional and more radical modern identities – aggressive competitor on the pitch, loving husband, doting father and fashion model off it – have helped to give men a healthy role model' (Parker and Cashmore cited ibid.). In this same way, we are encouraged to believe that 'the player's popularity is so great that his enthusiastic embrace of family life and readiness to spend time at home with his wife and sons . . . could make such behaviour normal for men' (Parker and Cashmore cited ibid.). Existing literature makes it clear that Beckham's image as a loving and caring father will help to break down traditional attitudes regarding gender specific work and the distinction between the masculine public role and the feminine private sphere. After all, a recent survey by Norwich Union Healthcare found that Beckham is the number one role model for young fathers in the UK and a range of newspapers and magazine commentators suggest that his relationship with his sons must be seen as a positive one because 'while media manipulation may well be involved here, you could not fake the easy familiarity that he exhibits towards his child' (White 2001: 8). In short, Beckham's ability to challenge dominant hegemonic stereotypes is said to 'make the world a better, more tolerant place' (Parker and Cashmore cited in Campbell 2003: online).

Beckham's sporting fixtures are routinely presented on the small screen, with commentators presenting the footballer as a brave, heroic and dedicated player. *David Beckham's Soccer USA* presents all the best major league soccer from America with short commentaries from the English footballer who, although signed with Los Angeles Galaxy, is injured at the time of writing. And yet, the fact that Beckham is not physically playing does not demand a title change, demean his opinions on a particular game or question his dedication to the sport. Although Beckham's sporting presence might be predicted on the small screen, it is worth noting that the footballer appears in such a wide range of television texts that Jim White of the *Daily Telegraph* has proposed a new genre called the 'Becksdox' (White 2003: online). However, irrespective of whether he is advertising milk, Pepsi, Adidas, or whether he is being interviewed about his sporting prowess or private life, the man has continually used the medium to challenge football's core values. Beckham has used British national television to acknowledge his gay fans, to introduce his young son to his club and to offer his support to female footballers within and beyond the UK. The point here is that although football fans would recognise David Beckham as a talented player, his wider star image as a skilled professional and sensitive family man is made available to audiences by way of the small screen. It has been argued that the Beckham phenomena 'would simply not have been possible without television' (Cashmore 2004: 202).

In the last few years, the Beckham family in general and David Beckham in particular have appeared on an exhaustive range of television adverts, campaigns, chat shows, sports programmes and documentaries dedicated to creating and upholding brand Beckham. Even when interviewers seek to mock the man for offering such a sensitive and stylish portrayal of family life or fatherhood, the footballer refuses to make any concessions to traditional images of the sporting male. In *The Real David Beckham* (2000) documentary we are witness to both the private and professional life of the star, so that we see him relaxed at home with friends and family, house-hunting and plucking his eyebrows alongside more public images of him on modelling shoots, book signings, on the pitch and even receiving his OBE. While Beckham's role as a father and husband is central to his appeal, this caring and emotional side can be seen to extend beyond his own family as the footballer takes time to raise the profile and profits of UNICEF, offers himself up for interview during Comic Relief and even presents an appeal for the Madeleine McCann family. In fact, at a time in his career when most players are considering football management or commentary as a way to continue in their favoured sport, Beckham has made it clear that once he has retired from the professional game he will dedicate himself to working with the David Beckham Football Academy that he has helped to set up for young children. And although one might assume that this is a mere publicity exercise that continues to circulate the Beckham name, the footballer tells us that he is heavily involved with the exercise and that he has personally chosen those coaches who make up the training team. What is most interesting here is that Beckham is not simply training future football heroes, but using the sport to encourage young boys and girls to respect both the world of sport and their own bodies. Indeed, the man appears to offer a gracious model of contemporary masculinity that draws on the stereotypical strength, stamina and competition of the sporting male combined with more traditionally feminine traits such as sensitivity, empathy and emotional maturity. As such, it is as if Beckham has single-handedly disbanded traditional gender roles and offered audiences an empowered and empowering image of the contemporary male

CONCLUSION

This chapter has introduced a brief history of organised sports and drawn attention to the ways in which television actually controls and creates rather than simply covers particular sporting events. Moreover, it has illustrated the ways in which women are routinely trivialised, infantilised and sexualised in sports in general and television sports coverage in particular before examining the representation of masculinity in the sporting arena. The chapter went on to examine the ways in which male-appropriate sports tend to situate the hegemonic male as the site of heroic masculinity and the ways in which they then marginalise alternative images of the male. However, even though the world of sport seems to reinforce traditional masculine values such as strength, work, success and stoicism, the ways in which footballer David Beckham has since challenged the very foundations of the hegemonic hierarchy goes some way towards reminding us that the image of the dominant, aggressive and competitive male is merely a historical and cultural construct that can be exploited or negated.

10. REALITY TELEVISION: ORDINARINESS, EXHIBITIONISM AND EMOTIONAL INTELLIGENCE

INTRODUCTION

The term 'Reality TV' has been used by audiences and industry alike since the late 1980s to refer to a wide range of programmes that focus on non-professional actors in a range of both real-life and highly contrived situations. However, irrespective of the authenticity or artificiality of a particular stage or scenario, audiences have recently responded to the presentation of unscripted and ordinary people on television. Therefore, this chapter will briefly outline the changing nature of reality programming, drawing attention to the debates surrounding the genre's claims to the real before considering the representation of gender that is being presented here. I will look at the depiction of masculinities in *Big Brother 8* UK (2007), and examine the ways in which a number of contestants can be seen to construct and circulate specific representations of male identity for the attention of the viewing public. Moreover, because contestants get to nominate their least favourite housemate, and because audiences are invited to evict contestants week by week, we can examine those models of masculinity that are considered to be the most authentic, appealing or destructive here, concluding that the most popular housemates tend to be those who challenge the hegemonic model of the male. Although there are national variations of the programme, *Big Brother* remains a recognisable format in both Britain and America, and as such, I hope that readers will be able to draw their own conclusions in relation to my chosen case study here.

HISTORY OF THE GENRE

According to Jon Dovey, the term 'Reality TV' was first used in the late 1980s and early 1990s to categorise a range of magazine-format programmes that were based on crime, accident and health stories (Dovey 2002: 135). Indeed, although the genre began in America with shows such as *Unsolved Mysteries* (1987–2002), *Rescue 911* (1989–96) and *Cops* (1989–), this accident and emergency format was soon seen in Britain with shows such as *Emergency 999* (1992–), *Blues and Twos* (1993–) and *Police, Camera, Action* (1994–). These programmes can be characterised by their use of surveillance footage of real life traumas, eyewitness accounts, expert testimonies, dramatic recon- structions and authoritative presenter commentaries, and as such, they are seen to offer a 'compelling mix' of actuality, immediacy, tabloidisation and public service (ibid.: 135). However, since the mid-1990s, the meaning of the term 'Reality TV' has changed somewhat, so as to include those chat shows and constructed documentaries, talent contests and docu-soaps that are loosely based on the day-to-day lives of ordinary people (Murray and Ouellette 2004: 4). And although these programmes might vary in subject and scope, and can be understood as 'a relatively broad generic category' (Kilborn 2003: 55), they are all seen to 'package particular aspects of everyday life as entertainment' (Dovey 2002: 135). These programmes can all be seen to draw on documentary traditions, employ soap opera narratives, use voiceover com- mentaries, demand minimal writing, focus on real lives and engage with first person accounts. In fact, it is 'this fixation with "authentic" personalities, sit- uations, and narratives [that] is considered to be Reality TV's primary dis- tinction from fictional television and also its primary selling point' (Murray and Ouellette 2004: 4).

However, since the early 2000s, the chat show, docu-soap and dating series have been usurped by another 'Reality TV' phenomenon, namely the reality game show. Although America took a half-step towards creating the reality game show when MTV followed a group of young people living in a trendy Manhattan loft for *The Real World* (1992–), existing literature tends to present *Survivor* (2000–) as the show that augmented this wave of reality program- ming. *Survivor* puts a group of strangers on a desert island to compete for a £1 million cash prize, dividing them into different tribes for a number of endurance, problem-solving, teamwork, dexterity and will-power challenges. Participants are voted off the island during the tribal council that is held at the end of each episode and the overall winner of the programme is decided by a jury made up of those players who have previously been evicted. This new reality phenomenon proved so popular with audiences that it came to 'achieve the status of "landmark" television' (Kilborn 2003: 58). Unsurprisingly then, *Survivor* was soon imitated by *Shipwrecked* (2000– ; *Survivor* for teens), *Temptation Island* (2001–3; *Survivor* with a dating twist), *The Mole* (2001–5; *Survivor* with paramilitary adventure-chic), *The Amazing Race* (2001– ; *Survivor*, cross-country, against the clock), *Fear Factor* (2001–6; *Survivor* challenges with an extreme sports twist) and *Castaway* (2000, 2007; *Survivor* in the cold, without the challenges) to name but a few (Brenton and Cohen 2003: 5–6). What these programmes all had in common was their status as social experiments as they each sought to place ordinary people in controlled environments for the attention of the viewing public (Hill 2005: 24).

However, although *Survivor* is said to have inaugurated the new genre of reality programming, it is *Big Brother* that is often understood as the archetypal reality game show (Cummings 2002a: xii). After all, since the programme first aired in the Netherlands in 1999 it has been a prime-time success in more than seventy different countries, with the programme providing Channel 4 with 'the best Friday night ratings in its history' (Hill 2004: 27). The programme has proved to be 'one of the most successful franchises in television history' (Hill and Palmer 2002: 251) due in part to the ways in which it activates and orchestrates audience responses, particularly among members of the younger generation, by deploying multimedia and interactive technologies including live web transmissions, video streaming, internet chat rooms and text updates (Kilborn 2003: 18). In brief then, *Big Brother* features a group of contestants in a specially designed house fitted with cameras which monitor the housemates twenty-four hours a day, seven days a week. The participants are given a range of physical, mental and endurance tasks to perform every week in return for extra food, treats and immunity from nominations. Every week the participants nominate their least favourite housemates, who are then put up for a public vote, with the last remaining housemate being crowned the winner and rewarded with a cash prize.

BIG BROTHER: REALITY, DISTORTION AND AUTHENTICITY

Much critical writing on *Big Brother* tends to focus on the programme's presentation of reality, either to champion the show for its 'pore close' (Jones 2003: 401) depictions of ordinary people or to condemn the artificiality and construction of this particular production (Holmes and Jermyn 2004: 11).

Big Brother contestants are non-actors chosen from the British public who, once they are inside the house, are filmed every minute of the day. Their every waking (and sleeping) moment is subject to scrutiny as audiences can choose to watch not only the edited highlights of the show, but also the 'rushes' on the web and the digital channel E4. With this in mind, any claims of the participants 'acting up' for cameras or performing a part in order to appeal to both their housemates and the wider viewing audience might be open to question. While the executive producer of the first British *Big Brother* (2000) tells us that 'nobody can keep up an act all the time in front of the cameras – the world was going to see them as they really were' (Ritchie 2000: 26), the presenter of *Big Brother's Little Brother* (2001–) echoes this sentiment by informing us that 'no one can act for 24 hours a day, or indeed, for 24 minutes an hour, so we know the housemates' reactions are genuine' (*heat* cited in Hill 2005: 71). Therefore 'the persistent gaze of the camera becomes a guarantor of realness' (Jones 2003: 409). Because *Big Brother* is set up to focus on the most trivial and mundane 'simulation of the everyday' (Roscoe 2001: 483), from cooking and eating to sunbathing and sleeping, the programme offers us a rare and extremely intimate insight into the behaviours of others. This point is made in existing audience research because the majority of viewers are said to watch the programme because it gives them an 'insight into people's behaviour' (Jones 2003: 407). Although one might argue that taking participants out of their everyday work, home and social settings and placing them in a highly artificial environment cannot possibly encourage real relations and authentic personalities, it is worth noting how the artificiality of the house can be seen to foster 'real life' exchanges. Cummings makes this point when he tells us that 'when you strip away the trappings of civilisation, responsibility and social expectations, you are left with the real person' (Cummings 2002b: 68). Even those participants who are keen to put on a public façade and construct a media friendly persona 'let their guard slip in moments of boredom, frustration or drunkenness' (Lavender 2003: 22). Therefore, even though *Big Brother* is staged in a specially designed house with obtrusive cameras, this does not detract from the actuality that takes place inside those mirrored walls. The programme operates its claims to the real within a fully managed artificiality so that 'everything that might be deemed to be true about what people do and say is . . . predicated on the larger contrivance of them being there in front of the camera in the first place' (Corner 2002: 256). Hence, even though the programme cannot, and does not, lay claim to the kinds of 'field naturalism' associated with the documentary tradition, *Big Brother* can make claims to the real due to its use of non-actors, its lack of scripting, its incessant cameras and the focus on everyday scenarios and interpersonal relationships. The former chairman of Endemol summarises the argument when he informs us that the programme is 'the launch pad for a new form of television culture which is "more real, real people and real language" than its predecessors' (Biressi and Nunn 2005: 26). That said, for every argument that leads critics to conclude that *Big Brother* is presenting a mode of 'real' behaviour there are counter-claims concerning the way in which the programme actually distorts reality.

Although housemates are chosen from the British public, critics routinely comment that these contestants are anything but ordinary. While some talk about a 'combustive and varied mix of personalities' (Brenton and Cohen 2003: 92) others have noticed that an exhibitionistic streak is an advantage in the series because 'contestants know very well that the celebrity they crave is directly proportionate to the exhibitionism they display' (Jagasia cited in Palmer 2002: 306). More cynical commentators go on to inform us that participants are chosen 'with their potential future celebrity in mind' (Lavender 2003: 22). Susan Murray and Laurie Ouellette make this point when they comment that

> the fifteen minutes of fame that is the principal material reward for participating on the programs limits the selection of 'real people' to those who make good copy for newspaper and magazine articles as well as desirable guests on synergistic talk shows and news specials.
>
> (Murray and Ouellette 2004: 8)

There is much evidence to support this claim due to the fact that a large number of *Big Brother* participants remain in the public eye for a short period after their summer spent in the house. For example, nine of the ten contestants of the original British *Big Brother* were working in the media nearly a year after leaving the programme (Bignell 2005: 96). There are examples of contestants remaining in the public eye long after their eviction. For example, Brian Dowling, the winner of *Big Brother 2* (2001), became a presenter on shows such as *SMTV: Live* (2002–3) and *Brian's Boyfriends* (2003) and remains a popular figure on programmes such as *Hells Kitchen* (2004–). Likewise, Jade Goody, a contestant on *Big Brother 3* (2002) continues to star in a number of cable and satellite shows such as *Jade's Salon* (2005), *Jade's PA* (2006) and more recently *Celebrity Big Brother* (2007). The point here is that participating in the programme can be seen to 'provide a continuation of the observed life, as former . . . players' offscreen behaviours are tracked by the media even after their show airs' (Murray and Ouellette 2004: 8). Even though digital television and the internet provide seemingly unlimited access to the housemates all day every day, the reality is that the vast majority of the *Big Brother* audience watch the edited highlights, and are therefore privy only to those narrative arcs, friendships and sexual flirtations that are presented here. Likewise, although common sense demands that these participants will have to show their real selves because no one could possibly perform for the duration of the show, the fact that the housemates talk to both the mounted cameras and the one-way mirrored glass suggests that they rarely forget that they are subject to surveillance. It is not that these people have discovered the cameras, but rather that 'they have actively sought them out' (Mapplebeck 2002: 23). Rather than suggest that it is precisely the construction of the artificial environment that reveals the truth about a particular individual, it has been argued that the 'high-pressure environment of penal chic in which subjects were given few physical or psychological comforts' (ibid.: 26) actually encourages housemates to perform. After all 'we are only truly ourselves in the familiar circumstances of our daily life, and preferably behind closed doors, when we no longer play the game of social behaviour' (Ryan 2004: online). And likewise,

> when you create a microcosmic world, replete with roles, rules and rituals, and all existence outside them is blocked out, you create unpredictable and extreme situations, in which people, with alarming rapidity, cease to be as they know themselves to be.
>
> (Brenton and Cohen 2003: 109)

And although the programme seems to be presenting an unmediated account of individual and group behaviour, the ways in which the house is designed, the ways in which the challenges are set and the number of activities available means that there is a finite number of responses and reactions that are available to the participants. Or rather 'rats can tackle a maze through a number of routes, but there are in the end only so many corridors' (ibid.: 54–5). Therefore, although *Big Brother* has been applauded by some for its unscripted dialogue, use of non-actors and focus on the everyday, the programme is routinely derided for its managed artificiality. Bernard Clark makes this point when he tells us that the words 'Reality TV' are mutually exclusive at the most basic level (Clark 2002: 6).

Irrespective of whether one chooses to view reality programming in general and *Big Brother* in particular as a site of authentic and real performances, staged and manipulated personalities or a balance of the two, it is important to examine the representations of gender that are being presented in the genre. If the contestants of such shows are being held up as 'ordinary' and 'average' members of the public, then it is relevant to explore what representations are standing in for, and appealing to, the wider society.

Vain and vacuous: reality television's representations of women

Existing work on the representation of gender in reality television programming tends to critique the genre for its misogynistic images of 'hot, desperate and dumb' women (Pozner 2004: online). After all, programmes such as *The Bachelor* (2002–5) show women competing for a marriage proposal, *The Swan* (2004–) presents women who are keen to alter their physical appearance and *Meet My Folks* (2002) chastises those women who are unable to answer common sense and general knowledge questions. Jennifer Pozner makes the point that viewers may be drawn to such programmes due to the 'poisonous' representations of women being presented in the genre, representations that teaches us that 'no matter their age [women are] "hot girls", not self-aware or intelligent adults' (ibid.). She goes on to inform us that phrases such as 'bitch' and 'beaver' are not uncommon in programmes such as *Average Joe* (2003–5) and that the promotion of *Joe Millionaire* (2003) tends to rely on the stereotypical image of 'money-grubbing, gold-digging whores' (ibid.). The point then is simply that the women that are cast for these shows are stereotypically attractive, passive and intellectually unchallenging, or rather what Pozner terms 'hot, dumb and licentious' (ibid.). Indeed, these programmes go as far as to suggest that anyone who dares to challenge the stereotypical image of female beauty is not worthy of love, attention, affection or happiness. After all, it is as if 'the most stereotypically beautiful, least independent women with the lowest-carb diets will be rewarded with love, financial security and the ultimate prize of male validation' (ibid.). In order to provide evidence to support her thesis she refers to one of the contestants on *The Swan* who, after announcing that she was once abused by her partner, was told that liposuction would help to 'break the cycle of violence' (ibid.).

Although *Big Brother* is not pitting women against one another for a wedding proposal nor outwardly ridiculing those females who do not conform to the stereotypical beauty myth, it is worth noting that the programme routinely includes a range of young, slim and attractive women in its line-up. *Big Brother 8* UK began as an all female house with 'a sea of lipgloss and hair straighteners' (*Big Brother* 2007: online) and the programme habitually depicted the attractive bikini-clad women in its edited highlights, situated either in the shower, outdoor pool or sunbathing. According to the official *Big Brother* website, the housemates included 19-year-old twins Sam and Amanda Marchant who are 'addicted to boys, partying, shopping and all things pink and fluffy' and 19-year-old Chanelle Hayes who is obsessed with the lifestyles of the rich and famous and who refuses to watch the news because 'there's too much bad stuff going on in the world'. Likewise, we are introduced to 19-year-old Emily Parr who would like to write for *Vogue* and who is 'hoping to find a gorgeous . . . man in the house', 22-year-old Charlie Uchea who 'likes shopping, money and going clubbing at celebrity hangouts' and 22-year-old Shabnam Paryani who is 'a self-confessed princess'. The website presents 28-year-old Nicky Maxwell who, as a 'girl's girl . . . takes up to four hours to get ready for a night out', and even 21-year-old Amy Alexander who joined the cast later in the series is a working glamour model who dreams of becoming a television presenter (ibid.). Therefore, these women all adhere to a narrow version of youthful, svelte and attractive femininity, and their respective dreams, aspirations and inspirations all go some way towards confirming Pozner's image of the 'hot, desperate and dumb' depiction of women in the reality television genre. With this cast in mind, one might suggest that the programme reasserts patriarchal gender roles by representing such a stereotypical, or even 'Stepford' depiction of modern young women. The edited highlights of the show repeatedly fetishise these women by paying particular attention to their bikini-clad bodies and clothing changes. However, this is not to suggest that these women are necessarily innocent victims of the show, after all, as other commentators have suggested 'some female contestants use these commodified body parts as survival tools' to keep both the man in the house and the man in the audience interested in her physical presence so as to stave off eviction (Moorti and Ross 2004: 204).

MONEY AND MISOGYNY: REALITY TELEVISION'S REPRESENTATIONS OF MEN

While Pozner condemns reality television for presenting contemporary young women as desperate WAGs and gold-digging whores, she goes on to argue that the depictions of the male in shows such as *Who Wants to Marry a Multi-Millionaire* (2000) and *For Love or Money* (2003) are equally as problematic. We are told to 'forget about decency, honesty or intelligence [because] the primary criteria to qualify as a reality-TV Prince is a firm ass and a firmer financial portfolio' (Pozner 2004: online). Reality television makes it clear that men must be, or must at least appear to be, wealthy in order to be successful with the women in the show and those women in the audience. The very fact that these programmes tend to present ordinary men posing as wealthy studs and playboys goes some way to demeaning both the man in question and his subsequent dates. As such, reality programming can be said to thoroughly underestimate 'men's inherent worth as people' (ibid.). After all, this representation makes it clear that qualities such as respect, sensitivity, loyalty and tolerance are neither desired nor rewarded in the genre, as long as they ride in on (quite literally in some cases) a white horse or an expensive sports car.

Big Brother is not asking the male to choose from a bevy of gold-digging beauties or requiring that he pose as a knight in shining armour, rather, the programme demands a degree of personality and 'ordinariness' from all contestants. As such, the show rarely depicts wealthy studs or precocious playboys, but instead chooses to cast affable, amiable and attractive working- and middle-class young men as company for those inside and beyond the enclosed environment. However, like the female housemates who entered before them, those men that were introduced into *Big Brother 8* UK tended to fit a rather narrow version of contemporary manhood. For example, the official website informed us that 20-year-old Brian Belo is a 'self confessed Jack-the-lad . . . with lots of sex appeal', 23-year-old Liam McGough is a tree-surgeon and 'a bit of a ladies man', 25-year-old Billi Bhatti is a model who says that 'gorgeous girls, money and attention make him happy' and 26-year-old Ziggy Lichman is a fashion-conscious model and ex-boyband member who dreams of working with Hugh Hefner and introducing 'a National Short Skirt Day' (*Big Brother* 2007: online). Therefore, the vast majority of men who enter the *Big Brother* house adhere to a rather stereotypical image of handsome, muscular and youthful masculinity, and all draw attention to their interest in and success with the opposite sex. In this way, the participants seem to provide evidence of the ways in which their handsome appearance, heterosexuality and sexual availability is of more interest to both viewers and *Big Brother* producers than any emotional responses or intellectual thought processes here. This is not to say that *Big Brother* only provides audiences with such stereotypical characters, but rather, that viewers and producers seem to favour them. After all, the majority of housemates fit this profile and it is these non-threatening and beautiful young women and traditionally attractive young men who routinely make it to the final week in the house, with the most recent series of the programme as a case in point. What is even more striking in the history of the programme in the UK is the number of men who have won the prize money. Six out of eight winners of the British version of the show have been male, with one transsexual and one female taking first place.

MASCULINITY AND THE FEMALE AUDIENCE

Annette Hill's seminal work on the first series of *Big Brother* in the UK tells us that 28 per cent of men and 34 per cent of women watched the show, that the programme proved most popular with the 16–34-year-old demographic and that the majority of viewers had a college education (Hill 2002: 331). However, what is most interesting here is the fact that female viewers are more likely to vote in weekly evictions, more likely to vote more than once a week and more likely to vote for men to stay in the house (Jones 2003: 420). While 71 per cent of men voted for male housemates, 76 per cent of women were also voting for the male (ibid.: 420). Although this research challenges much work on audience identification by demonstrating that audiences, and especially female audiences, are able to identify with and then vote for the opposite sex, it actually supports claims made by psychologists that 'girls tend to "identify" with both male and female performers [while] boys, on the other hand, tend to identify only with male heroes' (Noble 1975: 53).

Either way, what is clear is that women are the voice of *Big Brother*, and their vote is crucial if a participant wants to avoid eviction. Therefore, one might go as far as to suggest that those men who make it to the final week of the programme are those same men who are most appealing to the female in the audience. With this in mind, this chapter will now look at the runners-up and the eventual winner of *Big Brother 8* UK, and consider the representation of masculinities that are being offered here, irrespective of how authentic or manipulated, real or staged readers believe these representations to be. The programme chose a range of male stereotypes or 'more charitably . . . a range of representative characters' (Biressi and Nunn 2005: 28) in its casting process, and the three men who made it to the final week can be identified (in order of evictions) as an ex-boyband stud (Ziggy), a rugged labourer (Liam) and an Essex lad (Brian) respectively. I will now go on to examine the ways in which the programme presented these men for the viewing public, concluding that the most sincere, sensitive and emotionally responsive male was seen to both appeal to the female audience and win the series.

ZIGGY: ATTRACTION, MEDIA ATTENTION AND SELF-IMAGE

Twenty-six-year-old Ziggy, the model and Northern Line singer used his audition tape to tell the audience that he would like to try and date more than one girl in the house, preferably at the same time. And when the man entered an all-female house on day three of the show, he was soon heard telling the diary-room camera that 'every day just gets better and better' (*Big Brother* 08/08/07: Channel 4). And yet, when Ziggy was set the task of dating all of the female contestants in the house, he was seen to show a romantic interest in 19-year-old Chanelle, and just days after entering the house the couple (nicknamed 'Chiggy' in the popular British press) were seen cuddling in bed and spending much of their time together.

However, a number of housemates were soon heard commenting that although Chanelle's feelings appeared genuine, Ziggy's were rather more calculated (*Big Brother* 01/07/07: Channel 4). Indeed, if one considers that the programme appeals to a majority female audience, and that those 'females want to see the romance' (Moorti and Ross 2004: 203), then Ziggy's advances might be understood as a clever tactical move to keep him from eviction. Either way, by the fifth week the relationship was becoming strained, with Chanelle making demands on her partner and Ziggy becoming paranoid about the way the relationship was being presented to the outside world. The crux of the problem seemed to be that while Ziggy was telling Chanelle that their relationship was something special that would last beyond their time in the house, he was simultaneously telling male contestants 'if things do or don't happen on the outside we've had a good time in here' (*Big Brother* 03/07/07: Channel 4). In fact, he is heard telling one man that Chanelle's vision of their relationship 'is just so far from me it's unfunny, she's on about after, all this after, after, after and after, and it's like shit . . . why is there all this pressure about after, I just feel trapped' (*Big Brother* 03/07/07: Channel 4). When he talks about his relationship with Chanelle he starts by commenting 'I've been stuck in . . .' (*Big Brother* 03/07/07: Channel 4) before seeming to correct himself and saying 'I've been with someone' (*Big Brother* 03/07/07: Channel 4) and such slips seem to be rather telling here.

When the time came for Ziggy to finally end the relationship he tells Chanelle that he was depressed in the house and that 'I'm afraid to say it's got something to do with us' before going on to mouth those fatal words 'it's not you, it's me' (*Big Brother* 27/07/07: Channel 4). However, what is interesting here is not necessarily how or why the relationship ended, but what happened after the breakup. Chanelle makes it clear that after such humiliation and heartbreak she would be unable to stay in the house with Ziggy, to which our housemate agrees that one of them should leave the show (*Big Brother* 27/07/07: Channel 4). And yet, although Ziggy starts by saying that it should be him who leaves the house, this gesture soon turns into him simply offering to spend time out of her way in the garden caravan (*Big Brother* 29/07/07: Channel 4). Therefore, although Ziggy was initially seen to make a courteous gesture he was never actually going to put his words into practice by leaving the house early, and it was not long before Chanelle had packed her bags and left the *Big Brother* premises (*Big Brother* 29/07/07: Channel 4).

After leaving the show Chanelle spoke openly to a range of news and magazine media about her experiences in the house, and routinely commented that she had to leave because she 'couldn't live with someone who pretended to like me loads just to look good on camera' and that 'when he . . . called me "Sarah", the name of his ex-girlfriend, I had to leave' (Waterlow 2007: 4). And when asked if Ziggy had ever cared for her she concluded that 'I don't think he ever did' (Pollen 2007b: 6). Women's magazines seemed to form a consensus as they accused the former boyband singer of creating his relationship for public approval (Harkness and Dunn 2007: 21). Although Ziggy looked appropriately tearful and tormented after Chanelle left the programme, housemates and commentators alike agreed that this was simply because he wanted to maintain his popularity with the public rather than because of any actual remorse over the situation. While one female contestant tells us that 'he wants to come across as the nice, cool, easy-going, jokey guy' (*Big Brother* 20/08/07: Channel 4), *Big Brother*'s behaviour expert Judy James notes that 'he likes to protect his image, he likes to be the good guy in the house' (*BB on the Couch* 19/08/07: Channel 4). Likewise, media commentators seemed to agree that his remorse was bogus. We are told that Ziggy is 'very good at turning events to his advantage, he always does this thing where after he does something horrible he goes into the diary room wearing his hoody top, looking very upset, he's agonised, he's really thinking about it . . .', as a way of manipulating the public (*BB on the Couch* 05/08/07: Channel 4). The *Big Brother* psychologists even went on to provide evidence that Ziggy neither cared for nor was considerate of Chanelle's feelings. After all, through what clinical psychologist Dr Cecilia d'Felice termed art therapy, they deduced that the housemate actually missed his dog more than he missed his ex-partner (*BB on the Couch* 29/07/07: Channel 4).

However, although Ziggy's behaviour suggests that he fashioned a relationship as a way of creating a romantic narrative arc that would appeal to the woman in the audience, this relationship can be seen to have provided further benefits to the male. After all, Ziggy's relationship with Chanelle could have acted as a way for the model to reassert his masculinity over the other men in the house because 'it is sometimes thought that competition for women is the ultimate source of men's competition with each other' (Pleck 2004: 63). And although Brian and Liam were not seen to show any romantic intentions towards Chanelle, Brian was unsuccessful in his attempts to woo one of the housemates while Liam's brief fling created awkwardness between contestants. Alternatively, one might suggest that Ziggy used his relationship to provide himself with a refuge from the dangers and stresses of relating to the other males in the house. After all

> traditional relationships with women have provided men a safe place in which they can recuperate from the stresses they have absorbed in their daily struggle with other men, and in which they can express their needs without fearing that these needs will be used against them.
>
> (Pleck 2004: 63–4)

Indeed, the amount of time that 'Chiggy' spent simply cuddling on sofas, holding one another in bed or whispering in the caravan might go some way to support this claim. Moreover, the fact that Ziggy was the only male housemate at the start of the series, and the fact that he admitted that he would be 'jealous if other men came into the house' (*Big Brother* 05/06/07: Channel 4) after him provides further evidence here. And finally, it could be argued that Chanelle's role in the relationship was 'to reduce the stress of competition by serving as an *underclass*' for the male (ibid.: 64). After all, 'under patriarchy women represent the lowest status, a status to which men can fall only under the most exceptional circumstances' (ibid.: 64). Therefore, on those occasions when we hear Ziggy make comments such as 'love, you may be nineteen but you ain't gonna give me the run-around' (*Big Brother* 26/06/07: Channel 4) and 'I learnt from my dad to stick my foot down' (*Big Brother* 10/08/07: Channel 4) it asks that we question his relation to women in general and Chanelle in particular here.

Whether it is because of or in spite of his liaison in the house, both Brian and Liam are seen to admire and respect the model. For example we hear Liam inform Ziggy that 'you're a bit cool' (*Big Brother* 26/08/07: Channel 4) and Brian tells him that 'you're a cool person . . . don't let me blow any more smoke up your ass, in all honesty you're someone I'd look up to . . . seriously, I've looked up to you in this house' (*Big Brother* 26/08/07: Channel 4). And again, the resident psychologists go on to provide evidence of this point when they comment that the other men 'really admire Ziggy . . . his studly ways and his boyband moments' (*BB on the Couch* 19/08/07: Channel 4). And although Ziggy seems rather self-deprecating when he tells the other men that 'some of the things I've done in here are extremely uncool . . . being a complete dick' (*Big Brother* 26/08/07: Channel 4), it seems slightly disingenuous as we have heard the housemate boasting about his queue-jumping in clubs and celebrity name-dropping based on his previous career (*Big Brother* 29/07/07: Channel 4). However, although Ziggy proved extremely popular with the other men in the house he did not secure the final vote, and as such, it is worth considering the ways in which Liam and Brian were seen to present a more open, honest and appealing image of masculinity for the woman in the audience.

LIAM: SEXISM, SENSITIVITY AND AUTHENTICITY

Twenty-two-year-old Liam is a laid-back tree-surgeon who used his audition tape to tell us that although he is currently enjoying playing the field and dating several women, he will dedicate himself to a wife and children at some point in his future. He includes time spent with family and nights out with friends as his favourite pastimes, and tells us that after two weeks of interviews on leaving the house he will be returning to his old home, job and lifestyle. Liam was so well-liked in the house that on day 22 when three of the contestants were asked to nominate one contestant to win £100,000 they all agreed that it should be the man in question (*Big Brother* 20/06/07: Channel 4).

However, Liam's popularity with female housemates and the college-educated women in the audience may not be immediately obvious. After all, this was a man who told a more mature female contestant to 'have your boobs out when you talk to me or don't talk at all' (*Big Brother* 26/06/07: Channel 4); a man who saw the weekly challenges as 'a complete test of my manhood' (*Big Brother* 07/08/07: Channel 4); a man who tried to make Ziggy feel better about Chanelle leaving by offering him a cigarette (*Big Brother* 29/07/07: Channel 4); a man who had a short fling with a housemate because 'I'm just craving a little cuddle' and she was 'the first slice of ass that's drove through the house for weeks' (*Big Brother* 31/07/07: Channel 4) and a man who thought that 'doing the lads' mags' (*Big Brother* 20/08/07: Channel 4) was a perfectly reasonable way for a female contestant to pay off her mounting student debts. One might read a vote for Liam as a 'form of resistance to the supposed tyranny of "political correctness" and female cultural power – a lads' mag-style two fingers up to notions of gender equality' (Tincknell and Raghuram 2004: 266). And *Big Brother* seems to be encouraging this reading because when it challenged the housemates to play word games, Liam was asked to 'say as many different words or phrases as you can possibly think of which have the same meaning as . . . breasts' (*Big Brother* 11/08/07: Channel 4). Perhaps predictably when *Big Brother* says 'Liam, your time thinking about breasts is now up' he responds with 'my time thinking about breast is never up' (*Big Brother* 11/08/07: Channel 4).

However, Liam must be understood as something more than a one-dimensional image of British laddishness here, after all, this is a man who seemed to cherish his female friends and make genuine connections with the other men in the house, a man who puts friends and family above celebrity, who appears genuinely self-deprecating, modest, and willing to modify his future behaviour based on his experiences in the house. On leaving the programme he announced that 'I've learnt that I'm a bit insensitive at times, I've learnt that it doesn't matter where you are you can make pals, you've got to put a positive spin on everything and people are nice' (*Big Brother* 31/08/07: Channel 4). Indeed, if we go back to look at these first charges, Liam is not necessarily the figure of laddish sexism that he may at first seem.

When he asked a female housemate to have her 'boobs out' it was a deliberately tongue-in-cheek comment during a conversation about the sheer volume of gossip and bitching that seemed to be taking place in the female-dominated house. When the woman came over to join in the boys', conversation Liam confessed that 'we're being chauvinistic pigs' (*Big Brother* 26/06/07: Channel 4) and it was only when the female contestant said 'I'm OK with that' that Liam made the fateful comment. Therefore, it is as if the comment could be understood as part of a wider postmodern irony in contemporary lad culture whereby young males can appear sexist without ever having to apologise (Whannel 2002: 199). Likewise, when *Big Brother* asked the contestants to erect a wooden contraption and start a fire as part of a time-travelling task, Liam wanted to be seen to make it, not he hastened to add because he was being a Neanderthal or because he thought that the female contestant was not capable, but rather because he thought that 'it would be more embarrassing if I was to fail . . . given the job that I do' (*Big Brother* 07/08/07: Channel 4). Admittedly, offering Ziggy 'a tab' rather than having a more meaningful conversation about his feelings after Chanelle left the house may have seemed rather lacking in emotional sensitivity, however, the offer comes only after they have already had such discussions, and on the back of many similar ones that have occurred since they both entered the house. When Liam made it clear to his fellow housemates that he wanted to have a short fling with a female contestant who had entered the half-way house because he was sexually frustrated rather than because he had any deeper attraction to this particular woman, one might suggest that his behaviour was both misogynistic and disrespectful. However (perhaps unsurprisingly if we consider Pozner's work on the representations of women in the reality television genre), it was the woman who was vilified for using Liam in order to create a new romantic storyline for the attention of the viewing public. After all, unlike Ziggy, Liam made no attempt to suggest that the fling would be anything more than a physical release, even going as far as telling the woman that 'I just can't be assed to be all smooth with you tonight' before they kiss (*Big Brother* 31/07/07: Channel 4). The difference here then is that Liam is being honest about his intentions (however crude or base the viewing public may find them) rather than deceiving the woman about his thoughts and feelings here. Furthermore, the woman in question makes it clear that she only wants to have some fun in the house, telling another housemate that she likes Liam 'only as much as it's for while we're in here' (*Big Brother* 03/08/07: Channel 4) and going on to comment that she's 'really sexually frustrated' because she is 'a three- or four-times-a-day girl on the outside' (*Big Brother* 31/07/07: Channel 4).

On several occasions in the show we see Liam both reduced to tears and embarrassed by his emotional outpouring. For example, when he receives a letter from home and we find out that his family love him, miss him and are proud of him, he finds himself close to tears. However, rather than let the other housemates see him cry he covers his face with a sofa cushion and walks to the bathroom where we see him wipe away the tears. This appears to be evidence of real behaviour and a real emotion, however, rather than discuss it with the housemates in any real depth, he mocks himself by later telling Brian that 'you look at people crying on the telly, and you just think stop being so soft' (*Big Brother* 23/07/07: Channel 4) but admits that he can now understand the tearful release. Moreover, on hearing that he has won £100,000 he cries, falls to his knees and then leaves the crowded living room for the (relative) privacy of the bedroom. And when in his after-show interview he was asked why he never talked about the win with the other housemates he said it was '100 grand, I've nowt had 100 pounds, I didn't feel like I deserved it' (*Big Brother* 31/08/07: Channel 4) and when asked how he will spend the money we are told it will be on 'my dad, brother, mam, everybody I care about' (*Big Brother* 31/08/07: Channel 4). He tells us that he hopes to help out his family financially and only then if there is any money remaining 'possibly start my own business firm up, Liam's trees' (*Big Brother* 31/08/07: Channel 4).

When *Big Brother* asked Liam who he was closest to in the house, it was clear that he valued his new male friendships with Ziggy and Brian. He tells us

> Zig, I've grown really close to . . . I just think he's sound, he's on a similar level to myself, he's very funny I enjoy his company, he's quite interesting, he's just a nice lad . . . Brian's cool I've always got on with him.
> (*Big Brother* 10/08/07: Channel 4)

In one task where the housemates are meant to be demonstrating how to waltz, Liam and Ziggy abandon their female partners in order to dance together in a display of what appears to be genuine affection (*Big Brother* 21/08/07: Channel 4). Likewise, after being separated from Ziggy for a few days due to the introduction of a half-way house, he seems truly happy to be reunited with his friend. Even though the woman to whom Liam has admitted having an attraction is in the same house he simply says 'nice to see you' before asking her 'where's Zig?', because it is the company of his male friend rather than any chance of sexual fulfilment that is of importance to him here (*Big Brother* 31/07/07: Channel 4). On the last day of the show Liam tells Ziggy and Brian that he wants to 'say something really profound that you'll remember for the rest of your lives, but I really can't think of anything. So I'll just say I think the world of you' (Pollen 2007a: 5).

The point here is that Liam presents a rather complicated image of masculinity. After all, here is a man who makes seemingly sexist and borderline-misogynistic remarks and who appears unable to express his feelings to others in the house, and yet both housemates and the wider viewing public voted Liam the runner-up in the programme based on his kind, caring and considerate nature (*Big Brother* 31/08/07: Channel 4). As such, Liam might be seen to represent a version of contemporary young masculinity that is both aware of the limitations of the stoic, taciturn male, but who has not yet found the strength to break through such stereotypes.

BRIAN: SENSITIVITY, INSECURITY AND CONTEMPORARY MASCULINITY

Twenty-year-old Brian is a data-entry clerk who lists clubbing, shopping and drinking among his favourite pastimes. Indeed, perhaps Brian says it best when he says that 'I'm not really that complicated, I like to get pissed, hang out with my mates and go down Lakeside shopping' (Big Brother 2007: online). However, before we assume that Brian fits a stereotypical image of laddish youth, it is also worth noting that he considers himself a 'sexual novice' and 'would like to think of himself as a wild child, even though the thought of leaving home for university scares him' (ibid.). As such, we are being presented with an image of masculinity that cannot be obviously pigeon-holed or reduced to type here. Therefore, although his blurb on the official *Big Brother* website tells us that he considers himself a bit of a 'jack-the-lad', it is soon clear that this is something akin to wish-fulfilment as we later find out that he 'talks to imaginary hot girls' in his quieter moments (ibid.). Even though Brian looks like what both Ziggy and Liam refer to as 'a handsome lad' (*Big Brother* 06/08/07: Channel 4) he is sexually inexperienced, somewhat insecure and longing for a meaningful rather than just a sexual relationship.

Although in the first few weeks of the programme the female housemates and popular media alike seemed more interested in the traditionally handsome model and tree-surgeon, both came to focus on Brian as a more honest, open and sensitive image of masculinity in the final weeks of the show. Hannah Perry of *heat* magazine makes this point when she tells us that

> Brian came across as your standard loveable fool, and was quickly over-shadowed by the laddish hunkiness of Liam and the smooth charm of Ziggy. But, as the weeks wore on, our affections for the more conventional boys thawed, and our attentions turned to dopey old Brian.
>
> (Perry 2007: 6)

The reason why Brian proved so popular with the British public in general and the majority female audience in particular was because he seemed to be the most unerringly honest, open and emotionally sensitive of the young men in the house, and his relations with the female contestants seemed both considerate and respectful. Although he would routinely comment on the physical appearance of particular housemates, it was not always in line with the traditional lad-mag ethos. After all, he was often heard praising one young woman for her intelligence and elegance, commenting that 'the way she holds herself . . . that's quite a rarity in this day and age' (*Big Brother* 03/08/07: Channel 4).

It was not long before female housemates and the wider audience were aware of Brian's feelings towards Amanda, and it was his stolen shy glances towards her that endeared him to these women. After all, while Ziggy was making claims about having slept with Chanelle and Liam was heard telling others about his desire for a fling, the way in which Brian spoke about his fellow housemate provided evidence of heartfelt emotions not shared or spoken by the other men. When *Big Brother* asked him to talk about his fellow contestants he soon found himself talking about Amanda, telling us that 'having sex with someone like Mand would be like aaahhh, like a really nice experience, like angels playing on harps and stuff, and women with violins . . . like sitting on a fluffy cloud' (*Big Brother* 31/07/07: Channel 4). And when the couple shared a solitary kiss after many weeks in the house, Brian tells *Big Brother* that 'I'm walking on air right now, I don't normally get this feeling' (*Big Brother* 06/08/07: Channel 4). While the other men seem incapable of expressing genuine emotion, Brian is often heard telling Amanda that she is 'the nicest girl, you're so pretty Mand . . . you should know it sometimes . . . so beautiful Mand seriously . . . you deserve everything . . . so gorgeous' (*Big Brother* 06/08/07: Channel 4). And even after he left the house he was heard informing the popular media that Amanda is 'an amazing girl who makes me feel so special. I get butterflies in my stomach when I'm with her' (Boulos 2007: 9). Therefore, even though Brian may not necessarily be the most eloquent of speakers, the most stereotypically handsome of men or the most educated member of the house, he does seem to be the most considerate, authentic and sensitive. So much so, in fact, that the resident psychologist had a tendency to refer to him as 'the emotional barometer of the house' (*BB on the Couch* 05/08/2007: Channel 4). It was his emotional intelligence that proved popular with housemates and 'that genuine emotion that made us vote for him in our droves' (Perry 2007: 8).

Brian's emotions came to the fore on a number of occasions, for example when Liam left to enter the half-way house Brian was seen crying in the toilet after having to say goodbye to his friend, however, rather than hide his tears from the group he welcomed the hugs and consoling words from fellow housemates (*Big Brother* 31/07/07: Channel 4); when he received a message from home he was clearly overwhelmed at how proud his mother was of his behaviour in the house (*Big Brother* 24/07/07: Channel 4) and when Amanda told Brian that she just wanted to remain friends while they were in the house it was clear that he was emotionally distraught (*Big Brother* 18/08: Channel 4). At any point in the series when one of the other men looked ashamed of their tears, Brian told them quite plainly 'don't worry about crying son, I've done it, I've mugged myself off' (*Big Brother* 20/06/07: Channel 4) with no recourse to embarrassment or judgement. Although it was not uncommon to hear the young women on the programme commenting that Brian is 'a really really nice guy' and 'really really sweet' (*Big Brother* 06/08/07: Channel 4), his sensitivity did not mean that he was any less popular with the men in the house. Liam in particular considered Brian a good friend, telling him that 'you are cool, you're a nice lad . . . you're sound' (*Big Brother* 26/08/07: Channel 4) and later informing others that 'Brian's the main man, how can you not like Bri' (*Big Brother* 31/08/07: Channel 4). The most scathing thing that any contestant ever said about Brian was that he was 'normal', which in *Big Brother* folklore tends to mean judgement, boredom and eviction. However, although 'to appear too dull, too isolated, too introverted is to invite banishment' (Biressi and Nunn 2005: 151–2) in the house, Liam was the first to make it clear that 'there's nowt wrong with normal Bri' (*Big Brother* 31/07/07: Channel 4).

Brian went on to prove that there is nothing wrong with normal when he won *Big Brother 8* with 60.3 per cent of the final vote (*Big Brother* 31/08/07: Channel 4), and a vote for Brian might be understood as a vote for sensitive, honest and respectful masculinity. Therefore, even though it has been suggested that 'men's patriarchal competition with each other makes use of women as symbols of success, as mediators, as refuges, and as an underclass' (Pleck 2004: 64), and that Ziggy and (to a lesser extent) Liam have been seen to use women to play a role in those male relations in the *Big Brother* house, Brian appears to offer an alternative image of male–male and male–female relations for the contemporary audience.

Conclusion

This chapter has outlined the ways in which 'Reality TV' has been seen to develop from the crime, accident and health programmes of the 1980s to those popular reality game shows that dominate contemporary television schedules, paying particular attention to the issues of authenticity and artificiality that populate much writing on the genre. The chapter goes on to consider the traditional gendered stereotypes that dominate reality programming, concluding that existing research on the representations of gender in shows such as *The Swan* and *Average Joe* are at best problematic and at worst poisonous. However, rather than take such stereotypical representations at face value, I went on to consider a more detailed examination of the representation of gender in *Big Brother 8* UK. The programme did include a wealth of traditionally young, muscular and handsome cast-members and such men were, on occasion, seen to present manipulative and borderline-misogynistic behaviours. However, what is most important here is that those men who were most popular with the viewing public were also those men who showed tolerance of other housemates, consideration to alternative masculinities, respect for female participants and genuine outpourings of emotion. Indeed, one might suggest that it is the programmes combination of public audience and private space that encouraged the representation of a contemporary masculinity that challenges the traditional hegemonic stereotype.

11. LIFESTYLE: DOMESTIC LABOUR AND LEISURE ACTIVITIES

INTRODUCTION

Lifestyle programming has its roots in the hobbyist or enthusiast strand of television that was popular in 1960s Britain, when daytime schedules were keen to focus on a range of minority interests for 'the jazz fancier or the pigeon fancier . . . the fisherman or cyclist or collector of LP records . . . the bridge player or the naturalist, the more sophisticated film-goer, the ardent motorist or the enthusiast for amateur dramatics' (*Radio Times* cited in Brunsdon 2003: 6). However, due in part to an increase in home ownership and the continued inflation of house prices, the 1990s witnessed an increase in those prime-time 'infotainment' or 'factual entertainment' programmes that focused on fashion, style and grooming, gardening, property development, home improvement, travel, cookery and other food and drink topics, or what has been more concisely referred to as 'our most popular obsessions' (Moseley 2000: 299). While the genre was once dedicated to female experts talking to and instructing the female viewer, contemporary shows frequently present the male as client and expert respectively. Therefore, this chapter will introduce the history of lifestyle programming before focusing on the representations of masculinity in these narratives of transformation. After all, if one considers that the domestic space has been conventionally coded as the women's realm, then it is relevant to examine those programmes that present 'men . . . engaging in traditionally feminine activities – cooking, decorating, designing – prompting consideration of how men might be using domestic spaces and activities to generate new masculine identities which contest gendered and sexualized norms' (Gorman-Murray 2006: 244). By looking at the presentation of the food and fashion expert in programmes such as *The Naked Chef* and *Queer Eye for the Straight Guy*, this work will consider the role of consumerism in contemporary masculinity and pay particular attention to the ways in which domestic labour is being reclaimed as a masculine leisure activity.

History of the genre

Enthusiast or hobbyist programming has a long history on British daytime television, whereby programmes such as *Clothes that Count* (1967) showed its predominantly female audience how to make a particular item of clothing from week to week. Although the programme was keen to include 'fashion-show like segments in which the garment is modelled, made up in a range of fabrics', it was rather more committed to presenting close-up shots of the sewing machine and the dressmaker's hands at work (Brunsdon 2003: 10). After all, such shows were dedicated to informing and educating their viewers, and committed to providing them with useful skills. However, while *Clothes that Count* was keen to focus on the dressmaker's hands as she showed her audience how to make their very own piped buttonhole in a coat (ibid.: 10), more recent fashion-related texts tend to overlook any audience interest in making their own clothes in favour of receiving a hair, beauty and fashion makeover. Daytime programmes such as *This Morning* (1988–) and *GMTV* (1993–) have routinely presented a range of makeovers in their magazine formats, while prime-time shows such as *Looking Good* (1997–2000), *She's Gotta Have It* (1998–2000) and *What Not to Wear* (2002–), are dedicated to transforming the sartorial practices of their female audience. This narrative of transformation can be understood as 'a staple of US talk shows which have often devoted entire [programmes] to making over audience members' (Moseley 2000: 304). In this way, we can see a clear shift from enthusiast to lifestyle television. After all, while *Clothes that Count* treated its audience as enthusiasts who wanted to make their own garments, more recent fashion programming treats its audience as keen consumers who are dedicated to shopping for the latest trends as they have been introduced by the expert. Indeed, contemporary clothing, beauty and fashion texts have no interest in teaching their audience a particular craft or skill, but rather, they seek to instruct their audience on where, when and how to consume particular fashion items. Thus, when we witness a particular makeover we are not being shown how to reproduce the perfect blow-dry or how to dress for success for example, but rather, we are told about a particular product range to purchase or a particular high-street store to peruse in order to enable us to successfully alter our surface appearance.

Although one might charge fashion and beauty programmes with triviality and superficiality based entirely on their ephemeral subject matter, it is worth noting that this trajectory from enthusiast to lifestyle programming, from instruction to consumption, is not confined merely to fashion and beauty shows. This shift can also be seen in all manner of lifestyle programming including the ostensibly more worthy gardening and cookery shows. For example, in the same way that *Clothes that Count* focused on the acquisition of skill, so too, early garden productions such as *Gardener's World* (1969–) were keen to educate their viewers on 'spring pruning, how to divide herbaceous perennials and the planting-out of hardened seedlings' (Brunsdon 2003: 10). Whereas early episodes of *Gardener's World* were keen to focus on teaching the skills required to transform a garden, and used lengthy close-ups of the grounds being cultivated, more recent programmes such as *Ground Force* (1998–2005) seem interested in the spectacle of transformation, focusing on the banter of the celebrity presenter and the reactions of the garden's owner. While early examples of the genre used to show up to twenty minutes of continuous address by the expert, more recent shows are seen to offer both instruction and spectacle to their viewers as they are seen 'designing the new garden, clearing the old one, and then planting purchased mature specimens' (ibid.: 10). Therefore, in the same way that fashion and beauty programmes inform their audience of the ways to transform their appearance with the latest clothes and beauty products, so too, contemporary gardening programmes seem far more attuned to contemporary lifestyles as they offer their audiences advice on where to find established plants, specialist tradespeople and equipment-hire companies for their very own garden makeover (ibid.: 10).

Likewise, early cookery programmes such as *Family Fare* (1973–5) and *Delia's Cookery Course* (1982) were keen to show audiences how to cook by demonstrating basic techniques in the kitchen. Delia Smith, the presenter of the aforementioned shows, is said to pride herself on 'testing her recipes over and over again to make them easy to follow, simple and achievable' so that 'anyone who follows a Smith recipe can do so with confidence' (BBC 2007a: online). In fact, Smith is so committed to educating and even nurturing her viewers regarding the skills necessary for good basic cooking that she has been seen to instruct viewers on how to boil an egg (BBC 2003: online). However, while Smith was seen to show her viewers how to make simple nutritious meals for themselves and their families, recent television chefs appear more interested in presenting the location of the programme or in demonstrating a particular celebrity lifestyle than they do on demonstrating a tried-and-tested recipe to the viewer.

For example, Keith Floyd is a culinary adventurer who travels the world in order to introduce audiences to both foreign cuisines and exotic locations. However, although Floyd is understood as a celebrity chef, it is worth noting that in programmes such as *Far Flung Floyd* (1998) the camera is routinely focused on the chef's surroundings rather than on the food preparation so that 'cookery is not the focal point' of the programme (Strange 1998: 303). Likewise, in *Rhodes Around Britain* (1995), Gary Rhodes, a television chef well-known for reinventing popular and traditional British recipes such as faggots and leek pies spends as much screen time presenting 'the iconography of British heritage' (ibid.: 306) as he does actually informing the audience about how to make a particular dish. While Keith Floyd and Gary Rhodes are seen to combine cookery instruction with more anthropological insights into particular local communities, Nigella Lawson is seen to combine an educational remit with a taste of celebrity lifestyle. After all, while programmes such as *Nigella Bites* (2001), *Nigella Feasts* (2006) and *Nigella Express* (2007) educate audiences about how to make classic comfort food, devilish chocolate deserts and festive meals, the chef in question also reveals details about her private life. Therefore, it is not unusual for reviewers of such shows to comment on Nigella's magnetism beyond the kitchen space. For example, we are told that these programmes are 'a showcase for her personality . . . she's like the best female friend you ever had . . . she seems to be someone you'd really want to get to know and hang out with, not just cook with' (Magic 2007: online). And as such, these comments go further to put the skill and craft of cooking in the background here.

<h2 style="text-align:center">AN EQUAL OPPORTUNITIES EMPLOYER</h2>

One might look to argue that lifestyle programming is an equal opportunities employer due to the fact that fashion and beauty shows such as *What Not to Wear* have been seen (on occasion) to focus on male makeovers, shows such as *Looking Good* and *She's Gotta Have It* have both presented male transformations and *Trinny and Susannah Undress* . . . (2006–) has recently offered an emotional and sartorial makeover to both partners in a heterosexual couple. While the fashion and beauty show is happy to introduce male makeovers and highlight the benefits of style and grooming for the man in the audience, gardening programmes such as *Ground Force* present both male and female gardening experts, tradespeople and homeowners in need of assistance, with little distinction being made between male and female labour, skills or interest. In this same way, cookery programmes routinely focus on both male and female cooks, celebrity chefs, customers and audiences respectively. It is worth noting as Andy Medhurst does that 'these are refreshingly macho-free series, which is no surprise given their debt to the predominantly feminised aesthetic of daytime TV' (Medhurst 2003: 27).

This is not necessarily to say that lifestyle television has feminised the primetime schedules, but rather that the appearance of those programmes that focus on fashion, style and grooming, gardening, property development, home improvement, travel, cookery and other food and drink topics during the evening slot has gone some way towards negotiating the issue of gender on the small screen. Rachel Moseley makes this point when she comments that the saturation of lifestyle programming on the evening schedules 'is surely less a feminization of primetime programming than an ungendering of the discourses and spaces which have traditionally occupied daytime and primetime British television' (Moseley 2000: 309). With this in mind, it is worth noting that makeover shows 'articulate not just changes in the broadcasting climate and the move towards consumer-driven programming, but also shifts in discourses of gender and their television representation' (ibid.: 304). After all, lifestyle television makes it clear that the traditionally feminised 'worlds of fashion, beauty and the home are being opened up to men' and that our homes and our bodies are 'an important site of self-expression for both women and men' respectively (Attwood 2005: 97). In short, lifestyle programming 'helps to shape a . . . discourse in which it is acceptable for both men and women to express views on light furnishings and to share traditionally 'masculine' tasks such as DIY' (Palmer 2004: 175).

However, before applauding the genre for challenging stereotypical representations of gender, for 'outstepping traditional gender roles' (Taylor 2002: 492) and for negotiating the longstanding and negative link between daytime television and the female viewer, it is worth looking again at the presentation of gender in lifestyle programming. After all, although fashion and beauty programmes have been seen to focus on male makeovers, and instruct the male audience 'to tolerate and even appreciate grooming essentials such as facials, manicures, and nose-hair trimmings' (Hart 2004: 245), these programmes remain largely dedicated to a female audience and a feminine transformation from week to week. Moreover, on those rare occasions where a male makeover is the focus of the show, it is clear that the man in question is encouraged to negotiate his seemingly feminine position by talking at length about his work and his public role over and above any notion of domestic responsibilities or the private realm (Moseley 2000: 311–12). Therefore, one might question the progressiveness of a programme that cannot show a man being moisturised without encouraging him to talk about his working life, with all of the stereotypical connotations of breadwinner, provider and authority figure that this presents to the viewer. When watching a male makeover, one cannot help but think of Andrew Billen's comment concerning the contemporary male and his current interest in styling and grooming practices, as he asks 'what is the precise ratio between machismo and moisturiser that will get me laid?' (Billen 2006: online). Therefore, the suggestion that the presence of such programming goes some way towards 'ungendering' the television schedules may be compromised.

Although the *Ground Force* gardening team does include Charlie Dimmock as the water-feature expert on the programme, and even though the show makes no attempt to show her doing less physical work than her male co-presenters, it is worth noting that she is one of very few female garden experts on contemporary lifestyle programming. So much is made of Dimmock's role that her presence simply goes to remind audiences of the lack of other female gardeners on the small screen. The very fact that audiences and critics alike seem more interested in the woman's bust measurements than they ever have been in her water-features is very telling here. Internet sites dedicated to the presenter tend to focus more on her dress size than on her gardening expertise, more on the fact that she gardens without wearing supportive underwear than on her weekly garden transformations and more on the fact that she has won the Redhead of the Year 2000 award over and above her garden design achievements (Beautiful Britain 2007: online). Therefore, the fact that there are so few female gardening experts and that those with a celebrity profile are set up as exhibitionistic objects for the male gaze again does little to challenge stereotypical representations of gender.

Likewise, although male and female chefs are both visible on prime-time schedules, it soon becomes clear that the ways in which they present their culinary programmes differs dramatically. After all, whereas Delia Smith and Nigella Lawson are both 'at ease in their educative and nurturing role', Keith Floyd and Gary Rhodes seem so desperate to negotiate the traditionally feminised position and the stereotypically domestic space that they are seen 'using emphatic gestures, physical display and an irreverent approach . . . to ensure that their role as cooks does not undermine their manly status' (Geraghty and Lusted 1998: 299). After all, Floyd cooks in a range of outdoor ad-hoc kitchens, and as such, one might consider the man less a celebrity chef than a *'male* adventurer' due to his 'dynamic journey through the public sphere' (Strange 1998: 305). In this same way, Rhodes spends time not only hunting for food but acting 'like a lad on a package holiday [as he] flirts outrageously with the women he meets on his travels' (ibid.: 307). Again, one must be seen to question the ways in which such programming negotiates traditionally gendered stereotypes when they present the female nurturer in the domestic kitchen and the male adventurer cooking in the public sphere.

However, rather than blithely critique lifestyle television for failing to challenge such gendered stereotypes, it is worth looking in further detail at those programmes that have been seen to negotiate the traditional male role. Therefore, I will now examine the representation of masculinities in *The Naked Chef* and *Queer Eye for the Straight Guy* as these shows have been said to negotiate hegemonic masculinity by depicting the male chef and style guru in both the public and private spheres. After all, it is this 'relationship between inside and outside, domestic and public' (Moseley 2001: 38) or the 'play with private and public space' (Moseley 2000: 312) that can be seen to challenge dominant sex roles and negotiate the hegemonic male order.

THE NAKED CHEF

Television chef Jamie Oliver was discovered in the kitchens of the River Café in London before becoming the face of supermarket giant Sainsbury's and appearing in a number of his own culinary shows such as *The Naked Chef*, *Jamie's Kitchen* (2002), *Jamie's School Dinners* (2005) and *Jamie's Great Escape* (2005). So successful were his programmes and so powerful was Jamie's brand image that the young chef went on to sell his own range of tableware, cookware and live tour dates. And although Jamie is undoubtedly a British phenomenon, the chef has also achieved some success outside of the UK. For example 'the Food Network, a US cable channel, has now co-produced a 26-part series, *Oliver's Twist*, selling Jamie's cooking, lifestyle and London location to international audiences' (Hollows 2003b: 230).

NEGOTIATING THE DOMESTIC SPHERE

The kitchen has longstanding and somewhat negative connotations with femininity and a woman's role, with culinary skills being seen as 'integral to the image of the "happy homemaker" produced in cookbooks and women's magazines' (Hollows 2002: 143). However, Jamie is seen to challenge such traditional stereotypes as he presents the domestic kitchen as a masculine space, through the use of new lad language, the presentation of cooking as a leisure pursuit rather than a domestic chore and the depiction of a broader lifestyle image. In short, *The Naked Chef* can be seen to depict a fascinating and potentially positive representation of the contemporary male due in part to Jamie's ability to reconcile domestic cookery, youthful masculinity and public leisure activities.

MASCULINE LEISURE AND A LACK OF INSTRUCTION

While female cooks such as Delia and Nigella pride themselves on giving accurate and easy-to-follow guidelines in relation to particular recipes, Jamie (like Keith Floyd and Gary Rhodes before him) seems to make a conscious effort to be less prescriptive and therefore less instructive about the quantity of ingredients being presented in his dishes. For example, rather than talk about grammes, ounces, litres or pints, Jamie routinely asks viewers to 'chuck all your sugar in there' (*The Naked Chef* 1: 'The Chef's Night Off') and 'guess half of it, up or down, who really cares' (*The Naked Chef* 2: 'Hen Night'). Likewise, rather than educate his viewers about appropriate cooking techniques or relevant cooking times, Jamie seems rather vague. For example, we are asked to 'smash up' thyme (*The Naked Chef* 1: 'The Chef's Night Off'), 'squelch' butter (*The Naked Chef* 1: 'The Chef's Night Off'), 'pulverise' herbs (*The Naked Chef* 2: 'Hen Night'), 'bash' garlic (*The Naked Chef* 2: 'Hen Night'), and when talking about the quantities in question he simply tells us 'not to use garlic that's going to punch you round the face' (*The Naked Chef* 2: 'Hen Night'). We are given very few tips on food presentation, so that rather than be told how to present food in the same way as a professional restaurant, we are simply asked to tear rather than slice mozzarella because 'it looks a bit more funky' (*The Naked Chef* 5: 'Birthday Party'), to rip rather than slice a peach because that way 'it doesn't look commercial and horrible' (*The Naked Chef* 2 1: 'The Reunion') and to arrange the salad by 'just chucking it all over the place . . . no positioning . . . just scatter it . . . don't be fussy' (*The Naked Chef* 5: 'Birthday Party'). Indeed, the whole philosophy behind Jamie's cooking is that 'there are no bells and whistles' (*The Naked Chef* 2 6: 'A Bun in the Oven') and that 'you don't just do things because they're fashionable, or because you're told to, you do things because you like to eat things together' (*The Naked Chef* 6: 'Girlfriend'). Although such commentary may appear at odds with Jamie's training and continuing employment as a professional chef, it is clear that this use of language sets him apart from the more careful and controlled address of the female chef and from the labour associated with his profession.

Jamie can be seen to position himself in opposition to those female chefs who seek to educate and instruct their viewers about particular cooking techniques, and as such, he can be seen to distance his kitchen style from the chores of the domestic sphere. The chef is also seen to detach both himself and his cooking from the restaurant profession, again because he is seeking to position his culinary style as an enjoyable and entertaining leisure pursuit rather than hard work or paid employment. Frances Bonner makes this point when she tells us that within Jamie's televisual world 'food preparation must be fun; it is never presented as work' and that 'this is most clearly demonstrated in Jamie's separation of his being a cook on television from the serious business of being a professional chef' (Bonner 2005: 44). The very fact that *The Naked Chef* begins each episode with a relaxed-looking Jamie lounging on his sofa telling the viewer that 'what I cook in the restaurant isn't what I cook at home, cooking has got to be a laugh, got to be simple, got to be tasty, got to be fun' (*The Naked Chef* 1: 'The Chef's Night Off') is very telling in this regard. When Jamie is asked about how he likes to cook for his friends and family, he comments that 'the best thing about cooking for your mates is that you don't have to be flash. You're not making clever soufflés or putting things in a mould or balancing one thing on top of another. What I like doing is just slamming three big bowls of something hot and steaming on the table and telling everyone to tuck in' (Harrison 2000: 16). And such language goes further to present his time in the kitchen as a source of social pleasure rather than domestic labour.

ORDINARY MASCULINITY AND THE IDIOT IN THE KITCHEN

Jamie goes further to distance his cooking from both the feminised world of food preparation and the working world of the restaurant chef by routinely referring to himself as 'an idiot' in the domestic sphere, as someone with 'ordinary' tastes and as someone who will (on occasion) take short-cuts in the kitchen. So as not to alienate the viewer by drawing attention to his Smeg fridge, Dualit toaster and FrancisFrancis X1 coffee maker, Jamie only really comments on his kitchen appliances to tell us that 'I haven't got a lemon squeezer' (*The Naked Chef* 2: 'Hen Night'). When making a salad he tells us that 'what I like about this is that even an idiot like me can do it' (*The Naked Chef* 5: 'Birthday Party') and when showing school dinner-ladies how to make tomato bread he comments that 'any fucking idiot can do this, I can' (*Jamie's School Dinners* 1). Although Jamie does prepare some intricate looking meals for friends and family members, taking the time to make fresh pasta (*The Naked Chef* 3: 'Babysitting') and his own vanilla sugar (*The Naked Chef* 1: 'Chef's Night Off') we also see him making a 'bacon sarnie for brekkie' and refusing to eat brown bread (*The Naked Chef* 4: 'The Band'), using frozen peas (*The Naked Chef* 2 2: 'Girls, Girls, Girls'), buying supermarket puff pastry (*The Naked Chef* 2 4: 'Going to the Dogs') and making kebabs (*The Naked Chef* 5: 'Birthday Party'). In this same way, Jamie is more keen on 'normal beer and wine' (*The Naked Chef* 5: 'Birthday Party') than cocktails for his birthday party.

The chef positions himself alongside the male in the audience as he tells us that he loves thai green curry and that when he 'goes out with the boys and gets a bit bevoired . . . it has been known to turn into a competition who can handle the hottest curry' (*The Naked Chef* 4: 'The Band'). The chef even goes so far as to position himself alongside the audience as he refers to himself as 'us normal folk' in relation to his culinary expertise (*The Naked Chef 2* 4: 'Going to the Dogs'). He then takes this a step further when he regales us with tales of his culinary mishaps, telling the viewer that 'oh mate I've had so many disasters you wouldn't believe, I've lost count I've had so many bad ones' (*The Naked Chef* 6: 'Girlfriend'). We then see him making cheese on toast, boasting to us that 'this cheese on toast that I do, you'll love . . . I love breakfast like this, really really quick', before smelling burning, cremating his breakfast and mumbling 'fucking bollocks' for added effect here (*The Naked Chef 2* 6: 'A Bun in the Oven'). However, rather than comment on the seemingly schizophrenic image of a professional chef bumbling in the kitchen or a trained expert relating to a domestically challenged viewing audience, it is worth considering that Jamie is simply adhering to a popular image of the male in the kitchen. After all, 'cookbooks for men frequently present cooking as something easily mastered while maintaining that masculine incompetence in the feminine sphere of the kitchen is a virtue' (Hollows 2003b: 231).

COOKING, LEISURE AND LIFESTYLE

It is clear that Jamie presents cooking as a masculine leisure activity, far removed from the world of domestic chores and familial responsibilities, however, his programmes go further to position culinary skills as a fun masculine pastime by juxtaposing the chef's cooking sequences with a range of lifestyle segments. Joanne Hollows makes this point when she informs us that '*The Naked Chef* doesn't simply educate the viewer about "how to cook", but how to use food as one element "in an expressive display of lifestyle"' (Hollows 2003b: 230). The very fact that the visual style of the show draws on 'pop videos and employs "a grainy realist aesthetic"' (ibid.: 230) goes towards presenting the programme as a docu-soap about the life of the celebrity chef in question. For example, in the opening episode of the series we see Jamie leave his London home by sliding dramatically down his spiral staircase, and once outside his flat we see him admiring trainers in a trendy shoe store and chatting casually to local fishmongers, so that shopping for ingredients appears like a fun-packed day of leisure rather than a dull domestic chore (*The Naked Chef* 1: 'Chef's Night Off'). Therefore, even though there exists a longstanding link between femininity, domestic labour and the sphere of consumption, when we see Jamie shopping (be it in mainstream supermarkets, more traditional street markets, local grocers or specialist cheese stores) it is not necessarily to position him within a feminised space or to witness him negotiating the public and private realm, but rather to 'maintain a distance between [his] shopping practices and the more mundane aspects of feeding work' (Hollows 2003b: 241).

We routinely see Jamie shopping for ingredients, preparing food and serving a meal in between playing table football and listening to Brit-pop (*The Naked Chef* 1: 'Chef's Night Off'), drumming in a late gig (*The Naked Chef* 4: 'The Band'), go-carting (*The Naked Chef 2* 3: 'A Perfect Day'), visiting a dog track (*The Naked Chef 2* 4: 'Going to the Dogs'), admiring super-cars (*The Naked Chef* 4: 'The Band'), playing Scalextric (*The Naked Chef 2* 3: 'A Perfect Day') and riding his Vespa through London traffic (*The Naked Chef 2* 4: 'Going to the Dogs'). With this in mind, cooking is seen as just another enjoyable masculine pastime because there is no hint of domestic labour or tedious routine here. In short, *The Naked Chef* never shows Jamie make an effort to tidy the kitchen, wash-up or clean the oven because the programme is keen to overlook those mundane and repetitive aspects of domestic responsibility that 'cannot be recoded as leisure' (Hollows 2003b: 241). Therefore, rather than applaud *The Naked Chef* for presenting a positive image of masculinity that successfully spans both the public and private realms and thus renegotiate traditional images of the hegemonic male, the show might simply be seen to position the young chef as a 'cultural intermediary' who offers viewers the opportunity to transform both their culinary and wider lifestyle habits in order to achieve the Jamie lifestyle (Moseley 2001: 39).

By presenting recipe ideas in the home and active lifestyle sequences in the urban environment, *The Naked Chef* can be seen to offer an image of masculinity that could potentially reconcile both the domestic and the public sphere. In this same way, *Queer Eye for the Straight Guy* can be seen to present an image of contemporary manhood that reconciles such traditionally gendered spaces. Therefore, this chapter will now focus on the representation of masculinity in the 'head-to-toe' makeover show (Berila and Choudhuri 2005: 10), paying particular attention to those issues of paid labour, leisure and the masculine consumer that are exploited in this particular text.

QUEER EYE FOR THE STRAIGHT GUY

Queer Eye for the Straight Guy is a makeover, or what the presenters have termed a 'make-*better* show' (Allen *et al.* 2004: 13) that sees five gay men (Kyan Douglas, Jai Rodriguez, Ted Allen, Thom Filicia and Carson Kressley) transform a heterosexual male in the areas of grooming, culture, food and wine, home design and fashion. The programme shows the transformation of straight men from 'badly dressed, culturally illiterate, unhygienic slobs' (Kooijman 2005: 106) to metrosexuals who are highly versed in 'everything from hair products to Prada and Feng Shui to foreign films' (Berila and Choudhuri 2005: 10). However, although one would do well to praise the show for making positive images of homosexuality more visible in mainstream popular culture and for presenting such an 'easy fraternization' between gay and straight men in contemporary society (Westerfelhaus and Lacroix 2006: 431), this section will focus on the ways in which the programme begins to 'shift conventional images of home, and open up the domestic as a site of masculine activity' (Gorman-Murray 2006: 230).

TRANSFORMING LABOUR INTO LEISURE

Queer Eye for the Straight Guy can be seen, much like *The Naked Chef* before it, to ignore those repetitive and tedious aspects of domestic responsibility that are associated with the private sphere. Therefore, even though the programme presents a number of sartorial and cultural transformations, the audience only ever sees the fun, fashionable and consumer-driven sequences, with no attention being paid to the labour involved in such makeovers here. For example, much of the show is spent shopping in exclusive home, fashion and culinary locations with little interest in the heavy work involved in moving furniture, repainting an entire house or stocking an empty fridge. Dennis Allen makes this point when he informs us that

> what is unusual about the show is that we are not shown, as is typically the case on home renovation shows, at least some gestural series of steps in the process of transforming the straight guy's home. Here the living room or bedroom is magically renovated without any visible activity at all.
>
> (Allen 2006: 4)

Therefore, although we may see a man looking at beautiful furniture, we never have to watch him or any member of what popular media discourses refer to as the 'fab five' actually purchasing, organising delivery or moving said items. On the very rare occasion when we actually see any manual labour being done, it is only to draw our attention to the paid workers seen clearing out old furniture, stripping wallpaper and re-painting.

We tend to see the straight man being taken through a small sample of stylistically appropriate day and evening wear in a closed-off fashion store, with no acknowledgement of the many shopping expeditions and crowded outfitters the audience may have to trawl through to find a particular garment. Likewise, any food or wine that is mentioned by the culinary expert simply appears in the straight man's fridge, and is always accompanied by a full range of aesthetically pleasing table and cookware. Even though the programme includes various shots of the 'fab five' driving their pristine General Motors SUV through bustling metropolitan streets, and pulling up outside beautiful boutiques 'they never fill up with gas' (Berila and Choudhuri 2005: 12). Any efforts to encourage the straight man to sculpt or contour his body is presented as something other than work here. After all, because 'sheer physicality and the need to physically dominate women or other men is never mentioned as a desirable trait' in the programme, any mention of waxing, tanning or defining the body is purely for cosmetic purposes, for which one should read leisure purposes (Clarkson 2005: 239). Indeed, 'on *Queer Eye*, labor itself is completely erased. If there is any work, it is the work of consumption: shopping, grooming, and, usually, a bit of cooking or party preparation that is essentially recreational' (Allen 2006: 4).

In the same way that *Queer Eye for the Straight Guy* makes little effort to demonstrate the necessary labour involved in a style transformation, so too, the presenters of the show make no effort to introduce themselves as fashion, grooming or culinary professionals. Therefore, while Jamie made a concerted effort to distance himself from restaurant cuisine in order to present his style of cooking as a masculine leisure activity rather than a working practice, so too, Ted, Thom, Carson, Jai and Kyan seem to distance themselves from their professional roles here. And although details of their expertise, achievements and awards are available on the programmes official website, little is made of such knowledge in the show itself. Therefore, one might suggest that overlooking such training and skills in each field and presenting these gay men as seemingly 'natural' rather than 'trained' arbiters of good taste merely exploits existing stereotypes of the gay male as a domestic savant 'with inherent concern and flair for domestic styling' (Gorman-Murray 2006: 228). However, rather than view the 'fab five' as a predictable and problematic image of domestic homosexuality, one might acknowledge that the presenters have sought to distance themselves from their professional training in order to present their makeover skills as leisure rather than labour here.

Labour, leisure and the culture of consumption

Queer Eye for the Straight Guy is keen to present shopping as a masculine leisure activity rather than a laborious chore, and as such, one might suggest that the programme chooses to overlook the world of work in order to pick up on a shift in contemporary culture that has seen men define themselves less in relation to the world of work and more in relation to surface appearance and consumption practices. After all, we have witnessed a change in definitions of modern manhood 'from an emphasis on what a man produces to what he consumes' (Clarkson cited in Allen 2006: 5). Where 'we once lived in a society in which men . . . participated by being useful in public life . . . we now are surrounded by a culture that encourages people to play almost no functional public roles, only decorative or consumer ones' (Faludi 2000: 34–5).

However, rather than look to changing conceptions of the male as a shallow, superficial or ephemeral take on the future of masculinity, *Queer Eye for the Straight Guy* can be seen to applaud the decorative image of the male. After all, the programme can be seen to tame and retrain the straight man so that his polished floors and groomed facial hair is matched by his lack of aggression, his attentiveness to his partner, his dedication to his children and a respect for his friends and family network. Therefore, the show goes further than a fashion and beauty makeover because it grooms contemporary men to take a greater role in the domestic sphere, be it the bedroom, bathroom or kitchen. The show presents the male consumer as a positive figure of contemporary masculinity because this metrosexual is not established as an innate or natural model of the male, but rather, as an image that is highly constructed, deliberately calculated and leisurely shopped for. This male is said to 'endorse equal opportunity vanity through cosmetics, softness, hair care products, wine bars, gyms, designer fashion, wealth, the culture industries . . . cosmetic surgery, David Beckham and deodorants' (Miller 2005: 112), and as such, he can be seen to challenge the idea that masculinity is somehow fixed, unalterable and beyond enquiry. *Queer Eye for the Straight Guy* is acknowledging that masculinities, like femininities, are a construction, learned through social experience and presented through sartorial display. Thus, the programme makes it clear that 'choosing elements of one's lifestyle is often also choosing elements of one's identity, and vice versa' (Palmer 2004: 177), and as such, the 'fab five' can be seen to suggest that 'there is no such thing as "genuine" manliness or a stable subjective male position' beyond those created by fashion, culture and a particular historical period (Bruzzi 1997: 129). Therefore, while cultural critics may bemoan the fall of the modern man due to the fact that the 'internal qualities once said to embody manhood – surefootedness, inner-strength, confidence of purpose – are merchandised to men to enhance their manliness' (Faludi 2000: 35), my point is simply that these innate characteristics were nothing but a historical fabrication and a gendered construction in the first place.

It is not necessarily my point that ornamental culture demands consumer goods over inner resources, but rather, that it draws attention to the myth of hegemonic masculinity as an elite and unchanging image of the male. In this way, *Queer Eye for the Straight Guy* goes some way towards breaking down distinctions between alternative masculinities and erasing 'the imagined line between gay and straight male gender performances' (Clarkson 2005: 241). Even though critics of the show might choose to argue against the presentation of such market-driven representations, it is clear that these depictions can be seen to foreground the mutable and flexible status of contemporary manhood from beyond dominant cultural stereotypes. The very fact that the programme is dedicated to the makeover of a wide range of masculinities ranging from a fire-fighting hero with disfiguring burns (4:06 'Help Fireman Thank His Heroes'), an army soldier confined to a wheelchair (3:03 'Hero on Wheels'), a young transgendered individual (4:09 'Trans-form this Trans-Man') and a Buddhist hippie (2:03 'Dharma Dad'), alongside all manner of commitment phobes (3:12 'From the Doghouse to the Altar'), slobs (1:01 'Hair Today, Art Tomorrow'), dedicated husbands (4:08 'Give Newlyweds a New Lease of Life'), loving fathers (2:29 'An Overdue Reunion') and widows (2:08 'Senior Seeking Style') goes further to support the programmes central thesis regarding the fluidity of gendered identity in contemporary society.

Conclusion

This chapter has demonstrated the ways in which contemporary lifestyle television developed out of an earlier strand of hobbyist programming that has been popular on British screens since the 1960s, paying particular attention to the scheduling shifts of fashion, cookery and gardening shows from the supposedly 'feminised' world of daytime television to the more 'masculine' prime-time slots. The chapter went on to outline the potentially positive representations of masculinity and the male role that are displayed in such lifestyle productions, paying particular attention to the depiction of the food and fashion experts in *The Naked Chef* and *Queer Eye for the Straight Guy*. After all, these programmes can be seen to reconcile the public sphere with the domestic space, reclaiming shopping as a masculine leisure activity and negotiating the authority of the natural, unchanging hegemonic male.

12. ADVERTISING: SOCIAL LIFE, SOCIAL STANDING AND SEX

INTRODUCTION

In the UK, commercial channels air 12 minutes of adverts per hour, while in the US they show up to 16 minutes of national and local advertising in that same time. Moreover, because the British watch around 27 hours of television a week, and the ordinary American views for 31 hours, the average audience will be looking at between 5 and 8 hours of television commercials a week. Furthermore, if one considers that 'commercials offer an extremely concentrated form of communication about sex and gender' (Jhally 1990: 136) then it soon becomes clear that any examination of gender on the small screen must look at depictions of the male both in and between scheduled programming. Therefore, this chapter will introduce the ways in which representations of gender have changed in British and American television advertising from the 1950s to the present day, paying particular attention to the depiction of masculinity in a range of male grooming, car and beer commercials that have been created for a gender-balanced evening audience. By looking at the representations of masculinity in recent adverts for the Lynx, Volkswagen Passat, Golf and Budweiser brands, I hope to illustrate the ways in which these texts can be seen to negotiate early images of the competitive, hungry, individualist in favour of a softer, understated image of the male.

HISTORY OF SEX ROLES AND GENDER STEREOTYPES IN TELEVISION ADVERTISING

Television advertising has to communicate meaning at a glance, and as such, it tends to condense and concentrate stereotypical images from society at large. Indeed, although the industry can be seen to draw on all manner of class, age and racial distinctions to draw attention to a particular product, 'gender is probably the social resource that is used most by advertisers' (Jhally 1990: 135).

Steve Craig makes this point when he suggests that television 'commercials are designed to take maximum advantages of gender specific fantasies, myths, and fears' (Craig 1993: online). This is not to say that television advertising dictates societal sex roles, but rather, that they present the 'prevailing cultural values' about masculinity and femininity that dominate a particular period (Manstead and McCulloch 1981: 171). The ways in which advertisements 'emphasise some aspects of gender displays and de-emphasise others' (Jhally 1990: 135) makes it clear that such texts can only ever present 'ideology rather than social history' to the viewing public (MacKinnon 2003: 99).

Television advertising has a long history of reinforcing conventional sex role stereotypes whereby the representation of women is passive, nurturing and situated in the home whereas the representation of the male is physically active, assertive and seen beyond the confines of the domestic sphere. Since the early 1970s we have seen that 'women continued to clean house, launder, cook, serve meals, while men gave the orders, gave advice, and ate the meals' (Courtney and Whipple cited in Lovdal 1989: 717). We are informed that the representation of male characters routinely outnumber those of female protagonists in television advertising, and that the vast majority of voiceovers that are heard in such broadcasts are in fact male. The message here then is simply that television advertisers deem the male both more convincing and more authoritative than his female counterpart (Callan 1976: 76).

Leslie McArthur and Beth Resko's seminal work on sex role stereotyping in television advertisements found that the representation of men and women differs in several significant respects, paying particular attention to the fact that the male characters are presented as more knowledgeable, and experienced than their female counterparts, and many more men than women were depicted in an occupational setting (McArthur and Resko 1975: 217). And although one might suggest that such patriarchal representations of sex and gender was a simple reflection of a society struggling to keep up with the feminist movement, it is worth noting that such stereotypical portrayals were still in place throughout the 1980s and 1990s. A look at the representation of sex and gender in more recent television adverts make it clear that these texts are not only failing to reflect the reality of a society that includes working mothers and househusbands, but that they are continuing to depict some of the most stereotypical images of gender on the small screen.

For example, Daniel Bretl and Joanne Cantor's work on the representation of gender in American television commercials in the 1980s tells us that although 'males and females now occur approximately equally often as primary characters in prime-time television advertisements [they are] still different in terms of their level of employment' (Bretl and Cantor 1988: 606) with working men and the representation of the male outside the home greatly outnumbering that of women. We are informed that 'the most striking and persistent inequality in the data continues to be with regard to the sex of the narrators: Advertisers have continued to use male narrators approximately 90% of the time' (ibid.: 607).

Likewise, Adrian Furnham and Nadine Bitar's work on television advertising in Britain tells us that men dominate such media texts, with 134 male and 46 female characters being coded in their study (Furnham and Bitar 1993: 303). Because men were more likely to be portrayed as interviewers, narrators, or celebrities in occupational settings or in unspecified locations while women were most likely to be shown as dependent on others and at home with the children, this study concluded that 'sex role television stereotyping in Britain was more or less constant across time, compared to studies done 5 and 10 years ago' (ibid.: 297).

In this same way Lynn Lovdal's work on American commercials informs us that in the late 1980s, 90 per cent of voiceovers used were male and on those rare occasions when we heard a female tone, the woman in question was routinely 'speaking to something or someone in a subordinate position. For instance cats, dogs, and babies' (Lovdal 1989: 720). We are told that 'men are pictured in three times the variety of occupations and roles as are women', and that 'women were shown in a plethora of stereotyped roles, including wife, mother, bride, waitress, actress [and] dancer' (Lovdal 1989: 720, 721–2). Such results leave the author to conclude that such stereotypical representations of women in television commercials fail to reflect the reality of women's lived experience. If one considers that the representations of women in these texts lack a voice, are rarely seen outside of the domestic sphere and 'are not viewed in wider professional contexts' (ibid.: 722) then it is clear that they are either unable or unwilling to reflect the impact of the women's movement that emerged more than a decade earlier. In short, 'women today are not pictured any differently in television advertisements than they were pictured ten years ago' (ibid.: 722).

From this estimation then, it is perhaps unsurprising to find that 'various researchers have expressed concern about the roles portrayed by women in advertising' (Furnham and Bitar 1993: 298). However, rather than focus on the lack of women in television advertising and blithely ignore those representations of masculinity that are seen to dominate such texts, it is necessary to examine those images of the male that are being constructed and circulated by the advertising industry. According to Kenneth Allan and Scott Coltrane's work on the representation of gender in American television advertising, the representation of masculinity has changed little, if at all, in small screen commercials from the early 1950s to the late 1980s. After all, the authors 'found only a slight increase in the images of men parenting and an unexpected decrease in the images of men portrayed performing housework', and as such, they go on to conclude that 'commercial imagery has done little to change traditional expectations for masculine gender display' (Allan and Coltrane 1996: 200).

Much work on the representation of gender in television advertising argues that men continue to dominate through their visual and verbal presence on screen, and that the images being presented continue to hark back to an earlier generation of authoritative, competitive and emotionless breadwinners. Thereby, we discover that men are depicted as 'independent, intelligent, objective decision makers who demonstrated expertise and authority (Furnham and Bitar 1993: 299), as 'active, constructive, autonomous and achieving' (Hakala 2005: 7), as 'instrumental, inner-directed, and identified with power' (Wernick 1992: 63) and 'successful, unemotional, and prone to decisive action' (Allan and Coltrane 1996: 186–7). Indeed, Renee Meyers makes the point that 'men were less frequently seen in the home setting than females . . . lending confirmation to the stereotype which suggests that not only the care of the home, but the location itself is off limits to the male' (Meyers 1980: 14). In this way, we are told that 'television males are locked into certain recurrent images and roles and the existence of male sex role stereotyping is a reality' (ibid.: 12).

FROM FAMILY MAN TO MALE CONSUMER

Television adverts from the 1950s were dominated by representations of the family, or, to be more precise, dominated by representations of the white middle-class nuclear family with the father as family provider and mother as homemaker and nurturer. This image was so frequently drawn on that Andrew Wernick's seminal work on promotional culture has recently described it as the 'universal touchstone for defining social roles and identities' during that period (Wernick 1992: 51). Because both male and female consumers were assumed to belong to, or aspired to belong to, the nuclear family unit, characters in television adverts of the period 'were rarely presented outside its cheery frame' (ibid.: 51). However, although the 1950s tended to depict the male as a husband, father and career-focused breadwinner, 'the overall post-war trend has been away from depicting men in fixed family roles' (ibid.: 52).

Although the representation of the young heterosexual couple is now much more common in television advertising, they tend to be shown in the early stages of their romance 'or even at the moment of first encounter' so that issues of marriage, commitment, stability and responsibility are not in the equation here (Wernick 1992: 53). Likewise, the depiction of the homosocial group which has come to dominate these texts is even further removed from the image of the nuclear family unit (ibid.: 53). Therefore, where it was once the family that was seen to provide safety and sociability for an individual, the nuclear family has been sidelined in favour of a unigenerational peer group that is seen to act as the 'primary social anchor' for the viewing public (ibid.: 53). The point here is simply that the peer group does not have the same fixed roles as the nuclear family, and as such, the representation of the male can be seen to transcend his earlier paternal role in favour of a more flexible and free subject position. Removing the male from his rigid breadwinning responsibilities in contemporary television advertising 'highlights the fluidity of social bonding and associates the pleasures of consumption with the sexual, status or existential rewards to be obtained from exercising individual freedom in that setting' (ibid.: 53).

One might suggest that advertisers have stressed the unigenerational group over and above the nuclear family in order to reflect the reality of a society that is no longer dominated by this traditional unit. Such adverts might be seen to acknowledge the fact that women no longer act as the purchasing agent for the male, but rather, that men, both within and beyond the family frame, are making their own consumer choices. Therefore, although John Straiton informed us that 'women buy over 80 per cent of advertised products' (Straiton 1984: 21), more recent research suggests that there has been a growth in both the number of male consumers and in the number of commodities targeted specifically to the male. After all, 'the growth in the number of students, the rise in age at first marriage, the increase in divorce rates, and . . . gay households have enlarged the category of men who, from the standpoint of day-to-day consumption, effectively live apart from women' (Wernick 1992: 49). With this in mind, advertisers of all manner of household and leisure products are having to take into account the fact that men are powerful and self-directed consumers, and that their consumption practices are no longer 'confined to cars, alcohol, certain brands of cigarettes, mechanical tools, and life insurance' (ibid.: 49).

This chapter will now consider the representation of masculinity in contemporary male grooming, car and beer adverts in order to understand the key representations of masculinity that are depicted in such media texts, paying particular attention to those prime-time commercials that are seen to speak to both the male and female viewer. After all, while daytime schedules are aimed at the woman in the home and weekend afternoon television is targeted to a largely male audience, it is prime-time programming that assumes a less gender specific audience. Steve Craig makes this point when he comments that 'prime time commercials represent a more sophisticated and balanced portrayal of gender than either daytime or weekend ads' (Craig 1992a: 209). This is not necessarily to say that the products in question will be purchased by a balanced audience, but rather that such commercials are intended to create 'a pleasurable experience' for male and female viewers alike (ibid.: 208). Therefore, although one might assume that men routinely make the purchasing decisions concerning their grooming products, cars and alcoholic beverages (Wernick 1992: 49), it is worth noting that the representations of gender in such prime-time commercials are designed to appeal to a more balanced demographic.

I will be looking to examine the representation of masculinity by examining the male body and its surrounding environment, paying particular attention to ideas such as occupation, interests and activities, heterosexual and homosocial relations, props, settings and voiceovers (Hakala 2006: 85). After all, such depictions are 'rarely value-free' and each goes some way towards creating an image of contemporary masculinity (ibid.: 93). Moreover, I hope to demonstrate the ways in which the depiction of the male picks up on a range of gender characteristics that have previously been deployed in such research, including those supposedly masculine traits such as leadership, independence, aggressiveness and instrumentalism, and those ostensibly feminine traits that include dependence, passivity and emotional sensitivity (Allan and Coltrane 1996: 190). Last but not least, it is necessary to examine the ways in which such adverts entice the viewing public to consume. With this in mind, I will consider the ways in which contemporary commercials are seen to promise social approval, career advancement and self-enhancement for the male (Furnham and Spencer-Bowdage 2002: 464).

'SPRAY MORE, GET MORE': MEN'S STYLE, GROOMING PRODUCTS AND THE LYNX EFFECT

In recent years, increased efforts have been made by the advertising industry to sell men all manner of 'personal-care products and accessories, from jewellery . . . to bath-oil, deodorants, and hair-dye' (Wernick 1992: 49). Although women have been struggling with the objectification and dehumanisation of what has been termed the 'beauty myth' whereby they have felt pressurised into attaining a particular image of youthful, slender and attractive femininity, over the last two decades, men have also started to feel pressurised into enhancing their natural looks (Limpinnian 2002: online). If one considers that 'physically attractive people are perceived to be stronger, more sociable, more interesting, and more successful; they are considered to have an overall societal advantage in various fields of life – in marriage, getting jobs, and earnings' (Hakala 2006: 15) then it is little wonder that men are now succumbing to the 'beauty myth'. However, even though advertising in the early 1970s asked men to 'contemplate aftershaves and shifting paradigms in underwear' (Hunt 2001: 132), it is only more recently that we have seen a dramatic upturn in terms of product sales in the men's grooming industry. After all, since the early 1990s 'the sector encompassing male grooming products and toiletries [has been] one of the fastest growing of the whole toiletries market' (Sturrock and Pioch 1998: 338). Indeed 'in the US, sales of male-specific cosmetics and toiletries went up 37.3 percent between 1998 and 2003' (Ridder cited in Hakala 2005: 57) and are expected to increase by 2 per cent year on year (Lynx 2007: online).

The reason for the growing sales of men's grooming products can be attributed to the fact that men have become more 'comfortable with the ideas of purchasing toiletries, fragrances and skin care products for themselves' (Mintel cited in Sturrock and Pioch 1998: 339), and one might argue that they have become more comfortable with such products as the advertising of men's shower gels, shampoos and deodorants tend to depict 'the narcissistic pleasures of grooming and adornment' (Nixon 1996: 122). It is no coincidence that such texts tend to depict the freshly scented and carefully coiffured male as popular with the opposite sex. After all, 'if women's advertisements cry, "Buy this product and he will notice you" men's advertisements similarly promise that female attention will follow immediately upon purchase' (Barthel cited in Limpinnian 2002: online). However, this relationship between consumption and attraction is nothing new, after all, 'consumer culture had always promised much more than it advertised' (Ehrenreich 1984: 113) so in this instance a grooming product promises not just a fresh scent or close shave, but sexual excitement and adventure for the male.

Lynx body spray was launched in Britain in 1983 with 'distinctive black with silver lettering, giving it strong associations with maleness and sexual potency' (Lynx 2007: online). And today, over 8 million British men use Lynx products (ibid.). However, although the distinctive packaging might appeal to the male, Lynx advertising must be popular with a more balanced consumer market due to the fact that 'nearly half of all Lynx purchases are made by women' (ibid.). With this in mind, it is worth examining the representation of gender that is being presented in such advertising.

In recent years, Lynx has aired a number of television commercials for their deodorant, anti-perspirants and shower gels, with many of them adhering to similar codes and conventions of masculinity and the male body. Despite the plethora of masculinities available in contemporary society, these adverts tend to represent a very narrow image of the male. For example, commercials such as 'Hat Stand' (2005), 'Horse Riders' (2005) and 'Kitchen' (2006) all present a slim, lightly muscled, young, white, virile man in a leisure environment using the product in question in order to lure an attractive member of the opposite sex. The advert's emphasis on youth seems to coincide with John Fisher's thesis that 'youth equals popularity, popularity equals success, success equals happiness' (Fisher cited in Pollay 1986: 27). The first commercial watches one man spray his hat stand in order to encourage his half-naked girlfriend to pole dance for his viewing pleasure before turning the spray on his own body, another sees a man spraying the earth beneath his feet so as to encourage a mud fight between two passing female horse-riders who then beckon him to join their near-naked high jinks and a further advert depicts a young man strategically spraying a path through his flat in order to distract his girlfriend while he sneaks another woman out of his bedroom. What is relevant here is the fact that these men, although not unattractive, are not model-esque in either their facial looks, physiques or sense of fashionable dress, and as such, they are being presented as everyday and average figures of masculinity. Therefore, if Lynx can turn the 'normal' male into a magnet for the opposite sex, then it can perform this same feat for the male in the audience.

Although it has been suggested that television advertising tends only to depict 'particularly muscular . . . strong-jawed . . . sporty, successful . . . and ultimately sexy' (Edwards cited in Baker 2006: 68) images of masculinity, I would suggest that the Lynx adverts are doing something slightly different. After all, we are asked to see that it is the use of the product rather than the man himself that is attractive to women here. It is the task of the advert to get 'consumers to transfer the positive associations of the noncommodity material onto the commodity' (Fowles 1996: 11), so that Lynx products equal sexual magnetism in the mind of the viewer. In this way, when a man sprays Lynx, he is not simply using a deodorant, but is rather spraying 'better looks, success, love, respect and social approval' or in this case, sexual attraction (Hakala 2006: 16). In the advert that shows square-jawed hero Ben Affleck clicking to count how many admiring female glances (and gay male ones) he receives during the course of a day's shopping and socialising, the advert compares Affleck's 103 with a much more 'ordinary' looking bellboy who counts 2372 ('Click' 2006). The point is again quite clearly that it is the use of the product rather than the rugged good looks of the male that women respond to. Moreover, if the images were not clear enough in expressing the relationship between the product in question and the reward of sexual excitement, then recent straplines voiced by an anonymous male such as 'avoid sweat, attract women' ('Lynx Dry Anti-Perspirant' 2003), 'the girls are ready, are you?' ('The Lynx Effect' 2003) and 'Spray More, Get More' ('Beach Invasion' 2006) leaves little to the imagination here. The official Lynx website even refers to the 'unlimited powers of seduction' (Lynx 2007: online) of its new fragrances.

However, if such adverts strike the consumer as rather too predatory in their calculating use of the fragrance, then there are also those Lynx adverts which demonstrate a more innocent use of the product range. For example, commercials such as 'Shower Shakes' (2003) and the current 'Bom Chicka Wah Wah' series (2007) show the effect that the fragrances can have on women without the man in the advert even trying to create such a reaction. We see our stereotypical Lynx man in shock as he is being caressed rather than examined by a female doctor and a young male student being propositioned by a female teacher when he accidentally walks into her busy classroom. The women in these adverts are slim, young models whose role is simply to admire and respond to the product in question. From this perspective, these television commercials support Kenneth MacKinnon's point that 'in recent advertising . . . the purchase of particular consumer goods by the male will result in female attention to him' and that this provides a contrast with 'the advertising world of the 1980s and 1990s, where the male's authority preceded the promotion of a product, so that product might be recommended to . . . less confident, men' (MacKinnon 2003: 90).

Indeed, in order to understand the representations of gender in these adverts more fully, I hope to offer a more detailed analysis of one such advert. In 'Pulse' (2003), the most downloaded (and therefore, one might suggest, the most popular) of all Lynx commercials, we see a young, slim, white, clean-shaven man/Tom Godwin sitting at the counter of a coffee bar, wearing smart-casual jeans, shirt and blazer. Oliver Cheatham's 'Make Luv' tune starts up in the café, our man gives a mischievous grin and then takes it upon himself to start dancing in the middle of the establishment, combining air guitar with Saturday Night Fever movements, all under the watchful eye of more casually-dressed men playing pool. We see two attractive women admiring his disco technique before joining in as backing dancers on either side of our protagonist, and when these women end up in his arms, the other men look on amazed at the effect that this average-looking male is having on the opposite sex. The advert shows our hero drinking coffee in semi-casual clothes during the day and as such there is no indication of occupation or personal circumstances here, other than to note that he is not wearing a wedding ring in the sequence. Although we seem to learn little about our hero, the fact that he prefers coffee to alcohol, disco to pool, and is content both with his own company and the company of women, might suggest that he is a self-confident new man who transcends stereotypical images of aggressive masculinity. After all, he is happy to sit on his own in a café full of bustling groups and he seems totally unfazed by the slightly bemused glances of the other men in the bar. That said, although he does not seek the approval of other men and is not looking for career advancement in this situation, his reward for using the product is the attention of the attractive women in the establishment. And of course, the fact that these women are depicted outside of the home means that they are removed from the unglamorous chores associated with the domestic sphere. Even though there is only a hint of sexual availability in the advert, it is very clear that these females admire our hero throughout the short text, generally approving of his smile, his appearance and his dance moves, or what we understand to be 'the Lynx effect'. And predictably, the voiceover heard at the end of the advert is of course male. Therefore, one might suggest that the text is likely to appeal to the man in the audience due to the fact that it presents an image of masculinity that emphasises male freedom and leisure time, with no acknowledgement of domesticity or work responsibilities here. One might suggest that this image of youthful, vibrant masculinity is a welcome sight in relation to the humourless image of square-jawed masculinity that tends to occupy the mass media.

THE POWER OF UNDERSTATEMENT, CARS, CHARISMA AND SOCIAL STANDING

It has long been understood that 'automobiles are largely the male's province, and men are seen by the automotive industry as the primary decision makers when it comes to purchases' (Craig 1992b: online). However, recent statistics tell us that not only do women purchase 45 per cent of all motor vehicles, but they actually influence 85 per cent of all car buying decisions (Ford Motor Company 2007: online). Therefore, like the commercials for men's grooming products, contemporary car adverts must be seen to speak to both male and female audiences. With this in mind, I will examine the representation of masculinity as it is depicted in advertising campaigns, for the Volkswagen Passat saloon and Golf Match respectively, paying particular attention to these commercials due to the fact that they have been acclaimed by *What Car?* magazine as the best family car and best small family car of 2007.

Existing research tells us that the representation of masculinity in car commercials tend towards the competitive individualist due to the fact that 'automobiles are often seen as a key to masculinity and often denote success, achievement and wealth in our society' (Meyers 1980: 13). It has been suggested that these adverts depict men who are unencumbered by either work commitments or family responsibilities, with cars being presented as the means of freedom and escape. We are routinely presented with men who are 'on the move, untouched by the messiness of the everyday' (Gitlin cited in MacKinnon 2003: 95) and drivers who are 'always on the go, feel[ing] no connection with other people or with his environment' (MacKinnon 2003: 96). However, I would like to suggest that there is a rather different theme running through contemporary family car adverts. After all, not only do the current adverts for the Golf and Passat highlight the dignity and respect awarded to the understated everyman, but these same adverts are actually seen to mock the previous incarnation of competitive masculinity.

The current advertising campaign for the Passat presents a slim, white, attractive forty-something psychiatrist listening to the confessions of his middle-aged male clients, all of whom are acting out a predictable mid-life crisis. While one man tells us that he's taken up the electric guitar and written his first song, entitled 'hot-tub weekend', another is dating a 22-year-old, while a third has bought a boat. We then hear another protest too much about his youth, another seems keen to tell us that people at work 'definitely fancy me' before hearing how yet another is committing more time to clubbing at the weekend ('Volkswagen Passat – Mid Life Crisis' 2007). We are not asked to identify with the men on the couch, because as they reveal more and more details about their quest for youth, for younger women or for a motorbike, we are asked to see them as sad, insecure figures with little self-respect or self-awareness. Throughout the advert we see glimpses of the psychiatrist himself, dressed casually in a blue jumper and matching slacks, sitting comfortably in a leather chair in his classically styled office adorned with dark wood and stripped floorboards. This man listens to the mid-life crisis tales in his office, takes notes on each case and tries to conceal his amusement on hearing such stories. The advert ends as we discover that the understated Passat outside the office belongs to this particular character. The point here is simply that the traits of class, dignity, inner confidence and quiet self-assurance that belong to our central protagonist can be found in the car in question, and are therefore projected onto any man wishing to purchase this particular image of understated, reserved masculinity. After all, if one acknowledges that a strong relationship exists between self-concept and car preferences (Hogg and Garrow 2001: online), then it is clear that the car acts as the substitute for this particular image of the male. Although cars are primarily used for transportation, motor vehicles routinely hold a promotional role due to the fact that they 'project a sense of their owner's relative social standing [and] class/cultural identification' (Wernick 1992: 70).

In this same way, the current Golf advert makes it clear that cars can be understood as a marker of identity and as an indicator of the individuality and taste of a particular man. And, like the Passat advert before it, the image of masculinity being presented here is one of quiet understatement and inner confidence. We see a slim, white, clean-shaven young man dressed in a smart black suit and vibrant red shirt and tie giving a presentation in a trendy city office, over-gesticulating and laughing for his audience, we then see him walking through the busy office smiling, winking and giving high-fives to colleagues in the block. We cut to him pointing to his watch as if making plans with co-workers for the evening before seeing him running on a treadmill in a deserted, but no doubt exclusive, gym, eating a takeaway for one, being fitted for a bespoke suit, being the humorous entertainer at dinner with friends and driving an anonymous red sports car before literally throwing the keys at the doorman of his fashionable apartment block. Just as the man walks back through to his flat, he is passed by another, less gaudy, more understated version of himself who is wearing a simple grey pinstriped suit and white polo-shirt, who stops to speak to the same doorman before getting in to his Golf ('Volkswagen Golf – The Great Pretender' 2007). We are being asked to see the original gaudy presentation of masculinity as a vain and insecure image of the contemporary male with surface props such as a trendy home, loud suit and fast car, but with little in the way of confidence or self-assurance. In fact, it is as if the potency of this man depends on such surface appearances and social accessories, with no actual charisma, character or confidence beneath that shiny, thin veneer. So as to be sure that we mock, pity or even fear this particular image of masculinity, the advert shows us colleagues looking bored and dinner dates looking unimpressed as the man tries to entertain. Moreover, a male voiceover speaks the words from 'The Great Pretender' throughout the scene (The Platters 1956). Therefore, even though we see our central protagonist as a gregarious and fun-loving figure of masculinity, we hear about a far more lonely, insecure and troubled image of the male. As such, we are being asked to read the understated alter ego as the correct, pre-ferred version of contemporary manhood. And again, the quiet self-assurance of this man is equated with the car that he drives and vice versa, as if the car was 'a kind of third skin' (Wernick 1992: 70) that granted a material form to his 'par-ticular narrative of self-identity' (Giddens 1991: 81).

John Berger believes that 'men create a sense of identity by extending out from their body to control objects and other people' around them (Berger cited in MacKinnon 2003: 91), and nowhere is this more evident than in the car commercials outlined here. After all, these cars promise not just a smooth ride, five-star safety features or low-fuel economy for the male consumer, but self-assurance, quiet confidence and contentment. The traits of the character and the traits of the car are seen to be indistinguishable in these short texts, as if one can actually purchase the easy masculinity on offer here. Therefore, what is being advertised is not simply a stylish new car, but a 'perfected *condition* that is personally sought after but unlikely to be obtained in full' (Fowles 1996: 83). The car becomes a surrogate for a particular version of adult masculinity desired by the consumer, and whereas one cannot buy or trade mannerisms, attributes or charisma, they can own the commodity that promises them.

BEER, MATESHIP AND THE HOME

In both television advertising and the wider social context, beer drinking is understood as a 'central masculine activity' (Strate 1992: 79–80). The rela-tionship between manhood and drinking beer is so strong that beer advertise-ments are said to 'constitute a guide for becoming a man' (ibid.: 78). Therefore, it is interesting to examine this televisual 'manual on masculinity' (ibid.: 78) and examine the dominant cultural stereotypes that are represented in these texts, paying particular attention to a range of contemporary Budweiser commercials, due to the fact that Budweiser is the best-selling beer in America and the best-selling premium-packed lager in UK bars, pubs and restaurants (Budweiser 2007: online).

The beer industry has tended to rely rather heavily on hegemonic images of white masculinity in their television advertising. Lance Strate makes this point when he comments that 'no other industry's commercials focus so exclusively and so exhaustively on images of the man's man' (Strate 1992: 78). Beer commercials have routinely focused on those outdoor leisure pursuits that present a risk, challenge or threat of danger to the male, such as 'car and boat racing, fishing, camping, and sports' (ibid.: 81). Indeed, 'the central theme of masculine leisure activity in beer commercials, then, is challenge, risk, and mastery – mastery over nature, over technology, over others in good-natured "combat", and over oneself' (ibid.: 82). In this way, enjoying a beer acts as a reward for the male who has demonstrated his strength, endurance and mastery; or rather, a reward for the male who has demonstrated his very masculinity. It is rare to see a man drinking alone, or even with a female companion because beer commercials tend to 'feature men who are always in the company of other men' (MacKinnon 2003: 95). In short, 'beer becomes a symbol of group membership' and 'receiving a beer from one's peers acts as a symbol of other men's respect' (Strate 1992: 88, 80). It is said that it is the beverage itself that brings the all-male group together and acts as the common reference-point for the group, so much so in fact that a beer can be seen to substitute for more overt displays of affection between men (ibid.: 88).

Although men partaking in a range of challenging outdoor leisure activities is a regular feature in beer commercials, seeing the male group bonding in a bar setting is another popular theme. Strate suggests that many beer commercials 'seem to advertise bar patronage as much as they do a particular brand of beer' (Strate 1992: 84). The link between the all-male group and the bar becomes clear when one considers that 'the drinking hall has a venerable history in Western culture as a center for male socializing and tests of skill, strength, and drinking ability' (ibid.: 84). In this way, the bar of the beer commercial can be understood as a contemporary drinking hall that provides 'a controlled social context for the exchange of challenges and demonstrations of ego strength and self-control [and therefore] provides continuous reinforcement of the member's masculinity' (ibid.: 87). Although the beer commercial is resolutely a male reserve, on those rare occasions when we see a woman on screen, it is clear that she functions solely to marvel at the physical challenges being performed by the male. These women are 'conceived generally as an admiring audience for the male beer-drinker and for the feats which he is called on to perform' (MacKinnon 2003: 95). And yet, even though these women adhere to predictable sexual stereotypes, the men on screen must never appear distracted by their presence, in fact it is 'cool detachment' that is demanded here (ibid.: 95).

However, irrespective of the outdoor or indoor environment being presented, one might suggest that beer commercials depict a stereotypical image of hegemonic masculinity that leaves little room for alternative representations of a less physically forceful and more emotionally vulnerable male. And yet that said, the representation of masculinities in today's beer commercials can, on occasion, be seen to challenge such monolithic images of the male. After all, rather than focusing on either the great outdoors or the bar environment, many contemporary commercials are choosing to situate their male protagonists in the home. Such a change of setting could be seen to respond to changes in lifestyle patterns in the wider society due to the fact that 'drinking surveys have shown that about 60% of alcohol is consumed at home or in other people's homes' (Alcohol and Public Health Research Unit 2007: online). Therefore, rather than present the strength, and mastery associated with hegemonic masculinity, contemporary beer commercials can be seen to focus on friendship, male bonding and a 'softer' version of the male (ibid.).

Since 2000, the Budweiser 'True' campaign has focused on a diverse group of young urban black men in different domestic locations, phoning one another simply to find out that each in turn is simply 'watching the game, having a Bud' ('Budweiser True' 2002). This same group are seen spread out in one apartment, ordering pizza ('Budweiser Lager' 2002) and sitting round a dining-room table playing cards and drinking beer ('Budweiser True' 2002). The point here is that there are no outdoor leisure pursuits being played, no physical, technical or natural challenges to overcome and therefore no hegemonic rites of passage to perform. Alternatively, what we see is a group of friends just spending time together, without competition, individualism or any sense of physical activity, perhaps presenting a more realistic, or as the strapline puts it, a more 'True' image of male friendship and drinking patterns in contemporary society. In this way, the commercials can be seen to negotiate existing images of masculinity as they have been presented in earlier beer commercials due to the fact that these men are not slim, attractive white outdoorsmen partaking in challenging leisure pursuits, but young, humorous, ethnically diverse singletons simply relaxing in the company of other men. These men are not promoting sexual success, career advancement, self-enhancement or even respect from their peers, but rather a seemingly more genuine image of ordinary, average, somewhat mundane friendship. Although the adverts still suggest that 'beer brings peers together' (Limpinnian 2002: online) and that we find men 'in groups, as a "natural" part of male camaraderie and bonding' (Craig 1993: online), the way in which it presents this social group is quite distinct from the representation of homosociality and male bonding being offered in earlier commercials.

One might suggest that Budweiser has gone even further to challenge the 'manual of masculinity' by depicting men struggling to maintain a level of 'cool detachment' around beautiful females. For example, in 'Budwesier 10 o'Clock'

(2004) we see four young male friends sharing a drink at a bar when two attractive women walk in, one man tries to subtly signal this to his friends by discreetly saying 'guys, guys, guys, two hotties, ten o'clock'. After the friends look in what they assume is the direction of the women, they are told 'that's one o'clock', they try again, only to be told 'OK now, that's nine o'clock', after looking in the wrong direction once more they are told 'gentlemen, that's four o'clock'. The man at the bar is so desperate for his friends to see these women that he unwittingly finds himself saying rather too loudly 'there, over there, them' as he points unsurreptitiously at the women in question. As if the lack of 'cool detachment' was not obvious enough here, we hear the friends mock 'real, real smooth' as they shuffle uncomfortably in their seats under the watchful eyes of the women.

The ethnically diverse group of men at the bar are all young, slim, attractive, clean-shaven and wearing smart-casual eveningwear. Although there are no overt indicators of class, wealth or marital status, the fact that they are all without wedding rings, spending an evening together and freely noticing the attractive women in the room goes some way to suggest that they are without domestic commitments. The fact that they have seats at the bar, rather than standing-room only makes us think that they have been in the establishment for some time, perhaps for a post-work drink, and as such, the fact that they are smartly dressed and remaining in the venue leads us to believe that they are middle-class and financially stable. Moreover, like the 'True' adverts, there is no social enhancement or sexual advancement on offer as a reward here, and as such, the commercial can be seen to negotiate earlier representations of masculinity. This sequence presents a group of men who are laughing, joking and enjoying one another's company, and when they are faced with the prospect of addressing beautiful women, they are anything but 'cool, confident, and detached' (Strate 1992: 89). Because these men are not attempting to turn courtship into a masculine challenge, and because they look acutely embarrassed at being caught just looking in the direction of these women, one might suggest that the advert can be seen to challenge existing hegemonic stereotypes. Therefore, while existing research tells us that 'women often appear as . . . fantasy creatures made available only through the intervention of product' and that 'women in beer commercials always appear to be eager for male companionship' (Craig 1993: online) something else is clearly happening in these commercials.

CONCLUSION

This chapter has introduced those stereotypical representations of gender that have dominated television advertising since the 1950s, paying particular attention to the female as a passive sexual object, and the male as a rugged individualist. However, while the portrayals of men continue to outnumber that of women, and the use of male voiceovers continue to dominate the medium, the depiction of masculinities being presented has changed in recent years. Since the turn of the millennium, adverts for men's grooming products, cars and beer have all been seen to depict images of masculinity that challenge the competitive, physically powerful hegemonic male, and as such, they can be seen to respond to the multiple masculinities on offer in contemporary society. That said, the one thing that these advertisements all have in common is the representation of masculinity without domestic commitments or familial responsibilities. However, this may not necessarily be to dismiss or deride the paternal role *per se*, but rather, to try and reflect the wider social situation in which we see a growing number of men living apart from women.

13. CONCLUSION: THE FUTURE OF MASCULINITY ON TELEVISION

Although masculinity was 'once taken for granted as transparent, normal [and] too natural to require explanation' (MacKinnon 2003: 21), our understanding of manhood, machismo and the male sex role has recently been 'discovered, rediscovered, theorised . . . dislocated, unwrapped, unmasked, understood, embodied, fashioned, moulded, changed and put in perspective' (Whannel 2002: 20). With this in mind, this book set out to examine the ways in which masculinities are being constructed, circulated and interrogated in contemporary television programming, and to consider the ways in which such representations can be understood in relation to the 'common-sense' model of the hegemonic male that is said to dominate the cultural landscape.

In this way we have seen the soap opera blur the distinctions between the public and private realms and the situation comedy genre commit to the portrayal of intimate male friendships. We have witnessed prime-time animation depict problematic fathers and strained father–son relations and the supernatural teen drama foreground emotional connectedness as the key to successful male maturity. Likewise, we have observed science fiction and fantasy television position the American hero as a sensitive new man while both hospital and crime dramas have presented a hard-working male struggling to balance his personal and professional responsibilities. In this same way, we have explored the relationship between power, aggression and masculinity in sporting coverage and considered the link between masculinity and sensitivity in reality television. Last but not least, we have considered the ways in which lifestyle programming encourages men to take on a professional role within the domestic sphere and watched television advertising openly mock the hegemonic hierarchy.

Society has long been accustomed to the gendering of the public and private spheres, and the hegemonic model of masculinity remains dependent on the demarcation of such gendered spaces. However, the men in this volume can be seen to negotiate this rigid image of the male by forging a role in both the world of work and the private arena. This is not to say that these men are not dedicated to their professional lives, striving for dominance in the workplace or seeking to control the public sphere, but rather, that each man can be seen to create a relationship between masculinity and domesticity and thus signal the importance of the male role in the private realm. Therefore, even though television flow offers a multitude of different and alternating versions of masculinity, a wide range of British and American shows form a consensus as they present a challenge to the hegemonic male.

Only a small number of men in society ever reach what has been understood as the hegemonic ideal, and as such, only a small number could ever find themselves fully removed from the private sphere. As such, the contemporary male is said to be finding a variety of different ways in which to construct their gendered identities, to explore their personal relationships and to balance their working and domestic responsibilities. Donald Sabo makes this point when he comments that

> fewer and fewer men are protecting images of manhood that no longer fit the realities of their lives. They are slowly realizing that the old norms for manhood just aren't cutting it in the postmodern marriage and family, in the workplace [or] in government.

> (Sabo 1994: 210)

Therefore, the representation of masculinities that we have seen in contemporary television programming could be seen to exploit the experience of the modern male who 'exists in different spaces, sometimes simultaneously, and at various stages of the life course [who manages] transitions between work and home life, between being a colleague, friend, father and partner' (Hockey 2007: online). Indeed, it is the mobility of men's experiences and their desire to inhabit both the public world of work and the private domestic realm that appears as a common thread throughout these texts.

Although the representation of masculinities that have been presented here can be seen to negotiate traditional sex role stereotypes, some have been more successful than others in this regard. After all, while some men have found professional success in the domestic arena, others are struggling to move between public and private spaces, straining to find a balance between a successful professional role and a secure home life and feeling pressured into committing to either the traditionally masculine or feminine sphere. In this same way, some men are seen to embrace traditionally feminine qualities such as affection, sensitivity and emotionality while others are struggling to talk to male friends and family members, straining to secure intimate male friendships and desperately searching for new ways to bond with their children. And yet, the very fact that these men are attempting to find a role in the private sphere and embracing a softer and more reflexive notion of masculinity can be read as both enlightening and potentially empowering here.

However, in those cases where men are seen to find success in both areas, extant research questions whether these depictions of masculinity are in fact just another way of maintaining patriarchal rule, the idea here being that the modern male is looking to reinforce the 'existing power structure by producing a hybrid masculinity which is better able and more suited to retain control' (Rutherford cited in Crewe and Goodrum 2000: 40). Rowena Chapman makes this point when she tells us that 'if what we define as female qualities will be highly valued in our brave new future, then to maintain hegemony it is in men's interest to co-opt femininity . . . the future may be female, but I fear it will still belong to men' (Chapman cited ibid.: 40). Therefore, rather than praise these men for seeking to reconcile the public and private realm, it has been suggested that 'having secured the heartland of the public, men are now moving into the private' (White cited ibid. 40). In short, we are being asked to consider if these figures of masculinity are choosing to 'become less hegemonic precisely in order to stay hegemonic' (MacKinnon 2003: 73).

And yet, although feminism has carried out an invaluable task in the last thirty years by foregrounding the construction of gender and the political nature of sex role stereotyping, with feminist theory being crucial to the emergence of the sociology of masculinity and an understanding of men, manhood and machismo, to assume that men's interest in the private sphere is simply one more way in which to maintain patriarchal rule is problematic because it continues to reinforce hegemonic masculinity as the preferred model of the male. And it is this model of manhood which is currently being challenged; by feminist theory, the sociology of masculinity, by the representation of masculinities on the small screen and by a generation of men who were 'born and raised in a world already transformed by the feminist movement' (Huntley 2006: 47). In short, to encourage masculinities that transcend the narrow hegemonic stereotype means enabling these men to draw on traditionally masculine and feminine characteristics and allowing them to move freely between public and private spheres. Perhaps then we can talk about hegemonic masculinity as something that men should pity and fear rather than something they should be seen to aspire to.

The lived experience of masculinity will always be more complex and fluctuating than those representations of manhood and the male role being depicted in contemporary television programming, however, this does not detract from the power of the medium to define norms and conventions, to provide 'common-sense' understandings of gender and sexuality and to portray what is considered to be both 'appropriate' and 'inappropriate' social relations. However, no attempt has been made in this work to test out my interpretations through audience research, not because such research is unimportant, but rather because the scope of this particular book has been limited to an examination of the representation of masculinities on the small screen. In this same way, there is little in this volume about the economics, structure, organisation or production practices of the television industry in either the UK or the US, and again, this is not because such work is not relevant, but rather because of the scope of this volume. In short, I hope that readers will find the book a useful introduction to the representation of masculinities on television. Moreover, I would encourage future research in the field to draw on this work in relation to audience accounts and production-based scholarship. Furthermore, I would hope that future research will take into account those long-running programmes that I have included here such as *EastEnders*, *ER* and *24* in order to consider any changes to the representation of masculinities that I have outlined here, and consider the relevance of more recent programmes such as *Heroes* (2006–), *Skins* and *Men in Trees* (2006–) as they could prove invaluable for a further consideration of the depiction of masculinities in telefantasy, teen television and the comedy drama respectively.

BIBLIOGRAPHY

Abercrombie, Nicholas (1997), *Television and Society*, Cambridge: Polity Press.

Alberti, John (2004), 'Introduction', in *Leaving Springfield: The Simpsons and the Possibility of Oppositional Culture*, ed. John Alberti, Detroit, MI: Wayne State University Press, pp. xi–xxxii.

Alcohol and Public Health Research Unit (2007), 'A Review of Alcohol Advertising on Television', archived at: http://www.aphru.ac.nz/hot/adkit.htm

Allan, Kenneth and Scott Coltrane (1996), 'Gender Displaying Television Commercials: A Comparative Study of Television Commercials in the 1950s and 1980s', *Sex Roles* 35, 3/4, pp. 185–203.

Allen, Dennis (2006), 'Making Over Masculinity', *Genders Online Journal* 44, pp. 1–12.

Allen, Robert (2005), 'Soap Opera', The Museum of Broadcast Communications, archived at: http://www.museum.tv/archives/etv/S/htmlS/soapopera/soapopera.htm

Allen, Ted, Kyan Douglas, Thom Filicia, Carson Kressley and Jai Rodriguez (2004), *Queer Eye for the Straight Guy: The Fab 5's Guide to Looking Better, Cooking Better, Dressing Better, Behaving Better and Living Better*, London: Weidenfeld & Nicolson.

Andrews, Maggie (1998), '*Butterflies* and Caustic Asides: Housewives, Comedy and the Feminist Movement', in *Because I Tell a Joke or Two: Comedy, Politics and Social Difference*, ed. Stephen Wagg, New York: Routledge, pp. 50–64.

Anger, Dorothy (1999), *Other Worlds: Society Seen through Soap Opera*, Peterborough: Broadview Press.

Arundel, John and Maurice Roche (1998), 'Media Sport and Local Identity: British Rugby League and Sky TV', in *Sport, Popular Culture and Identity*, ed. Maurice Roche, Aachen: Meyer & Meyer Verlag, pp. 57–91.

Attebery, Brian (2002), *Decoding Gender in Science Fiction*, London: Routledge.

Attwood, Feona (2005), 'Inside Out: Men on the Home Front', *Journal of Consumer Culture* 5, 1, pp. 87–107.

Badley, Linda (2000), 'Scully Hits the Glass Ceiling: Postmodernism, Postfeminism, Posthumanism, and *The X-Files*', in *Fantasy Girls: Gender in the New Universe of Science Fiction and Fantasy Television*, ed. Elyce Rae Helford, Oxford: Rowman and Littlefield, pp. 61–90.

Baker, Brian (2006), *Masculinity in Fiction and Film: Representing Men in Popular Genres 1945–2000*, London: Continuum.

Baker, Robin (2008), 'DNA Paternity Testing Directory', archived at: http://www.australianpaternityfraud.org/statistics.htm

Banks, Miranda (2004), 'A Boy for All Planets: *Roswell*, *Smallville* and the Teen Male Melodrama', in *Teen TV: Genre, Consumption and Identity*, ed. Glyn Davis and Kay Dickinson, London: BFI, pp. 17–28.

Battis, Jes (2007), *Investigating Farscape: Uncharted Territories of Sex and Science Fiction*, London: I. B. Tauris.

Battles, Kathleen and Wendy Hilton-Morrow (2002), 'Gay Characters in Conventional Spaces: *Will and Grace* and the Situation Comedy Genre', *Critical Studies in Media Communication* 19, 1, pp. 87–105.

BBC (2003), 'Did Delia Teach the Nation to Cook?', BBC News, archived at: http://news.bbc.co.uk/1/hi/talking_point/2679611.stm

BBC (2007a), 'Delia Smith', BBC Food, archived at: http://www.bbc.co.uk/food/chef_biogs/s.shtml#delia_smith

BBC (2007b), 'Spooks Expert: Your Questions Answered', bbc.co.uk, archived at: http://www.bbc.co.uk/drama/spooks/spooksexpert_questions_1.shtml#2

BBC (2007c), 'Personnel Character Info: Adam Carter', bbc.co.uk, archived at: http://www.bbc.co.uk/drama/spooks/personnel_ac.shtml

BBC (2007d), 'Personnel Character Info: Fiona Carter', bbc.co.uk, archived at: http://www.bbc.co.uk/drama/spooks/personnel_fc.shtml

Beautiful Britain (2007), 'Charlie Dimmock' Beautiful Britain, archived at: http://www.charliedimmock.beautifulbritain.co.uk/charlie_dimmock_faq.htm

Becker, Ron (2004), 'Prime-Time TV in the Gay Nineties: Network Television, Quality Audiences, and Gay Politics', in *The Television Studies Reader*, ed. Robert Allen and Annette Hill, London: Routledge, pp. 389–403.

Bentall, David (2004), *The Company You Keep: The Transforming Power of Male Friendship*, Minneapolis, MN: Augsburg Books.

Benwell, Bethan (ed.) (2003), *Masculinity and Men's Lifestyle Magazines*, London: Blackwell.

Berila, Beth and Dibya Choudhuri (2005), 'Metrosexuality the Middle Class Way', *Genders Online Journal* 42, pp. 1–15.

Bick, Ilsa (1996), 'Boys in Space: *Star Trek*, Latency, and the Neverending Story', in *Enterprise Zones: Critical Positions on Star Trek*, ed. Taylor Harrison, Sarah Projansky, Kent Ono and Elyce Rae Helford, Oxford: Westview Press, pp. 189–210.

Big Brother (2007), 'The Official *Big Brother* Site', Channel 4, archived at: http://www.channel4.com/bigbrother/

Bignell, Jonathan (2004), *An Introduction to Television Studies*, London: Routledge.

Bignell, Jonathan (2005), *Big Brother: Reality TV in the Twenty-First Century*, London: Palgrave Macmillan.

Billen, Andrew (2006), 'Metrosexual RIP?', Timesonline, archived at: http://www.timesonline.co.uk/tol/life_and_style/article702600.ece

Bird, Sharon (1996), 'Welcome to the Men's Club: Homosociality and the Maintenance of Hegemonic Masculinity', *Gender and Society* 10, 2, pp. 120–32.

Biressi, Anita and Heather Nunn (2005), *Reality TV: Realism and Revelation*, London: Wallflower.

Bonner, Frances (2005), 'Whose Lifestyle Is It Anyway?' in *Ordinary Lifestyles: Popular Media, Consumption and Taste*, ed. David Bell and Joanne Hollows, Maidenhead: Open University Press, pp. 35–46.

Booker, M. Keith (2004), *Science Fiction Television*, London: Praeger.

Booker, M. Keith (2006), *Drawn to Television: Prime Time Animation from The Flintstones to Family Guy*, Westport, CT and London: Praeger.

Bordo, Susan (1999), 'Gay Men's Revenge', *Journal of Aesthetic and Art Criticism* 57, 1, pp. 21–6.

Bould, Mark (2003), 'Film and Television', in *The Cambridge Companion to Science Fiction*, ed. Edward James and Farah Mendlesohn, Cambridge: Cambridge University Press, pp. 79–95.

Boulos, Nick (2007), 'Brian: I Love Amanda to Bits: We're Going on a Date', *Star*, 10 September, pp. 8–10.

Boyle, Raymond and Richard Haynes (2000), *Power Play: Sport, the Media & Popular Culture*, London: Longman.

Brenton, Sam and Reuben Cohen (2003), *Shooting People: Adventures in Reality TV*, London: Verso.

Bretl, Daniel and Joanne Cantor (1988), 'The Portrayal of Men and Women in U.S. Television Commercials: A Recent Content Analysis and Trends over 15 Years', *Sex Roles* 18, 9/10, pp. 595–609.

Breward, Christopher (1995), *The Culture of Fashion: A New History of Fashionable Dress*, Manchester: Manchester University Press.

Brookes, Rod (2002), *Representing Sport*, London: Arnold.

Brown, Mary Ellen (1994), *Soap Opera and Women's Talk – The Pleasures of Resistance*, London: Sage.

Brunsdon, Charlotte (2000), *The Feminist, the Housewife, and the Soap Opera*, Oxford: Clarendon Press.

Brunsdon, Charlotte (2003), 'Lifestyling Britain: The 8–9 slot on British Television', *International Journal of Cultural Studies* 6, 1, pp. 5–23.

Bruzzi, Stella (1997), *Undressing Cinema: Clothing and Identity in the Movies*, London: Routledge.

Bruzzi, Stella (2005), 'Gregory Peck: Anti-Fashion Icon', in *Fashioning Film Stars: Dress, Culture, Identity*, ed. Rachel Moseley, London: BFI, pp. 39–49.

Buckingham, David (1987), *Public Secrets: EastEnders and Its Audience*, London: BFI.

Buckman, Peter (1984), *All for Love: A Study in Soap Opera*, London: Secker & Warburg.

Budweiser (2007), 'Anheuser-Busch Companies', archived at: http://company.monster.co.uk/anheuseruk/

Butcher, Jim (2005), 'Crackers Don't Matter', in *Farscape Forever! Sex, Drugs and Killer Muppets*, ed. Glenn Yeffeth, Dallas, TX: BenBella Books, pp. 67–72.

Butsch, Richard (2003), 'A Half Century of Class and Gender in American TV Domestic Sitcoms', *Cercles* 8, pp. 16–34.

Callan, Maureen (1976), 'Women Copywriters Get Better, but Male Chauvinism in Ads Rolls On', *Advertising Age* 4 October, pp. 75–6.

Campbell, Denis (2003), 'Beckham Is Most Influential Man in the UK', *Observer*, 2 February, archived at http://observer.guardian.co.uk/uk_news/story/0,,887176,00.html

Carrigan, Tim, Bob Connell and John Lee (1985), 'Toward a New Sociology of Masculinity', *Theory and Society* 14, 5, pp. 551–604.

Casey, Bernadette, Neil Casey, Ben Calvert, Liam French and Justin Lewis (2002a), 'Crime Series', in *Television Studies: The Key Concepts*, Bernadette Casey *et al.*, London: Routledge, pp. 44–8.

Casey, Bernadette, Neil Casey, Ben Calvert, Liam French and Justin Lewis (2002b), 'Science Fiction', in *Television Studies: The Key Concepts*, Bernadette Casey *et al.*, London: Routledge, pp. 207–9.

Cashmore, Ellis (1994), *And There Was Telev!s!on*, London: Routledge.

Cashmore, Ellis (2004), *Beckham – Fully Revised and Updated*, Cambridge: Polity.

Cashmore, Ellis (2005), *Making Sense of Sports* (4th edition), London: Routledge.

Cassidy, Jane and Diane Taylor (1997), 'Doctor, Doctor, Where Can I Get an Aspirin?', *Guardian* 12 December, p. 6.

Cavelos, Jeanne (2005), 'Down the Wormhole', in *Farscape Forever! Sex, Drugs and Killer Muppets*, ed. Glenn Yeffeth, Dallas, TX: BenBella Books, pp. 25–38.

Chow, Valerie (2004), 'Homer Erectus: Homer Simpson as Everyman . . . and Every Woman', in *Leaving Springfield: The Simpsons and the Possibility of Oppositional Culture*, ed. John Alberti, Detroit, MI: Wayne State University Press, pp. 107–36.

Christopher, Renny (2004), 'Little Miss Tough Chick of the Universe: *Farscape*'s Inverted Sexual Dynamics', in *Action Chicks: New Images of Tough Women in Popular Culture*, ed. Sherrie Inness, London: Palgrave Macmillan, pp. 257–82.

Church-Gibson, Pamela (2005), 'Brad Pitt and George Clooney, the Rough and the Smooth: Male Costuming in Contemporary Hollywood', in *Fashioning Film Stars: Dress, Culture, Identity*, ed. Rachel Moseley, London: BFI, pp. 62–74.

Clare, Anthony (2001), *On Men: Masculinity in Crisis*, London: Arrow.

Clark, Bernard (2002), 'The Box of Tricks', in *Reality TV: How Real Is Real?*, ed. Dolan Cummings *et al.*, London: Hodder & Stoughton, pp. 1–16.

Clarke, Alan (1986), 'This Is Not the Boy Scouts: Television, Police Series and Definitions of Law and Order', in *Popular Culture and Social Relations*, ed. Tony Bennett, Colin Mercer and Janet Woollacott, Milton Keynes: Open University Press, pp. 219–32.

Clarke, Alan (1992), 'You're Nicked!: Television Police Series and the Fictional Representation of Law and Order', in *Come on Down? Popular Media Culture in Post-War Britain*, ed. Dominic Strinati and Stephen Wagg, London: Routledge, pp. 232–53.

Clarke, Alan and John Clarke (1982), 'Highlights and Action Replays – Ideology, Sport and the Media', in *Sport, Culture and Ideology*, ed. Jennifer Hargreaves, London: Routledge & Kegan Paul, pp. 62–87.

Clarkson, Jay (2005), 'Contesting Masculinity's Makeover: *Queer Eye*, Consuming Masculinity, and "Straight Acting" Gays', *Journal of Communication Inquiry* 29, 3, pp. 235–55.

Clayton, Ben and John Harris (2004), 'Footballer's Wives: The Role of the Soccer Player's Partner in the Construction of Idealised Masculinity', *Soccer and Society* 5, 3, pp. 317–35.

Cobley, Paul (2001), 'Who Loves Ya, Baby?: *Kojak* and the Great Society', in *Action TV: Tough Guys, Smooth Operators and Foxy Chicks*, ed. Bill Osgerby and Anna Gough-Yates, London: Routledge, pp. 53–68.

Cohen, David (2004), 'Men, Empathy, and Autism', *The Chronicle of Higher Education* 50, 26, pp. 1–9.

Cohen, Theodore (1992), 'Men's Families, Men's Friends: A Structural Analysis of Constraints on Men's Social Ties', in *Men's Friendships*, ed. Peter Nardi, London: Sage, pp. 115–31.

Connell, R. W. (1995), *Masculinities*, Berkeley, CA: University of California Press.

Connell, R. W. (1998), 'Masculinities and Globalization', *Men and Masculinities* 1, 1, pp. 3–23.

Cooke, Lez (2002), 'The Police Series', in *The Television Genre Book*, ed. Glen Creeber, London: BFI, pp. 19–23.

Cooke, Lez (2003), *British Television Drama: A History*, London: BFI.

Corner, John (2002), 'Performing the Real: Documentary Diversions', *Television & New Media* 3, 3, pp. 255–69.

Cowan, Katherine and Gill Valentine (2006), 'Tuned Out: The BBC's portrayal of Lesbian and Gay People', London: Stonewall, pp. 1–25.

Craig, Steve (1992a), 'The Effect of Television Day Part on Gender Portrayals in Television Commercials: A Content Analysis', *Sex Roles* 26, 5/6, pp. 197–211.

Craig, Steve (1992b), 'Men's Men and Women's Women: How TV Commercials Portray Gender to Different Audiences', in *Issues and Effects of Mass Communication: Other Voices*, ed. Robert Kemper, San Diego, CA: Capstone Publishers, pp. 89–100, archived at: http://www.rtvf.unt.edu/people/craig/pdfs/menmen.pdf

Craig, Steve (1993), 'Selling Masculinities, Selling Femininities', *The Mid-Atlantic Almanack* 2, pp. 15–27, archived at: http://www.rtvf.unt.edu/html/craig/pdfs/gender.PDF

Creeber, Glen (2001), 'Cigarettes and Alcohol: Investigating Gender, Genre, and Gratification in *Prime Suspect*', *Television & New Media* 2, 2, pp. 149–66.

Creedon, Pamela (1994), 'Women, Media and Sport: Creating and Reflecting Gender Values', in *Women, Media and Sport: Challenging Gender Values*, ed. Pamela Creedon, London: Sage, pp. 3–27.

Crewe, Louise and Alison Goodrum (2000), 'Fashioning New Forms of Consumption: The Case of Paul Smith', in *Fashion Cultures: Theories, Explorations and Analysis*, ed. Stella Bruzzi and Pamela Church Gibson, London: Routledge, pp. 25–48.

Crotty, Mark (1995), 'Murphy Would Probably Also Win the Election: The Effect of Television as Related to the Portrayal of the Family in Situation Comedies', *JPC* 29, 3, pp. 1–15.

Cummings, Dolan (2002a), 'Introduction', in *Reality TV: How Real Is Real?*, ed. Dolan Cummings, Bernard Clark, Victoria Mapplebeck, Christopher Dunkley and Graham Barnfield, London: Hodder & Stoughton, pp. xi–xviii.

Cummings, Dolan (2002b), 'Afterword', in *Reality TV: How Real Is Real?*, ed. Dolan Cummings *et al.*, London: Hodder & Stoughton, pp. 67–70.

D'Acci, Julie (2005), 'Television, Representation and Gender', in *Popular Television Drama: Critical Perspectives*, ed. Jonathan Bignell and Stephen Lacey, Manchester: Manchester University Press, pp. 373–88.

Davis, Glyn and Kay Dickinson (2004), 'Introduction', in *Teen TV: Genre, Consumption and Identity*, ed. Glyn Davis and Kay Dickinson, London: BFI, pp. 1–16.

Deakin, Simon and Stephen Pratten (2000), 'Quasi Markets, Transaction Costs, and Trust: The Uncertain Effects of Market Reforms in British Television Production', *Television & New Media* 1, 3, pp. 321–54.

Delaney, Sean (2007), 'TV Police Drama: TV Cops from Fabian to Morse', Screenonline: The Definitive Guide to Britain's Film and TV History, archived at: http://www.screenonline.org.uk/tv/id/445716/index.html

Dickinson, Roger, Anne Murcott, Jane Eldridge and Simon Leader (2001), 'Breakfast, Time, and "Breakfast Time": Television, Food, and the Household Organization of Consumption', *Television & New Media* 2, 3, pp. 235–56.

Dolan, Deirdre (1999), 'WB Knows Its Teens', *The National Post*, archived at: http://www.geocities.com/Heartland/Valley/8414/wb.htm

Donnelly, Kevin (2002), 'Adult Animation', in *The Television Genre Book*, ed. Glen Creeber, London: BFI, pp. 73–5.

Dovey, Jon (2002), 'Reality TV', in *The Television Genre Book*, ed. Glen Creeber, London: BFI, pp. 134–7.

Dow, Bonnie (1996), *Prime-Time Feminism: Television, Media Culture and the Women's Movement Since 1970*, Philadelphia, PA: University of Pennsylvania Press.

Dow, Bonnie (2001), '*Ellen*, Television, and the Politics of Gay and Lesbian Visibility', *Critical Studies in Media Communication* 18, 2, pp. 123–40.

Dyer, Richard (1992), *Only Entertainment* (2nd edition), London: Routledge.

Edwards, Tim (1997), *Men in the Mirror: Men's Fashion, Masculinity and Consumer Society*, London: Cassell.

Ehrenreich, Barbara (1984), *The Hearts of Men: American Dreams and the Flight from Commitment*, New York and London: Anchor Books.

Elrod, Patricia Nead (2005), '*Farscape* Villains I've Known and Loved', in *Farscape Forever! Sex, Drugs and Killer Muppets*, ed. Glenn Yeffeth, Dallas, TX: BenBella Books, pp. 187–98.

Evison, Sue (1998), 'Grow Up You Pathetic Yobs', *The Sun* 10 June, p. 2.

Faludi, Susan (2000), *Stiffed: The Betrayal of the Modern Man*, London: Vintage.

Farley, Rebecca (2003), 'We Hardly Watch that Rude, Crude Show: Class and Taste in *The Simpsons*', in *Prime Time Animation: Television Animation and American Culture*, ed. Carol Stabile and Mark Harrison, London: Routledge, pp. 147–64.

Felperin, Leslie (1999), 'Animated Cool', *Sight and Sound* 9, 3, pp. 16–17.

Flood, Michael (2003), 'Men, Sex and Mateship: How Homosociality Shapes Men's Heterosexual Relations', paper presented at '(Other) Feminisms: An International Women's and Gender Studies Conference', University of Queensland, July, pp. 1–9.

Ford Motor Company (2007), 'For Fusion Puts Life in Drive for Women', archived at: http://media.ford.com/newsroom/feature_display.cfm?release= 22580

Fowles, Jib (1996), *Advertising and Popular Culture*, London: Sage.

Fradley, Martin (2004), 'Maximus Melodramaticus: Masculinity, Masochism and White Male Paranoia in Contemporary Hollywood Cinema', in *Action and Adventure Cinema*, ed. Yvonne Tasker, London: Routledge, pp. 235–51.

Furnham, Adrian and Nadine Bitar (1993), 'Stereotyped Portrayal of Men and Women in British Television Advertisements', *Sex Roles* 29, 3/4, pp. 297–310.

Furnham, Adrian and Sarah Spencer-Bowdage (2002), 'Sex Role Stereotyping in Television Advertisements: A Content Analysis of Advertisements from South Africa and Great Britain', *Communications* 27, pp. 457–83.

Gauntlett, David and Annette Hill (1999), *Television Living – Television, Culture and Everyday Life*, London: Routledge.

Geraghty, Christine (1991), *Women and Soap Opera: A Study of Prime Time Soaps*, Cambridge: Polity Press.

Geraghty, Christine (1995), 'Social Issues and Realist Soaps: A Study of British Soaps in the 1980s/1990s', in *To Be Continued . . . Soap Operas around the World*, ed. Robert Allen, London: Routledge, pp. 66–80.

Geraghty, Christine and David Lusted (1998), 'Introduction to Chapter 19', in *The Television Studies Book*, ed. Christine Geraghty and David Lusted, London: Arnold, pp. 299–300.

Giddens, Anthony (1991), *Modernity and Self-Identity: Self and Society in the Late Modern Age*, Stanford: Stanford University Press.

GLAAD (1998), '*Will & Grace* Come Out on Monday', GLAAD Alert, archived at: http://www.glaad.org/action/al_archive_year.php?year=1998

Gledhill, Christine (1997), 'Genre and Gender: The Case of Soap Opera', in *Representation: Cultural Representations and Signifying Practices*, ed. Stuart Hall, London: Sage, pp. 337–86.

Good, Glenn, Michael Porter and Mark Dillon (2002), 'When Men Divulge: Portrayals of Men's Self-Disclosure in Prime Time Situation Comedies', *Sex Roles* 46, 11/12, pp. 419–27.

Gorman-Murray, Andrew (2006), 'Queering Home or Domesticating Deviance?: Interrogating Gay Domesticity through Lifestyle Television', *International Journal of Cultural Studies* 9, 2, pp. 227–47.

Gray, Jonathan (2006), *Watching with the Simpsons: Television, Parody and Intertextuality*, London: Routledge.

Graydon, Jan (1983), 'But It's More than Just a Game: It's an Institution', *Feminist Review* 13, pp. 5–16.

Greenberg, Harvey (1984), 'In Search of Spock: A Psychoanalytic Inquiry', *Journal of Popular Film and Television* 12, 2, pp. 52–65.

Gregory, Chris (2000), *Star Trek Parallel Narratives*, London: Macmillan Press.

Gross, Larry (2001), *Up from Invisibility: Lesbians, Gay Men, and the Media in America*, New York: Columbia University.

Gwenllian Jones, Sarah (2002), 'Gender and Queerness', in *Television Studies*, ed. Toby Miller, London: BFI, pp. 109–12.

Hakala, Ulla (2005), *Yesterday's Breadwinners in Today's Mixed Salad: Cultural Representations of Masculinity in Advertising*, Tampere: Esa Print Tampere.

Hakala, Ulla (2006), *Adam in Ads: A Thirty Year Look at Mediated Masculinities in Advertising in Finland and the US*, Tampere: Esa Print Tampere.

Hallam, Julia (1998), 'Gender and Professionalism in TV's Medical Melodramas', in *Medical Fictions*, ed. Nickianne Moody and Julia Hallam, Wallasey: Eaton Press, pp. 25–47.

Hamamoto, Darrell (1989), *Nervous Laughter: Television Situation Comedy and Liberal Democratic Ideology*, New York: Praeger.

Hanke, Robert (1998), 'The Mock-Macho Situation Comedy: Hegemonic Masculinity and its Reiteration', *Western Journal of Communication* 62, 1, pp. 74–93.

Harkness, Justine and Karen Dunn (2007), 'Chanelle: Her First Real Interview', *Now* 13 August, pp. 20–3.

Harrison, Mark (2000), 'Look Who's Coming Over for Dinner', *Radio Times* 4–10 November, pp. 16–18, 21.

Hart, Kylo-Patrick (2004), 'We're Here, We're Queer – and We're Better Than You: The Representational Superiority of Gay Men to Heterosexuals on *Queer Eye for the Straight Guy*', *Journal of Men's Studies* 12, 3, pp. 241–53.

Hartley, John (2002), 'Situation Comedy, Part 1', in *The Television Genre Book*, ed. Glen Creeber, London: BFI, pp. 65–7.

Helford, Elyce Rae (1996), 'A Part of Myself No Man Should Ever See: Reading Captain Kirk's Multiple Masculinities', in *Enterprise Zones: Critical Positions on Star Trek*, ed. Taylor Harrison, Sarah Projansky, Kent A. Ono and Elyce Rae Helford, Boulder, CO: Westview Press, pp. 11–31.

Helford, Elyce Rae (2000), 'Introduction', in *Fantasy Girls: Gender in the New Universe of Science Fiction and Fantasy Television*, ed. Elyce Rae Helford, Oxford: Rowman and Littlefield, pp. 1–12.

Henry, Matthew (2003), 'The Triumph of Popular Culture: Situation Comedy, Postmodernism and *The Simpsons*', in *Critiquing the Sitcom: A Reader*, ed. Joanne Morreale, New York: Syracuse University Press, pp. 262–73.

Herbert, Susannah (2007), 'The Myth of Mars and Venus by Deborah Cameron', *The Sunday Times* 7 October, pp. 40–1.

Hill, Annette (2002), '*Big Brother*: The Real Audience', *Television & New Media* 3, 3, pp. 323–40.

Hill, Annette (2004), 'Watching *Big Brother*', in *Big Brother International: Formats, Critics & Publics*, ed. Ernest Mathijs and Janet Jones, London: Wallflower, pp. 25–39.

Hill, Annette (2005), *Reality TV: Audiences and Popular Factual Television*, London: Routledge.

Hill, Annette and Gareth Palmer (2002), '*Big Brother*', *Television & New Media* 3, 3, pp. 251–4.

Hilton-Morrow, Wendy and David McMahan (2003), '*The Flintstones* to *Futurama*: Networks and Prime Time Animation', in *Prime Time Animation: Television Animation and American Culture*, ed. Carol Stabile and Mark Harrison, London: Routledge, pp. 74–88.

Hobson, Dorothy (2003), *Soap Opera*, Cambridge: Polity Press.

Hockey, Jenny (2007), 'Symposium: Mobile Masculinities: Spatial, Intimate and Bodily Transitions', University of Sheffield, archived at: http://www.britsoc.co.uk/NR/rdonlyres/C21B59AA-A45E-43C7-A72B-F2FF316F7EDC/0/Mobile_masculinities_call_for_papers.pdf

Hogg, Margaret and Jade Garrow (2001), 'Gender Identity and the

Consumption of Visual Images in Television Advertising', paper presented at the 'Critical Studies Management Conference', Manchester, July, pp. 1–17, archived at: http://www.mngt.waikato.ac.nz/ejrot/cmsconference/2001/Papers/Marketing/Hogg.pdf

Hollows, Joanne (2002), 'The Bachelor Dinner: Masculinity, Class and Cooking in *Playboy*, 1953–1961', *Continuum: Journal of Media & Cultural Studies* 16, 2, pp. 143–55.

Hollows, Joanne (2003a), 'Feeling Like a Domestic Goddess: Postfeminism and Cooking', *European Journal of Cultural Studies* 6, 2, pp. 179–202.

Hollows, Joanne (2003b), 'Oliver's Twist: Leisure, Labour and Domestic Masculinity in *The Naked Chef*', *International Journal of Cultural Studies* 6, 2, pp. 229–48.

Holmes, Su and Deborah Jermyn (2004), 'Introduction', in *Understanding Reality Television*, ed. Su Holmes and Deborah Jermyn, London: Routledge, pp. 1–32.

Horrocks, Roger (1995), *Male Myths and Icons: Masculinity in Popular Culture*, London: Macmillan.

Hoynes, William (2003), 'Branding Public Service: The "New PBS" and the Privatization of Public Television', *Television & New Media* 4, 2, pp. 117–30.

Huffer, Ian (2003), 'What Interest Does a Fat Stallone Have for an Action Fan? Male Film Audiences and the Structuring of Stardom', in *Contemporary Hollywood Stardom*, ed. Martin Barker and Thomas Austin, London: Arnold, pp. 155–66.

Hunt, Leon (2001), 'Drop Everything ... Including Your Pants: *The Professionals* and Hard Action TV', in *Action TV: Tough Guys, Smooth Operators and Foxy Chicks*, ed. Bill Osgerby and Anna Gough-Yates, London: Routledge, pp. 127–42.

Huntley, Rebecca (2006), *The World According to Y: Inside the New Adult Generation*, Sydney: Allen & Unwin.

Iglebæk, Vegard (2000), 'What Kind of Male Friendship? A Case Study of Joey and Chandler in *Friends*', paper presented at the '4th European Feminist Research Conference', Bologna, October, pp. 1–10.

Jacobs, Jason (2002), 'Hospital Drama', in *The Television Genre Book*, ed. Glen Creeber, London: BFI, pp. 23–6.

Jacobs, Jason (2003), *Body Trauma TV: The New Hospital Dramas*, London: BFI.

Jancovich, Mark (2004), 'Dwight MacDonald and the Historical Epic', in *Action and Adventure Cinema*, ed. Yvonne Tasker, London: Routledge, pp. 84–99.

Jermyn, Deborah (2006), 'Bringing out the Star in You: SJP, Carrie Bradshaw and the Evolution of Television Stardom', in *Framing Celebrity: New Directions in Celebrity Culture*, ed. Su Holmes and Sean Redmond, London: Routledge, pp. 67–86.

Jhally, Sut (1990), *The Codes of Advertising: Fetishism and the Political Economy of Meaning in the Consumer Society*, London: Routledge.

Johnson, Catherine (2002), '*Buffy the Vampire Slayer*', in *The Television Genre Book*, ed. Glen Creeber, London: BFI, p. 42.

Johnson, Catherine (2005), *Telefantasy*, London: BFI.

Jones, Janet Megan (2003), 'Show Your Real Face', *New Media & Society 5*, 3, pp. 400–21.

Karpf, Anne (1988), *Doctoring the Media*, London: Routledge.

Kennedy, Eileen (2007), 'Watching the Game: Theorising Masculinities in the Context of Mediated Tennis', in *Sport & Gender Identities: Masculinities, Femininities and Sexualities*, ed. Cara Carmichael Aitchison, London: Routledge, pp. 22–33.

Kidd, Bruce (1990), 'The Men's Cultural Centre: Sports and the Dynamic of Women's Oppression/Men's Repression', in *Sport, Men, and the Gender Order: Critical Feminist Perspectives*, ed. Michael Messner and Donald Sabo, Champaign, IL: Human Kinetics Books, pp. 31–43.

Kiernan, Caitlin (2002), 'Worlds Glimpsed, Worlds Lost: Why *Farscape* Should be Saved', *SF Site*, archived at: http://www.sfsite.com/09b/far136.htm

Kilborn, Richard (2003), *Staging the Real: Factual Programming in the Age of Big Brother*, Manchester: Manchester University Press.

Kimmel, Michael (2004), 'Masculinity as Homophobia: Fear, Shame, and Silence in the Construction of Gender Identity', in *Feminism and Masculinities*, ed. Peter Murphy, Oxford: Oxford University Press, pp. 182–99.

Kooijman, Jaap (2005), 'They're Here, They're Queer, and Straight America Loves it', *GLQ: A Journal of Lesbian and Gay Studies* 11, 1, pp. 106–9.

Lavender, Andy (2003), 'Pleasure, Performance and the *Big Brother* Experience', *Contemporary Theatre Review* 13, 2, pp. 15–23.

Lavine, Howard, Donna Sweeney and Stephen Wagner (1999), 'Depicting Women as Sex Objects in Television Advertising: Effects on Body Dissatisfaction' *Personality and Social Psychology Bulletin* 25, 8, pp. 1049–58.

Lehne, Gregory (1989), 'Homophobia among Men: Supporting and Defining the Male Role', in *Men's Lives*, ed. Michael Kimmel and Michael Messner, New York: Macmillan, pp. 416–29.

Leverenz, David (1986), 'Manhood, Humiliation and Public Life: Some Stories', *Southwest Review* 71, Fall, pp. 442–62.

Lewis, Jon and Stempel, Penny (1999), *The Ultimate TV Guide*, London: Orion.

Liebes, Tamar and Sonia Livingstone (1998), 'European Soap Operas: The Diversification of a Genre', London: LSE Research Online, pp. 1–29, archived at: http://eprints.lse.ac.uk/archive/00000402

Limpinnian, Danielle (2002), 'The Portrayal of Men and Women in TV Ads', archived at: http://www.aber.ac.uk/media/Students/del0001.html

Lovdal, Lynn (1989), 'Sex Role Messages in Television Commercials: An Update', *Sex Roles* 21, 11/12, pp. 715–24.

Lynx (2007), 'Lynx', archived at: http://www.unilever.co.uk/ourbrands/personalcare/lynx.asp

McArthur, Leslie and Resko, Beth (1975), 'The Portrayal of Men and Women in American Television Commercials', *The Journal of Social Psychology* 97, pp. 209–20.

MacInnes, John (1998), *The End of Masculinity: The Confusion of Sexual Genesis and Sexual Difference in Modern Society*, Buckingham: Open University Press.

Mackenzie, Michael (2005), '*Spooks* Season Two', DVDTimes, archived at: http://www.dvdtimes.co.uk/content.php?contentid=58406

MacKinnon, Kenneth (2003), *Representing Men: Maleness and Masculinity in the Media*, London: Arnold.

MacMurraugh-Kavanagh, Madeleine (2000), 'What's All This Then?: The Ideology of Identity in *The Cops*', in *Frames and Fictions on Television: The Politics of Identity within Drama*, ed. Bruce Carson and Margaret Llewellyn-Jones, Exeter: Intellect, pp. 40–9.

McQueen, David (1998), *Television: A Media Student's Guide*, London: Arnold.

Madill, Anna and Rebecca Goldmeier (2003), '*EastEnders*: Texts of Female Desire and Community', *International Journal of Cultural Studies* 6, 4, pp. 471–94.

Magic, Lemon (2007), 'Nigella Bites' imdb.com, archived at: http://www.imdb.com/title/tt0285390/

Manstead, A. S. R. and Caroline McCulloch (1981), 'Sex-Role Stereotyping in British Television Advertisements', *British Journal of Social Psychology* 20, pp. 171–80.

Mapplebeck, Victoria (2002), 'Money Shot', in *Reality TV: How Real Is Real?*, ed. Dolan Cummings *et al.*, London: Hodder & Stoughton, pp. 17–34.

Mathijs, Ernest and Janet Jones (eds) (2004), *Big Brother International: Formats, Critics and Publics*, London: Wallflower.

Matthews, Nicole and Farah Mendlesohn (2000), 'The Cartesian Novum of *Third Rock from the Sun*: Gendering Human Bodies and Alien Minds', in *Fantasy Girls: Gender in the New Universe of Science Fiction and Fantasy Television*, ed. Elyce Rae Helford, Oxford: Rowman and Littlefield, pp. 41–60.

Mavis, Paul (2007), '*MI5*: Volume 4', DVDTalk, archived at: http://www.dvdtalk.com/reviews/read.php?ID=26001

Meân, Lindsey (2001), 'Identity and Discursive Practice: Doing Gender on the Football Pitch', *Discourse & Society* 12, 6, pp. 789–815.

Medhurst, Andy (2003), 'Day for Night', *Sight and Sound* 9, 6, pp. 26–7.

Merrick, Helen (2003), 'Gender in Science Fiction', in *The Cambridge Companion to Science Fiction*, ed. Edward James and Farah Mendlesohn, Cambridge: Cambridge University Press, pp. 241–52.

Messner, Michael (1992), *Power at Play: Sports and the Problem of Masculinity*, Boston, MA: Beacon Press.

Messner, Michael (1994), 'Sports and the Politics of Inequality', in *Sex, Violence & Power in Sports: Rethinking Masculinity*, ed. Michael Messner and Donald Sabo, New York: The Crossing Press, pp. 129–35.

Messner, Michael and Donald Sabo (1994), 'Sexuality and Power', in *Sex, Violence & Power in Sports: Rethinking Masculinity*, ed. Michael Messner and Donald Sabo, New York: The Crossing Press, pp. 33–5.

Messner, Michael, Michele Dunbar and Darnell Hunt (2000), 'The Televised Sports Manhood Formula', *Journal of Sport & Social Issues* 24, 4, pp. 380–94.

Meyers, Renee (1980), 'An Examination of the Male Sex Role Model in Prime Time Television Commercials', paper presented to the Speech Communication Association, New York, November, pp. 1–41.

Miller, Toby (2005), 'A Metrosexual Eye on Queer Guy', *GLQ: A Journal of Lesbian and Gay Studies* 11, 1, pp. 112–17.

Milligan, Andy (2004), *Brand It Like Beckham*, London: Cyan.

Mills, Brett (2005), *Television Sitcom*, London: BFI.

Mittell, Jason (2003), 'The Great Saturday Morning Exile: Scheduling Cartoons on Television's Periphery in the 1960s', in *Prime Time Animation: Television Animation and American Culture*, ed. Carol A. Stabile and Mark Harrison, London: Routledge, pp. 33–54.

Moody, Nickianne (2001), 'A Lone Crusader in the Dangerous World: Heroics of Science and Technology in *Knight Rider*', in *Action TV: Tough Guys, Smooth Operators and Foxy Chicks*, ed. Bill Osgerby and Anna Gough-Yates, London: Routledge, pp. 69–80.

Moody, Nickianne (2002), 'Displacements of Gender and Race in *Space: Above and Beyond*', in *Aliens R Us: The Other in Science Fiction Cinema*, ed. Ziauddin Sardar and Sean Cubitt, London: Pluto, pp. 51–73.

Moorti, Sujata and Karen Ross (2004), 'Reality Television: Fairy Tale or Feminist Nightmare?', *Feminist Media Studies* 4, 2, pp. 203–5.

Morreale, Joanne (ed.) (2003), *Critiquing the Sitcom: A Reader*, New York: Syracuse University Press.

Moseley, Rachel (2000), 'Makeover Takeover on British Television', *Screen* 41, 3, pp. 299–314.

Moseley, Rachel (2001), 'Real Lads do Cook . . . But Some Things Are Still Hard to Talk About: The Gendering of 8–9', *European Journal of Cultural Studies* 4, 1, pp. 32–9.

Moseley, Rachel (2002), 'The Teen Series', in *The Television Genre Book*, ed. Glen Creeber, London: BFI, pp. 41–3.

Mullen, Megan (2004), '*The Simpsons* and Hanna-Barbera's Animation Legacy', in *Leaving Springfield: The Simpsons and the Possibility of Oppositional Culture*, ed. John Alberti, Detroit, MI: Wayne State University Press, pp. 63–84.

Mumford, Laura Stempel (1995), *Love and Ideology in the Afternoon: Soap*

Opera, Women, and Television Genre, Bloomington, IN: Indiana University Press.

Murray, Susan and Laurie Ouellette (2004), 'Introduction', in *Reality TV: Remaking Television Culture*, ed. Susan Murray and Laurie Ouellette, New York: New York University Press, pp. 1–19.

Nardi, Peter (1992), 'Seamless Souls: An Introduction to Men's Friendships', in *Men's Friendships*, ed. Peter Nardi, London: Sage, pp. 1–14.

Neale, Steve (1995), 'Masculinity as Spectacle: Reflections on Men and Mainstream Cinema', in *Screening the Male*, ed. Steven Cohan, London: Routledge, pp. 9–22.

Newland, Martin (2006), 'Why Women Prefer Talking to Sex', *Daily Mail* 13 September, pp. 32–3.

Ney, Sharon and Elaine Sciog-Lazarov (2000), 'The Construction of Feminine Identity in *Babylon 5*', in *Fantasy Girls: Gender in the New Universe of Science Fiction and Fantasy Television*, ed. Elyce Rae Helford, Oxford: Rowman and Littlefield, pp. 223–44.

Nixon, Sean (1996), *Hard Looks: Masculinities, Spectatorship and Contemporary Consumption*, New York: St Martin's Press.

Noble, Grant (1975), *Children in Front of the Small Screen*, London: Constable.

O'Connor, Michael (1998), 'The Role of Television Drama *E.R.* in Medical Student Life: Entertainment or Socialization', *MS/JAMA: The Medical Student JAMA* 280, 9, pp. 854–5.

Ouellette, Laurie and Justin Lewis (2000), 'Moving Beyond the "Vast Wasteland": Cultural Policy and Television in the United States', *Television & New Media* 1, 1, pp. 95–115.

Palmer, Gareth (2002), '*Big Brother*: An Experiment in Governance', *Television & New Media* 3, 3, pp. 295–310.

Palmer, Gareth (2004), 'The New You: Class and Transformation in Lifestyle Television', in *Understanding Reality Television*, ed. Su Holmes and Deborah Jermyn, London: Routledge, pp. 173–90.

Palmer-Mehta, Valerie (2006), 'The Wisdom of Folly: Disrupting Masculinity in *King of the Hill*', *Text and Performance Quarterly* 26, 2, pp. 181–98.

Papp, Jeanette (2008), 'DNA Paternity Testing Directory', archived at: http://www.australianpaternityfraud.org/statistics.htm

Pasquier, Dominique (1996), 'Teen Series' Reception: Television, Adolescence and Culture of Feelings', *Childhood: A Global Journal of Child Research* 3, 3, pp. 351–73.

Pearson, Wendy (2003), 'Science Fiction and Queer Theory', in *The Cambridge Companion to Science Fiction*, ed. Edward James and Farah Mendlesohn, Cambridge: Cambridge University Press, pp. 149–62.

Perry, Hannah (2007), '*Big Brother*', *heat* 8–14 September, pp. 5–24.

Philips, Deborah (2000), 'Medicated Soap: The Woman Doctor in Television

Medical Drama', in *Frames and Fictions on Television*, ed. Bruce Carson and Margaret Llewellyn-Jones, Exeter: Intellect, pp. 50–61.

Pleck, Joseph (2004), 'Men's Power with Women, Other Men, and Society: A Men's Movement Analysis', in *Feminism and Masculinities*, ed. Peter Murphy, Oxford: Oxford University Press, pp. 57–68.

Pollay, Richard (1986), 'The Distorted Mirror: Reflections on the Unintended Consequences of Advertising', *Journal of Marketing* 50, 2, pp. 18–36.

Pollen, Lisa (2007a), '*Big Brother 8*! Amazing Final Night: Minute by Minute', *Star* 10 September, pp. 4–7.

Pollen, Lisa (2007b), 'Chanelle: The First Interview', *Star* 13 August, pp. 4–6.

Pozner, Jennifer (2004), 'The Unreal World: Why Women on Reality TV Have to Be Hot, Desperate and Dumb' *Ms. Magazine*, archived at: http://www.msmagazine.com/fall2004/unrealworld.asp

Projansky, Sarah and Leah Vande Berg (2000), 'Sabrina, the Teenage . . .?: Girls, Witches, Mortals and the Limitations of Prime Time Feminism', in *Fantasy Girls: Gender in the New Universe of Science Fiction and Fantasy Television*, ed. Elyce Rae Helford, New York: Rowman and Littlefield, pp. 13–40.

Richmond, Ray (1996), 'Toons Tune to Adult Auds', *Variety* 7–13 October, pp. 37, 40.

Ritchie, Jean (2000), *Big Brother: The Official Unseen Story*, London: Channel Four Books.

Roberts, Adam (2000), *Science Fiction: The Critical Idiom*, London: Routledge.

Roberts, Robin (1993), *A New Species: Gender and Science in Science Fiction*, Urbana and Chicago: University of Illinois Press.

Robson, Justina (2005), 'Frelling Fantastic', in *Farscape Forever! Sex, Drugs and Killer Muppets*, ed. Glenn Yeffeth, Dallas, TX: BenBella Books, pp. 1–14.

Root, Jane (1986), *Open the Box: About Television*, London: Comedia.

Roscoe, Jane (2001), '*Big Brother* Australia: Performing the Real Twenty-Four-Seven', *International Journal of Cultural Studies* 4, 4, pp. 473–86.

Rowe, David (1995), *Popular Cultures: Rock Music, Sport and the Politics of Pleasure*, London: Sage.

Rowe Karlyn, Kathleen (2003), 'Television, New Media and Feminism's Third Wave', paper delivered at the 'Media in Transition Conference', Massachusetts Institute of Technology, Cambridge, MA.

Russo, Vito (1987), *The Celluloid Closet: Homosexuality in the Movies*, New York: Harper Row.

Rutherford, Leonie (2004), 'Teen Futures: Discourses of Alienation, the Social and Technology in Australian Science Fiction Television Series', in *Teen TV: Genre, Consumption and Identity*, ed. Glyn Davis and Kay Dickinson, London: BFI, pp. 29–40.

Ryan, Marie-Laure (2004), 'From *The Truman Show* to *Survivor*: Narrative Versus Reality in Fake and Real Reality TV', *Intensities: The Journal of Cult Media* 2, archived at: http://davidlavery.net/Intensities/Intensities_2.htm

Sabo, Donald (1994), 'Different Stakes: Men's Pursuit of Gender Equity in

Sports', in *Sex, Violence & Power in Sports: Rethinking Masculinity*, ed. Michael Messner and Donald Sabo, New York: The Crossing Press, pp. 202–13.

Sandler, Kevin (2003), 'Synergy Nirvana: Brand Equity, Television Animation, and Cartoon Network', in *Prime Time Animation: Television Animation and American Culture*, ed. Carol Stabile and Mark Harrison, London: Routledge, pp. 89–109.

Sawyer, Jack (2004), 'On Male Liberation', in *Feminism and Masculinities*, ed. Peter Murphy, Oxford: Oxford University Press, pp. 25–7.

Seidler, Victor (1992), 'Rejection, Vulnerability, and Friendship', in *Men's Friendships*, ed. Peter Nardi, London: Sage, pp. 15–34.

Shugart, Helene (2003), 'Reinventing Privilege: The New (Gay) Man in Contemporary Popular Media', *Critical Studies in Media Communication* 20, 1, pp. 67–91.

Sloane, Robert (2004), 'Who Wants Candy? Disenchantment in *The Simpsons*', in *Leaving Springfield: The Simpsons and the Possibility of Oppositional Culture*, ed. John Alberti, Detroit, MI: Wayne State University Press, pp. 137–71.

Spadoni, Mike (2006), 'Medical Dramas in the US', Teletronic, archived at: http://www.teletronic.co.uk/usmeddrama.htm

Sparks, Richard (1992), *Television and the Drama of Crime: Moral Tales and the Place of Crime in Public Life*, Buckingham: Open University Press.

Straiton, John (1984), *Of Women and Advertising*, Toronto, ON: McClelland and Stewart.

Strange, Niki (1998), 'Perform, Educate, Entertain: Ingredients of the Cookery Programme Genre', in *The Television Studies Book*, ed. Christine Geraghty and David Lusted, London: Arnold, pp. 301–12.

Strate, Lance (1992), 'Beer Commercials: A Manual on Masculinity', in *Men, Masculinity and the Media*, ed. Steve Craig, London: Sage, pp. 78–92.

Sturrock, Fiona and Elke Pioch (1998), 'Making Himself Attractive: The Growing Consumption of Grooming Products', *Marketing Intelligence & Planning* 16, 5, pp. 337–43.

Svetkey, Benjamin (2000), 'Is Your TV Set Gay?' *Entertainment Weekly* 6 October, pp. 24–8.

Swain, Jon (2000), 'The Money's Good, The Fame's Good, The Girls Are Good', *British Journal of Sociology of Education* 21, 1, pp. 95–109.

Sweeney, Gael (1994), 'The Face on the Lunch Box: Television's Construction of the Teen Idol', *The Velvet Light Trap* 33, pp. 49–59.

Taylor, Lisa (2002), 'From Ways of Life to Lifestyle: The "Ordinari-ization" of British Gardening Lifestyle Television', *European Journal of Communication* 17, 4, pp. 479–93.

Tetreault, Mary Ann (1984), 'The Trouble with *Star Trek*', *Minerva* 22, 1, pp. 119–29.

Theberge, Nancy (1981), 'A Critique of Critiques: Radical and Feminist Writings on Sport', *Social Forces* 60, 2, pp. 341–53.

Tincknell, Estella and Parvati Raghuram (2004), '*Big Brother*: Reconfiguring the Active Audience of Cultural Studies', in *Understanding Reality Television*, ed. Su Holmes and Deborah Jermyn, London: Routledge, pp. 252–69.

Tropiano, Stephen (2002), *The Prime Time Closet: A History of Gays and Lesbians on TV*, New York: Applause.

Tueth, Michael (2003), 'Back to the Drawing Board: The Family in Animated Television Comedy', in *Prime Time Animation: Television Animation and American Culture*, ed. Carol Stabile and Mark Harrison, London: Routledge, pp. 133–46.

Turnbull, Sue (2006), '*The O.C.*, Masculinity and the Strategies of Teen TV', paper presented at MeCCSA Women and Media Studies Network, Oxford Brookes University, June, pp. 1–18.

Turner, Chris (2005), *Planet Simpson: How a Cartoon Masterpiece Documented an Era and Defined a Generation*, London: Ebury Press.

Turow, Joseph (1989), *Playing Doctor: Television, Storytelling and Medical Power*, Oxford: Oxford University Press.

Walker, Karen (1994), 'Men, Women, and Friendship: What They Say, What They Do', *Gender and Society* 8, 2, pp. 246–65.

Walters, Suzanna (2001), *All the Rage: The Story of Gay Visibility in America*, Chicago: University of Chicago.

Walton, Chris, Adrian Coyle and Evanthia Lyons (2004), 'Death and Football: An Analysis of Men's Talk about Emotions', *British Journal of Social Psychology* 43, pp. 401–16.

Waterlow, Lucy (2007), '*Big Brother 8*', *New* 13 August, pp. 4–6, 8.

Wells, Martha (2005), 'Don't Make me Tongue You', in *Farscape Forever! Sex, Drugs and Killer Muppets*, ed. Glenn Yeffeth, Dallas, TX: BenBella Books, pp. 73–82.

Wells, Paul (1998a), *Understanding Animation*, London: Routledge.

Wells, Paul (1998b), 'Where Everybody Knows Your Name: Open Convictions in Closed Contexts in the American Situation Comedy', in *Because I Tell a Joke or Two: Comedy, Politics and Social Difference*, ed. Stephen Wagg, New York: Routledge, pp. 180–201.

Wernick, Andrew (1992), *Promotional Culture: Advertising, Ideology and Symbolic Expression*, London: Sage.

West, Peter (1996), 'Why Men Play Sport' Manzine, archived at: http://www.manhood.com.au/Manhood.nsf/3d17d03aceb6903f4a256a74002329aa/53ac35230f8bf0f64a256a7b0034d7af!OpenDocument

West-Burnham, Joss and David Roberts (1998), 'Love and Death in the Emergency Room', in *Medical Fictions*, ed. Nickianne Moody and Julia Hallam, Wallasey: Eaton Press, pp. 249–60.

Westerfelhaus, Robert and Celeste Lacroix (2006), 'Seeing "Straight" through *Queer Eye*: Exposing the Strategic Rhetoric of Heteronormativity in a Mediated Ritual of Gay Rebellion', *Critical Studies in Media Communication* 25, 5, pp. 426–44.

Whannel, Garry (1995), *Fields in Vision: Television Sport and Cultural Transformation*, London: Routledge.

Whannel, Garry (1998), 'Individual Stars and Collective Identities in Media Sport', in *Sport, Popular Culture and Identity*, ed. Maurice Roche, Aachen: Meyer & Meyer Verlag, pp. 23–36.

Whannel, Garry (2002), *Media Sports Stars: Masculinities and Moralities*, London: Routledge.

White, Jim (2001), 'Over'Ere Son, on Me Arm', *Guardian*, 14 March, pp. 8–9.

White, Jim (2003), 'Sport on TV: Beckham's All Too Familiar', telegraph.co.uk, archived at: http://www.telegraph.co.uk/sport/main.jhtml?xml=/sport/2003/11/06/sotv06.xml

Whitehead, Stephen (2002), *Men and Masculinities*, Cambridge: Polity Press.

Wilcox, Rhonda (2000), 'Lois's Locks: Trust and Representation in *Lois and Clark: The New Adventures of Superman*', in *Fantasy Girls: Gender in the New Universe of Science Fiction and Fantasy Television*, ed. Elyce Rae Helford, Oxford: Rowman and Littlefield, pp. 91–114.

Yeates, Helen (2001), 'Ageing Masculinity in *NYPD Blue*: A Spectacle of Incontinence, Impotence and Mortality', *Canadian Review of American Studies* 31, 2, archived at: http://www.utpjournals.com/product/cras/312/yeates.html

Zoglin, Richard (1992), 'Where Fathers and Mothers Know Best', *Time* 1 June, 33.

INDEX